# Culture and Consensus in European Varieties of Capitalism

*International Political Economy Series*

General Editor: Timothy M. Shaw, Professor and Director, Institute of International Relations, The University of the West Indies, Trinidad & Tobago

*Titles include*:

Andreas Bieler and Adam David Morton (*editors*)
SOCIAL FORCES IN THE MAKING OF THE NEW EUROPE
The Restructuring of European Social Relations in the Global Political Economy

Ian Bruff
CULTURE AND CONSENSUS IN EUROPEAN VARIETIES OF CAPITALISM
A "Common Sense" Analysis

Steve Chan and A. Cooper Drury (*editors*)
SANCTIONS AS ECONOMIC STATECRAFT
Theory and Practice

Aldo Chircop, André Gerolymatos and John O. Iatrides
THE AEGEAN SEA AFTER THE COLD WAR
Security and Law of the Sea Issues

Chad Damro
COOPERATING ON COMPETITION IN TRANSATLANTIC ECONOMIC RELATIONS
The Politics of Dispute Prevention

Diane Ethier
ECONOMIC ADJUSTMENT IN NEW DEMOCRACIES
Lessons from Southern Europe

Jeffrey Henderson (*editor*)
INDUSTRIAL TRANSFORMATION IN EASTERN EUROPE IN THE LIGHT OF THE EAST ASIAN EXPERIENCE

Jacques Hersh and Johannes Dragsbaek Schmidt (*editors*)
THE AFTERMATH OF 'REAL EXISTING SOCIALISM' IN EASTERN EUROPE
Volume 1: Between Western Europe and East Asia

Peadar Kirby
THE CELTIC TIGER IN DISTRESS
Growth with Inequality in Ireland

Anne Lorentzen and Marianne Rostgaard (*editors*)
THE AFTERMATH OF 'REAL EXISTING SOCIALISM' IN EASTERN EUROPE
Volume 2: People and Technology in the Process of Transition

Gary McMahon (*editor*)
LESSONS IN ECONOMIC POLICY FOR EASTERN EUROPE FROM LATIN AMERICA

Árni Sverrison and Meine Pieter van Dijk (*editors*)
LOCAL ECONOMIES IN TURMOIL
The Effect of Deregulation and Globalization

---

International Political Economy Series

Series Standing Order ISBN 978 0–333–71708–0 hardcover
Series Standing Order ISBN 978 0–333–71110–1 paperback
(*outside North America only*)

You can receive future titles in this series as they are published by placing a standing order. Please contact your bookseller or, in case of difficulty, write to us at the address below with your name and address, the title of the series and one of the ISBNs quoted above.

Customer Services Department, Macmillan Distribution Ltd, Houndmills, Basingstoke, Hampshire RG21 6XS, England

---

# Culture and Consensus in European Varieties of Capitalism

## A "Common Sense" Analysis

Ian Bruff
*Research Officer*
*Edge Hill University, UK*

palgrave
macmillan

First published 2008 by
PALGRAVE MACMILLAN

Palgrave Macmillan in the UK is an imprint of Macmillan Publishers Limited, registered in England, company number 785998, of Houndmills, Basingstoke, Hampshire RG21 6XS.

Palgrave Macmillan in the US is a division of St Martin's Press LLC, 175 Fifth Avenue, New York, NY 10010.

Palgrave Macmillan is the global academic imprint of the above companies and has companies and representatives throughout the world.

Palgrave® and Macmillan® are registered trademarks in the United States, the United Kingdom, Europe and other countries.

ISBN-13: 978–0–230–54932–6 hardback
ISBN-0: 0–230–54932–2 hardback

This book is printed on paper suitable for recycling and made from fully managed and sustained forest sources. Logging, pulping and manufacturing processes are expected to conform to the environmental regulations of the country of origin.

A catalogue record for this book is available from the British Library.

A catalogue record for this book is available from the Library of Congress.

10 9 8 7 6 5 4 3 2 1
17 16 15 14 13 12 11 10 09 08

Printed and bound in Great Britain by
CPI Antony Rowe, Chippenham and Eastbourne

*To Laura, the light of my life*

# Contents

# Acknowledgements

While significantly different in many respects, this book is an updated and revised version of the PhD thesis I completed in 2005. Therefore, my first acknowledgements must go to my PhD supervisors in the School of Politics and International Studies at the University of Leeds, Christine Harlen and Charlie Dannreuther, for their patience, perseverance and advice. In addition, several people from within the School were helpful in a variety of ways: Hugo Radice, Ricardo Blaug, Stuart McAnulla, Victoria Honeyman, Caroline Wise and, at undergraduate and MA level at Leeds, Phil Cerny. Hugo Radice was also the internal examiner of the thesis; together with the equally commendable Colin Hay, my external examiner, they made a great team for my viva. As for the research itself, I am grateful to the individuals who agreed to be interviewed and their organizations for responding to my letters and emails. Some of the interviewees were contacted directly: for this I am thankful for Mara Yerkes' and Johannes Kandel's efforts. Finally, Linde Vereecke was an excellent and hospitable host during my time in the Netherlands.

Away from Leeds, I can never thank enough Nicola Smith and Paul Dixon for their unending enthusiasm and support for myself and my work – this was especially helpful when it appeared that the Research Assessment Exercise would sabotage any hope I had of a career in academia. For short-term positions which helped me keep my foot in the door, I am grateful to James Wickham, Richard Gillespie, Jocelyn Evans, James Newell, Paul Reynolds and David Farrell. As for my present post, Katherine Straker has been very supportive, and I am forever indebted to my department head Alistair McCulloch for taking a chance on me. I am also grateful to Palgrave Macmillan for doing the same upon receiving my book proposal. Philippa Grand and Hazel Woodbridge, editor and editorial assistant for the first half of the writing process, and Alexandra Webster, Matthew Hayes and Gemma d'Arcy Hughes, my editor and editorial assistants during the second half, were consistently supportive and helpful. In addition, Shirley Tan was efficient and informative in preparing the manuscript for production.

My intellectual debts range far and wide, but, in addition to those in Leeds during my PhD, I am particularly grateful for discussions, suggestions and constructive criticism from Colin Hay, Nicola Smith, Andreas Bieler, Adam Morton, Christina Rowley, Penny Griffin and Jan Drahokoupil. In addition, the Critical Political Economy Research Network of the European Sociological Association has provided an excellent forum for intellectual and social engagement with like-minded individuals: Jan Drahokoupil and Laura Horn deserve a medal (and several pints) for their efforts.

I may not have seen my friends as frequently as I would have liked – and my excuses for being anti-social seem to go a long way back in time – but they knew why I was shutting myself away for weeks on end and were never judgemental in that respect. Neither were my family, and none of this would have been possible without their support. They consistently went well beyond the call of duty to help me through my degrees, and also when an academic career seemed to be slipping away. In particular, my parents consistently put my needs before theirs, and I hope that this book is the first of many ways in which I can show that it has all been worth it.

Finally, by the time this book is published I will be married to Laura Chambers. The most amazing person I have ever met, words can't describe how important she is to me. This book is dedicated to Laura for her support, love, encouragement and companionship.

# List of Abbreviations or Acronyms and Table

| | |
|---|---|
| BDA | Bundesvereinigung der Deutschen Arbeitgeberverbände (Confederation of German Employers' Associations) |
| BDI | Bundesverband der Deutschen Industrie (Federation of German Industries) |
| CDA | Christen Democratisch Appèl (Christian Democratic Appeal) |
| CDU | Christlich Demokratische Union Deutschlands (Christian Democratic Union of Germany) |
| CME | Coordinated Market Economy |
| CPB | Centraal Planbureau (Central Planning Bureau) |
| CSU | Christlich-Soziale Union in Bayern (Christian Social Union of Bavaria) |
| D66 | Democraten D66 (Democrats 66) |
| DGB | Deutsche Gewerkschaftsbund (German Federation of Labour) |
| EMU | European Economic and Monetary Union |
| EU | European Union |
| FDP | Freie Demokratische Partei (Free Democratic Party) |
| FNV | Federatie Nederlandse Vakbeweging (Federation of Dutch Trade Unions) |
| GRN | Bündnis 90/Die Grünen (Alliance '90/The Greens) |
| IAB | Institut für Arbeitsmarkt- und Berufsforschung (Institute for Employment Research) |
| INSM | Initiative Neue Soziale Marktwirtschaft (New Social Market Economy Initiative) |
| IPE | International Political Economy |
| LME | Liberal Market Economy |
| LPF | Lijst Pim Fortuyn (Pim Fortuyn List) |
| OECD | Organisation for Economic Cooperation and Development |

| | |
|---|---|
| PDS | Partei des Demokratischen Sozialismus (Party of Democratic Socialism) |
| PvdA | Partij van de Arbeid (Labour Party) |
| PVV | Partij voor de Vrijheid (Party for Freedom) |
| SER | Sociaal Economische Raad (Social and Economic Council of the Netherlands) |
| SGP | Staatkundig Gereformeerde Partij (Reformed Political Party) |
| SP | Socialistische Partij (Socialist Party) |
| SPD | Sozialdemokratische Partei Deutschlands (Social Democratic Party of Germany) |
| STAR | Stichting van de Arbeid (Foundation of Labour) |
| UK | United Kingdom of Great Britain and Northern Ireland |
| US | United States of America |
| VNO–NCW | Vereniging VNO–NCW (Confederation of Netherlands Industry and Employers) |
| VVD | Volkspartij voor Vrijheid en Democratie (People's Party for Freedom and Democracy) |

## Table

# 1
# Introduction

As Nicola Smith (2006: 519) argues, '[t]he trajectory of contemporary European political economies remains the subject of enormous academic and political controversy.' Nevertheless, while certainly true, one common theme in the discussions is the need for a consensus to exist across different actors in order for the economy to perform well. This is necessary in European political economies, because they are characterized by a compromise between capital and labour (underwritten by the state), in which labour accepts the market economy, and capital the need for the market economy to be embedded in institutions which cushion the population from the damaging impact of economic change. As a result, an essential prerequisite of the economy performing well is the presence of a consensus across the state, employers and trade unions – the tripartite actors – on economic and social policy. This is because institutions tend, over time, to become dysfunctional owing to the effects of economic, social and political change. Overcoming such dysfunction in European varieties of capitalism requires agreement on how to proceed. Thus institutional dysfunction, and economic underperformance, perpetuates in conditions of no consensus, and can potentially be overcome in conditions of consensus.

This book's primary concern is to provide a framework for analysing the role of consensus in European political economies that goes beyond the hitherto dominant varieties of capitalism literature, whose explanations centre on the institutional environment across different countries. While these contributions are frequently given different labels, '[f]rom the standpoint of comparing national capitalisms, the extent of an institutionalist common ground within the social sciences is striking.' (Radice 2004: 188; see also Campbell 2004: 9). Thus research on European varieties of capitalism encompasses a considerably wider range of scholars than the term might suggest, particularly given its association with the narrower Varieties of Capitalism framework (as espoused by Peter Hall and Soskice 2001b).

Debate in the literature has revolved around differences between contrasting institutionalisms (see Campbell and Pedersen 2001 for an excellent overview). Regardless of the institutionalism adhered to by the scholar, the focus on institutions makes it necessary for consensus to be produced *internal* to the institutional environment. In consequence, institutions are separated from the society they are part of. My point of departure is that the role of consensus in the trajectories of European varieties of capitalism can be analysed adequately only with recourse to a discussion of culture. This entails an acknowledgement of the tightly connected relationship between state and society while remaining aware of their methodological distinctiveness. Institutions are intrinsically rooted in the society they are part of, giving them a social content which is nationally distinct. Although this is often discussed *in principle* in varieties of capitalism texts – especially in the discursive institutionalism corpus (see Schmidt 2000) – *in practice* there is a retreat to the institutions. As a result, the social content of any consensus that may form is neglected.

Perhaps the most lucid and persuasive commentaries in the varieties of capitalism literature have concerned the trajectories of the Dutch and German political economies. The Netherlands has often been portrayed as an example of how institutions can be mobilized effectively when responding to socioeconomic challenges such as high unemployment (Visser and Hemerijck 1997; Hemerijck *et al.* 2000). In contrast, Germany is more likely to be cited as an example of how institutions can fail to meet these challenges (Manow and Seils 2000; Kitschelt and Streeck 2003). Symbolizing the difference in economic performance are two milestones in the trajectories of the Dutch and German varieties of capitalism – the Wassenaar and Alliance for Jobs processes. Briefly, when facing considerable challenges such as high unemployment and economic recession, the Dutch were in the early 1980s able to forge a long-lasting consensus on reform which enabled institutional dysfunction to be overcome. In contrast, the Germans were in the late 1990s unable to do the same, despite the years of mass unemployment and low economic growth that preceded Alliance for Jobs.

Through providing a more persuasive explanation of Wassenaar and Alliance for Jobs than has hitherto been the case, this book confronts the varieties of capitalism literature where it is at its strongest. In particular, I question the literature's ability to analyse the issue of consensus formation – which extends to consensus not being formed – in European varieties of capitalism. I argue that a persuasive analysis is possible only through the utilization of Antonio Gramsci's notion of "common sense", which captures both culture and consensus in one conceptual apparatus. This is possible through his focus on the role of the material basis for existence in shaping how humans view the world. Interview data, presented in Chapters 5 and 6, demonstrate the existence of shared perspectives on economic "reality" in the Netherlands – most notably the assumption of economic vulnerability – which stands in contrast to the distinctive outlooks articulated by the German interviewees. Because of this common denominator, it proved easier for tripartite actors in the Netherlands to form a consensus in the early 1980s than their equivalent in Germany in the late 1990s. In addition, Chapter 7 shows how the radicalized political environment of the early 2000s in both countries reinforces my position, despite the challenge to my case that this seems to pose.

The rest of this chapter, because of the above assertion that to analyse consensus we must consider culture, will focus on culture. The next section highlights the shortcomings of the varieties of capitalism literature on this issue, before discussing the value of Gramsci's writings on common sense and also the contributions of the neo-Gramscian literature more generally.

## The varieties of capitalism literature and culture

"Culture" has become one of the most important reference points across the social sciences in recent years. Indeed, along with other closely-related "turns" (such as the constructivist, the linguistic and the ideational), the "cultural turn" signifies an increasing willingness to take seriously the role of culture in social science research (for example, see Chaney 1994; Hunt and Bonnell 1999; Crothers and Lockhart 2000; Slater and Tonkiss 2001; Lawson 2006). This has enabled studies of culture to escape from their traditional home in anthropology, cultural studies and sociology and penetrate hitherto more resistant areas of social science such as International Political Economy (IPE). This shift took place, probably uncoincidentally, at the same time as a corresponding debate within IPE about the impact of "globalization" on the nation-state (for a review of the debate, see Bruff 2005). Those arguing against the notion that globalization is destroying national autonomy frequently invoked the specificities of national varieties of capitalism, and did so on an ostensibly institutionalist basis: that is, each country's institutional environment generates a path-dependence to the trajectories of national political economies that resists global pressures (see Weiss 1998; Garrett 1998; Hirst and Thompson 1999).

Out of such contributions emerged the varieties of capitalism literature, which provides a sophisticated theoretical basis for analysing the 'differences in economic and political institutions that occur across countries.' (Peter Hall and Soskice 2001b: 1). This extends to institutional adaptation as well as stability, since the former takes place in a path-dependent manner (see also Peter Hall and Soskice 2001a; Swank 2002; Weiss 2003). Such institutionalist explanations have been particularly effective in analysing the evolution of European varieties of capitalism, which assume a privileged position in the literature by way of continental Europe's status as the symbol of a more humane, egalitarian and consensual capitalism (frequently in contrast to the US version) (see Albert 1993; Scharpf and Schmidt 2000a, 2000b; Hemerijck 2002; Campbell *et al.* 2006).

Nevertheless, the literature's inadequate conceptualization of the role of culture in European varieties of capitalism renders it unable to incorporate the analytical potential generated by the "cultural turn". This is most apparent when the literature considers the role of consensus in European varieties of capitalism, for the fortunes of the varieties have been linked by many to the presence or absence of consensus across policymakers – principally the state, the employers' associations and the trade unions – on how to adjust to economic change (Hemerijck *et al.* 2000; Campbell and Pedersen 2007). However, the presence or absence of consensus across policymakers is often connected to societal factors. The attempt by the varieties of capitalism literature to incorporate the linkages between state and society is laudable, and terms such as culture, identity and norms are often used. Despite such attempts, one of the main consequences is for culture to be conflated with institutional norms and conventions.

To give an example from the literature, Peter Hall and Soskice (2001b: 13) argue that 'the institutions of a nation's political economy are inextricably bound up with its history in two respects... [one] formal institutions and their operation procedures...[two] repeated historical experience [that] builds up a set of common expectations'. Regarding the latter, 'the shared understandings that accumulate from this experience constitute something like a common culture.' (*ibid.*: 13). Thus consensus – the shared understandings – is in effect *the same* as culture, a key consequence of the conflation of culture with institutional norms of appropriateness (cf. March and Olsen 1989, who are cited by Hall and Soskice despite their different brand of institutionalism). However, elsewhere Hall concedes that '[s]ome attitudes have a more exogenous character in the sense that they derive from fundamental beliefs about politics or economics whose origins are not to be found in any immediate institutional situation' (Peter Hall 1986: 278), and that the state is exposed to societal influences in the way it relates to institutional networks which have deep roots in society (*ibid.*: 17).

At a stroke the genie escapes from the lamp, for if culture and consensus are *not* conflated then it becomes impossible to account for culture's role in the political economy by way of the continued focus on institutions. However, varieties of capitalism scholars who acknowledge society more explicitly fare little better. For some, culture is now merely one variable among others, introduced by the author when other frameworks appear limited in their explanatory power. Characteristic is Schmidt's (2002a: 7–8) admission that she finds cultural explanations to be useful only when asking certain research questions. This fails to acknowledge the fact that *culture is embodied in all human social practice.*

I do not want to appear in favour of one-dimensional explanations, but such epistemological opportunism is surely something that we need to avoid. It should be stressed the Schmidt is far from alone in this respect, but she is one of the few to acknowledge openly this position (as do other discursive and constructivist institutionalists, who will be considered below). Instead there is usually a discussion of the need to incorporate a myriad of factors into a framework which, in consequence, faces in many directions at the same time. Campbell and Pedersen (2001) argue that this is a strength of the "new institutionalism" underpinning the varieties of capitalism literature's approach (see Chapter 2 for more on this), but it also means that interminable discussions on when to use which variables, and in what sequence, have taken on the status of "defining debates" that ultimately generate much heat but little fire (a rare example to the contrary is Kenworthy 2006; compare with some of the symposia in the same journal which published this article).

Another approach taken by varieties of capitalism scholars who acknowledge society more explicitly is to relegate culture to the status of a vague umbrella term. A recent example is Streeck and Thelen's (2005b) attempt to formulate a theory of institutional change. In this important chapter they redefine an institution as a "social regime" consisting of rules made by rule makers with which rule takers are expected to comply. Yet they then make the somewhat bizarre move of, on the one hand, asserting that institutional regimes depend on societal legitimacy for its rules to be enforced, and on the other, claiming that '[i]n order not to make our Figure [summarizing institutions as regimes] too confusing, we have decided not to indicate the relations between both rule makers and rule takers with the surrounding society and the values the latter enforces on them.' (14). This closure of the opportunities afforded by their redefinition of institutions is breathtaking, and is inadequately addressed in the following paragraphs which attempt to shore up their position.

A seemingly more appropriate version of institutionalism has come to prominence in recent years, going beyond the rational choice and historical institutionalisms of Hall and Soskice and Streeck and Thelen, is discursive or constructivist institutionalism (see Schmidt 2002b; Hay 2006; Kjær and Pedersen 2001; Robert Henry Cox 2001; Blyth 2002).[1] Its point of departure is the belief that other institutionalisms are better at explaining institutional stability than institutional change. Secondly, in order to explain institutional change we need to consider the role of ideas and discourse in articulating the need for, and winning support for, change. Discourse thus matters when we come to consider substantial policy change (or lack of), because 'its ability to convince of the necessity *and* appropriateness of a policy program' (Schmidt 2001: 250; emphasis added) is crucial to any story of successful or stillborn reform processes.

The emphasis on dynamism and the role of discourse in framing how people think and act is laudable, as are the discussions of the extent to which ideas and discourses resonate with society. Nevertheless, although superficially in accord with the neo-Gramscian approach I outline below, the belief still is – to quote an eminent scholar who highlights the role of ideas – that '[i]nstitutions are the foundation of social life.' (Campbell 2004: 1). In other words, these authors are just as committed to institutions, at the expense of the society they are part of, as the institutional perspectives that they seek to go beyond. In consequence, the ideas and discourses are formulated *from within the confines of the institutional environment* – hence the epistemological opportunism discussed above. Yet again, there is an inability to conceptualize the relationship between state and society.

To summarize, it is clear that varieties of capitalism scholars believe the link between state and society to be important. However, in practice the literature retreats to institutions as the basis for their explanation. To give an illustration of the problems this causes, Fritz Scharpf (2000: 120), when accounting for the willingness of the Dutch government of the early 1990s to press ahead with disability benefit reforms, remarks that it was such a controversial step that there could only have been an 'extremely strong cognitive orientation' towards reform. However, he fails to elaborate, and it is clear that he is unable to provide an explanation beyond an inadequate "they must have really believed in the reform" statement. As I will now outline, such abstention from formulating a plausible explanation allows him, along with the rest of the literature, to avoid discussing the elephant in the room: *capitalism.*

## Conceptualizing culture in capitalist society

The core of the book's argument is that Antonio's Gramsci's notion of "common sense" provides us with the conceptual tools necessary for understanding and explaining the role of consensus in European varieties of capitalism. This is because Gramsci theorized culture as a political issue (Anderson 1976: 78), and thus a means by which state and society could be considered as intimately linked without losing sight of their distinct analytical importance (cf. Gramsci 1971: 159–60). Two elements of Gramsci's writings are of great significance for this book: one, all humans are philosophers because everyone holds conceptions about the world, or common sense, no matter how fragmentary and uncritical; two, these conceptions of the world are embodied in all human social practice (*ibid.*: 323, 344, 357).

This enables us to define culture in a particular way, which is a precondition of conceptualizing the role of consensus in the trajectories of European varieties of capitalism. 'Culture is one of the two or three most complicated words in the English language' (Williams 1983: 87), and thus open to contestation. In my view, culture must be viewed as an irreducible and universal aspect of human existence if it is to be called culture at all, which immediately rules out one of the traditional conceptualizations of culture – culture as "the arts".[2] It is true that Gramsci tended to focus on "the arts" in his writings on culture, with a particular emphasis on literature and education (Forgacs and Nowell-Smith 1985: 13). Nevertheless, the editors of his *Cultural Writings* (Gramsci 1985) volume note:

> In all cases his interest is not so much in the object itself as in the place it occupies within a range of social practices. The writings on philosophy, for example, rarely enter in detail into philosophical arguments as such; their concern is with the place of philosophical thinking and of particular philosophies within social life. In other words, with the "culture" of philosophy...The fundamental concepts in play in Gramsci's observations on cultural themes are those which inform his writings generally – state and civil society, intellectuals, hegemony and so forth. (Forgacs and Nowell-Smith 1985: 14).

Hence Gramsci's (1985: 25) declaration that culture is the 'exercise of thought, acquisition of general ideas, habit of connecting causes and effects. For me, everybody is already cultured because everybody thinks, everybody connects causes and effects.' Moreover, the conglomeration of each person's thoughts about the world is their own version of common sense. Thus there are many different versions of common sense within any one society, but these conceptions can only be recognized as part of a culture if they are intersubjective rather than merely subjective, and thus embodied in persistent *collective* patterns of human activity and thought (cf. Robert W. Cox 1996d: 514). Furthermore, there may be several different versions of culture co-existing at any one point in time, but, crucially, each version is a version of culture in *capitalist society*. Hence Gramsci's (1996: 233) opinion that the rise of capitalism signalled 'a phase [in human history] that would completely transform all modes of existence and radically upset the past.'

Two decades ago, Robert W. Cox (1987: 1, 13) defined production as the material basis for all human existence, for we need to produce in order to satisfy our needs for food, shelter, clothing and so on. Moreover, this need to produce must be organized in one way or another in order to produce anything at all. As Cox puts it, 'the ways in which human efforts are combined in productive processes affect all other aspects of social life' (Robert W. Cox 1987: 1). Therefore, if culture is an irreducible and universal aspect of human existence, our conceptions of the world will surely be saturated by references to the need to produce and its organization, or, to take the two together in one term, to the mode of production. Given that European varieties of capitalism, as the phrase suggests, are part of a capitalist mode of production – characterized by the predominantly private ownership of productive activity in a market-based system of exchange and distribution – then culture in these societies can be conceptualized as intersubjective *capitalist* conceptions of the world. As Coates (2000: 142) argues, '[c]apitalism comes in certain "models"...but all of the models are recognizably capitalist.'

Thus while the state, as the juridically sovereign set of institutions in European varieties of capitalism, should be the focal point of analysis, the varieties of capitalism literature neglects the fact that it is a *capitalist state*. As a result, culture cannot be conflated with institutional norms, bracketed off as a variable or viewed as a vague umbrella term: it traverses all parts of the social world – including state and society. This last point leads the discussion towards the next part of the chapter: the state itself. Having established the means by which we can conceptualize the role of culture in European political economies without committing the errors made by the varieties of capitalism literature, it is now necessary to explain why the state will be, as just asserted, the focal point of the analysis.

Chapter 3 argues that the way in which a version of common sense can come to predominate is through its connection to social groups who promote such a version. What Gramsci terms a "fundamental social group" – one of the major social classes – will be at the head of any alliance of social groups seeking societal hegemony, owing to the fact that human existence is rooted in production and its organization. Key to the success of these groups in securing societal support for their agenda is the ability to transcend their core economic interests and construct a worldview – or hegemonic project – which takes 'into account the popular and democratic aspirations and struggles of the people which do not have a necessary class character.' (Simon 1991: 43).

If these groups are able to gain the support and consent of enough of society in order to achieve societal leadership (or hegemony), then their version of common sense, as expressed through the articulation of their hegemonic project, has the opportunity to become the dominant worldview in that society at that point in time. This is because the reshaping of the legal framework institutionalizes and entrenches this version of common sense – or culture – in the framework, and the coercive legal status of state policies and institutions insulates this version from challenges by way of their "natural" appearance (cf. Robert W. Cox 1996d: 517–19). This is not to say that there will be no modification to state policies and institutions in the future; more that they acquire a durability which can be difficult to overcome.

The state's sovereign status makes it necessary for competing social groups to seek societal leadership on its administrative terrain, meaning that state and society are, while analytically distinct – in Gramsci's terminology they are "political society" and "civil society", together forming the "integral state" – they are tightly interlinked (Bieler and Morton 2003: 492, n.9). However, this means that any version of common sense that has come to predominate at a particular point in time will come into contact with earlier versions of common sense which had led that society. Therefore, any social groups seeking to attain societal hegemony must engage with the sediments of thought which have built up over time in that society, in order to gain support *vis-à-vis* other groups.

Furthermore, any social groups seeking to entrench their version of common sense in the legal framework – that is, to attain political hegemony – must engage with the sediments of thought ingrained in existing policies and institutional arrangements on the state's administrative terrain. In consequence, while the present and future evolution of common sense within any country is an open empirical question, 'the contemporary world [is] a synthesis of the past...which projects itself into the future' (Gramsci 1971: 34–5). Therefore, different societies, and their state policies and institutions, exhibit path-dependent trajectories which can be observed and analysed over time.[3] Hence it is possible to conceive theoretically and observe empirically both the changes taking place in the given society and the path-dependent elements which distinguish one society from the next.

## Methodological issues

From a research design perspective, the role of culture in the trajectory of the national variety of capitalism can be most clearly observed and analysed at the state level, because elites are a rarefied embodiment of their society's culture. As Chapter 3 explains, each version of common sense has the chance of leading the society the more successfully it moves from fragmentary, contradictory, uncritical everyday conceptions of the world in society to the opinions expressed and promoted by elite actors at the level of the state. This process is driven by organic intellectuals – such as political parties, trade unions and employers' associations – who represent and stem from each social group. Organic intellectuals clarify, renovate and shape the everyday conceptions into a synthesis of ideas which seek to mobilize and rally society around their vision. As a result, given this book's focus, organic intellectuals are conceptualized as 'institutional frameworks within and through which different class fractions [or components] of capital and labour attempt to establish their particular interests and ideas as the generally accepted, or "common sense", view.' (Bieler 2000: 13).

As a result, the closer common sense moves to the state level the more coherent, consistent and lucid it becomes. This does not mean that it is an internally consistent body of thinking when expressed in state policies, because synthesizing different ideas together in order to gain support from different social groups often entails a certain organizational coherence at the expense of ideological clarity.

However, because the elite have more time to think about issues such as the economy, and receive policy and intellectual advice from many sources, these different ideas will be most clearly expressed at the state level. Gramsci (1971: 331) described the art of politics as the intermediary between everyday life and philosophy, which enables elite common sense to be relatively coherent and sophisticated without being abstract or disconnected from the "real world". Therefore, while elite common sense is analytically distinct from everyday common sense, they are two ends of the same continuum rather than separate categories. For the purposes of this book, elite common sense will be focused on because it is articulated at a level – the state – whereby its expression through policies and institutions could have real and lasting significance for that society. Secondly, elite common sense is more empirically accessible in both organizational and observational terms: certain actors (in this book's case the tripartite actors) can be identified for the purposes of research, and their versions of common sense will be more amenable to analysis than everyday versions.

This is not to say that non-elite common sense is unimportant (see Motta 2006 for an important corrective to notions of statism), but that the state, as a juridically sovereign set of institutions, provides the terrain upon which predominant versions of common sense can become the basis for a hegemonic order in that society. Regarding the second point, everyday common sense is not too difficult an object of study, but it is more fragmented in both organizational and observational terms. My approach is thus infused with a certain pragmatism, and this is because one must keep in mind at all times the research agenda. This book's point of departure is from discussions of consensus in European political economies by the varieties of capitalism literature. Key to my position is the belief that we can study the same aspects of the political economy as this literature – national-level tripartite actors and institutions (Gramsci's "integral state") – and arrive at a considerably more persuasive analysis through the utilization of a neo-Gramscian framework. In particular, I will demonstrate that the potential for synthesis between different cultures, or versions of common sense, shapes whether consensus is present or absent across the tripartite actors. In other words, *the source of consensus is not the institutional environment; it is culture.*

In addition, the study is comparative, and my conceptualization of culture in capitalist society enables us, again, to confront the varieties of capitalist literature on its own terrain, for many of its most famous outputs are comparative studies. Indeed, the utilization of comparisons is central to its explanatory power, because it exposes less rigorous analyses to forensic and damning examination (such as Ohmae 1990; Barnet and Cavanagh 1994; Friedman 2005), forcing scholars to be more cautious and sensitive when undertaking their research. Thus there is little point in talking past the literature you are departing from: far better is to demonstrate that *in and of itself* it is inadequate.

As Sassoon (2000: 10) says, comparison is useful not just because it widens one's horizons, which is important for any researcher, but also due to the critical approach to the world that it encourages: '[comparative perspectives] are a prerequisite for acquiring an appreciation of the specificities of any single society and for denaturalising what appears unproblematically "normal" or "natural".' Thus this study will, unlike the varieties of capitalism literature, utilize comparisons and contrasts in order to enquire into the basis for the opinions and actions of Dutch and German actors. In so doing capitalism is brought back into focus, thus correcting the uncritical studies of capitalist institutions prevalent in the varieties of capitalism literature.

In terms of research methods, this study utilized semi-structured qualitative interviews with a range of elite actors – some of whom were politically involved at the time of the Wassenaar and Alliance for Jobs processes, and some of whom gave comments from a more personally detached perspective (thus providing for a balance between those on the inside of the negotiations and those who were not).[4] Qualitative methods, of which interviews are the primary example, 'are most appropriately employed where the goal of research is to explore people's subjective experiences and the meanings they attach to those experiences...[They] are good at capturing meaning, process and context' (Devine 2002: 199). In terms of the interviews themselves, '[t]he very strength of the interview is its privileged access to the common understanding of subjects, the understanding that provides their worldview' (Kvale 1996: 291). Therefore, qualitative interviews are appropriate for a study of this kind, for they seek to bring to light the assumptions underlying the interviewees' opinions. This way 'it becomes possible to uncover the social, structural and cultural bases of choices and actions that might appear natural or predetermined.' (Gerson and Horowitz 2002: 206).

In consequence, the data was analysed via an inspection of the language the interviewees used. Language is important, for it reveals assumptions which tell us something about how people view the world in which they live – it is an 'expression of a conception of the world.' (Gramsci 1996: 384). As stated above, because the common sense opinions were expressed relatively coherently and clearly by the elite actors, it was possible to analyse what this meant for the role of consensus in the Dutch and German varieties of capitalism – both in and of themselves and also in comparison to each other. In so doing a close connection between theory and practice is achieved: theoretically it has been posited that the source of consensus is culture because every human is cultured by way of holding thoughts about the world, and empirically the interviews sought to gain access 'neither to a subjective relativity of interpretations, nor to an absolute objective knowledge, but to knowledge produced and tested intersubjectively through conversations.' (Kvale 1996: 297).

## Gramsci removed from his context?

Before we go any further it is necessary to consider two challenges to the book's application of Gramsci's work on common sense. The first one relates to the utilization of any of Gramsci's concepts; the second to how Gramsci himself viewed common sense. Regarding the first issue, it has been argued that there is a need for reflection on the extent to which contemporary scholars should employ concepts – such as common sense – for analyses of societies very different from the one in which Gramsci lived. Space precludes anything more than a brief overview, but there is concern that the Italian context – taken in both the national–territorial and the historical senses of context – is too specific for scholars not of the place or era to apply his concepts elsewhere in space and time (Bellamy 1990; Bellamy and Schecter 1993). There is also the argument that Gramsci's concepts, because of the appalling prison conditions in which he was writing, are so open to radically different interpretations that their application is fraught with difficulty (Germain and Kenny 1998).

In a manner similar to Stuart Hall (1988: 161–73; 1997) and Adam David Morton (2003a, 2007a), this book occupies a middle ground between rejecting the notion that Gramsci's ideas are applicable to contemporary societies and utilizing them uncritically. For example, Hall (1997) admits that he finds some of Gramsci's writings relatively uninteresting, and the aspects most relevant for his own work are Gramsci's discussions of ideology. Similarly, Morton (2003a, 2007a) argues that Gramsci's ideas can be situated in and beyond their context through a critical appreciation of what might be limited as well as relevant in his work when applying it to different social conditions (see also Sassoon 2000; Femia 1981). The book's utilization of common sense is an example of this, and will be considered below when discussing Andrew Robinson's position.

Before that I wish to add to Morton's (2003a) excellent riposte to what he terms the "austere historicism" of scholars such as Bellamy and others. Gramsci's notes are full of fertile theoretical and conceptual possibilities: it is precisely the incompleteness of the *Prison Notebooks* that provides us with the multiple horizons that are still being explored. The benefits of an unfinished theoretical framework in and of itself *have* been noted by other scholars, albeit reluctantly (presumably for fear of being derided for not being rigorous enough). For example, Stuart Hall (1996b: 146) "confessed" to 'an alarming tendency in myself to prefer people's less complete works to their later, mature and complete ones...where they have gotten over their adolescent idealism but their thought has not yet hardened into a system'. Elsewhere, Hall (1980: 68) praised the 'theoretical unevenness' of Poulantzas' (1978) final work for providing 'the stimulus of the book, its generative openness'. Similarly to how I read Gramsci, I read some of Poulantzas' work – particularly in the headlong rush that is *State, Power, Socialism* – as suggestive rather than definitive, as will be demonstrated in Chapter 3 in particular (see also Bruff 2007).

Therefore, there is much to be said for acknowledging the potential of Gramsci's writings rather than their limitations (Morton 2003a: 129). And, equally significantly, Gramsci's incompleteness leaves room for empirical research to fill in the gaps. No theoretical schema can adequately explain the social world in all of its complexity, dynamism and spatio-temporal variability, and it is through rigorous attention to the research question that a persuasive argument can most effectively be made. Indeed, one of the great advantages of Stuart Hall's (1996a: 45) formulation of the 'economic in the *first* instance' is that, through positing the constraints on and not the contents of our conceptions of the world, he leaves space for empirical research to establish the content of the thoughts, and also the biases within the content. The potential of the conceptual apparatus provided by "common sense" to connect theory and practice will be demonstrated in Chapters 5–7, which consider the interview data generated by this study.

It is now time to deal with the powerful argument made by Andrew Robinson (2006) regarding common sense. Robinson criticizes the relative absence of reflection in the secondary literature on Gramsci on:

> his critique of common sense. This is crucial, because this critique was a central part of his conception of revolutionary change. It is clear from the *Prison Notebooks* that Gramsci was opposed both to everyday "common sense", the philosophy of the masses, and to the manipulative and passivity-inducing effects of elite-dominated politics. He was therefore an advocate of a revolution in everyday life...he has in mind a thoroughgoing transformation and development of people's ways of thinking and acting in everyday life (75, 76; original emphasis).

Robinson cites many examples, several of which revolve around Gramsci's desire for organic intellectuals to enable the masses to raise their intellectual level in order for them to become an active historical force. A collective will can then be articulated, enabling the dominated sections of society to break free of the conceptions of the world which imprison them in their subordination. It is a compelling argument, and one which needs to be taken seriously. In response, I believe it is of great significance to acknowledge that Gramsci was not the only writer to argue for the need for intellectual enlightenment. This may seem an obvious point, but if we consider the following quote then we can see that, depending on the writer's perspective, an emphasis on intellectual enlightenment of the masses could lead to very different conclusions than Gramsci's, or indeed those of any other historical materialist:

> The despotism of custom is everywhere the standing hindrance to human advancement, being in unceasing antagonism to that

> disposition to aim at something better than customary, which is called, according to the circumstances, the spirit of liberty, or that of progress or improvement...The progressive principle...in either shape...is antagonistic to the sway of Custom, involving at least emancipation from that yoke; and the contest between the two constitutes the chief interest of the history of mankind. (Mill 1991: 78).

John Stuart Mill's polemic in *On Liberty* against the dangers of the "tyranny of the majority" is hardly complementary to Gramsci's commitment to a future communist society, yet their radically differing agendas stem from the same source, at least with regard to intellectual emancipation from custom, or common sense. Therefore, depending on the author the masses could be enlightened, and thus free themselves from intellectual enslavement, in a range of ways. Thus historical materialist analysis must incorporate the fact that various social groups struggling for societal leadership may well, *in their own terms*, be pushing for intellectual enlightenment of the masses. This may be an uncomfortable proposition for historical materialists, but the point is this: Mill believed in human progress as much as Gramsci, and so may different social groups seeking to achieve societal hegemony.

The emphasis here is on the contingent – different social groups *may* believe in human progress – but this theoretical shift would accomplish two things. One, it would enable historical materialism to engage more constructively with other critical theories, such as those which study the gendered, racialized and heteronormative nature of contemporary societies, when seeking to achieve human progress on a collective basis (see Rupert (2005) for an account of how his historical materialist outlook has engaged with other critical theories). Two, which is of central importance for this book, it would enable historical materialists to view common sense opinions *in and of themselves* as important (see also Crehan 2002). Common sense is of supreme political significance by the time it has made its journey from uncritical, amorphous philosophies in everyday life to relatively coherent, clear conceptions of the world articulated by elite actors. The study of common sense is an essential part of political economy analysis *per se*, not least because it enables the study of European varieties of capitalism to acquire a critical edge. This, rather than emancipatory concerns, is at the heart of the book.

## Outline of the book

In keeping with the above discussion of the need to consider culture in order to arrive at an adequate analysis of the role of consensus in the trajectories of European varieties of capitalism, Chapter 2 reviews a range of literatures for their conceptualization of culture. The first part of the chapter provides an in-depth critique, via a discussion of the relationship between state and society, of the varieties of capitalism literature's inability to incorporate culture into its framework. The second part reviews five broad perspectives on culture: political culture; webs of meaning in the local context; cultural embeddedness and cultural constitution; culture industries in and the culturalization of "late capitalism"; and power. I contend that none of these positions captures adequately the role of culture in national varieties of capitalism, because they say little about the material basis for human existence, and thus the connection between capitalism and the contents of our thoughts about the world.

Chapter 3 outlines an alternative, neo-Gramscian framework, utilizing the conceptual apparatus provided by Antonio Gramsci's discussions of "common sense". It is argued that in all aspects of life common sense shapes how humans make sense of the situation they find themselves in. The aim is to chart theoretically the journey made by common sense from the conceptions of the world in everyday life to its embodiment in national institutions in European varieties of capitalism. I do this through considering the material structure of common sense, the role of organic intellectuals, the versions of common sense promoted by different social groups, the different versions of common sense inscribed into the state apparatus, and the necessary international element of any version of common sense.

Chapter 4 provides an overview of the historical trajectories of the Dutch and German political economies. The 1980s and 1990s in the two countries, and the analysis provided by the varieties of capitalism literature – especially its utilization of the concepts of social learning and path-dependence – are concentrated on. I outline how the Wassenaar and Alliance for Jobs processes are excellent illustrations of, respectively, social learning and path-dependence. Nevertheless, I argue that although the literature is thorough and comprehensive in its *description* of the trajectories of the Dutch and German political economies, an alternative framework is necessary for *analysing* the trajectories. Only when armed with a neo-Gramscian approach can the role of consensus in the Dutch and German varieties of capitalism be adequately explained.

Chapter 5 utilizes interview data, allied with the theoretical framework outlined in Chapter 3, to argue that Dutch actors share the assumption of economic vulnerability, providing an anchor for the different versions of common sense that exist in the Netherlands. As a result, there is considerable overlap between the different versions, and thus considerable potential for a synthesis of these versions in a consensus on how to overcome economic difficulties. I concur with the varieties of capitalism literature that Wassenaar is an excellent example of consensus formation, but go further by arguing that Wassenaar also witnessed the asymmetric exchange of concessions between capital and labour. In short, Wassenaar was capital's moment of power in the Netherlands, with the trade unions forced to acquiesce reluctantly to wage moderation and, subsequently, to reforms such as the flexibilization of the labour market.

Chapter 6 also utilizes interview data, allied with the theoretical framework outlined in Chapter 3, to argue that in contrast to the Netherlands there was less potential for synthesis between the different versions of common sense in Germany. Moreover, this inability to forge a consensus on how to overcome economic difficulties was driven by the different views on economic "reality". Again, I concur with the varieties of capitalism literature that the Alliance for Jobs process is an excellent example of consensus not being formed, but go further by showing how German trade unions were more able to demand the symmetric exchange of concessions than their counterparts in the Netherlands. Nevertheless, the growing transnationalization of German capital in the 1990s made it increasingly possible that its new (modified) version of common sense would prevail post-Alliance for Jobs.

Chapter 7 discusses the post-2001 period, which appears to pose a significant challenge to the case established in the previous chapters. The Dutch seemed to abandon consensus in the face of economic crisis, and the German institutional machinery was mobilized in an unexpected way in order to implement a programme of substantial reform. I argue that both countries actually exhibited greater continuity than has been perceived. In the Netherlands there was a swift return to consensus by acquiescence in 2003–4, and the apparent consensus which facilitated the Agenda 2010 reforms in Germany quickly unravelled. I conclude that while it is possible for common sense opinions to fragment in the Netherlands and cohere in Germany, over time the reverse is more likely to be the case.

Chapter 8 summarizes the book's argument before discussing its relevance for the IPE literature as a whole. In particular, I take issue with how the literature has received and applied Robert W. Cox's work, appropriating his writings on modes of thinking while simultaneously rejecting his work on production, class and social forces. In consequence, "critical" scholarship has come to be defined as, and defines itself as, an enquiry into the role of ideas in constituting interests, identities and institutions. This separation of ideas from the conditions out of which they emerged ignores the material basis for existence, enabling such scholars to regard historical materialism as useful only when subsumed into other frameworks or, more brazenly, as dogma. I contend, in contrast, that historical materialism is central to the study of capitalist societies and must be taken seriously in its own right.

# 2
# Culture in the Literatures

> Culture is one of the two or three most complicated words in the English language. This is so partly because of its intricate historical development, in several European languages, but mainly because it has now come to be used for several important concepts in several distinct intellectual disciplines and in several distinct and incompatible systems of thought. (Williams 1983: 87).

As stated in the previous chapter, the route to an adequate conceptualization of the role of consensus in the trajectories of European varieties of capitalism is via an adequate conceptualization of the role of culture. Therefore, this chapter will be concerned with culture. As can be seen from the above opinion of one of the most respected commentators on culture, there is substantial disagreement about what "culture" is, with many different emphases and loci. Perhaps unsurprisingly, this chapter will not cover the multitude of positions and conceptualizations in their entirety, instead focusing on those literatures of potential relevance for the conceptualization of culture articulated and defended from Chapter 3 onwards.

The first half of the chapter focuses on the varieties of capitalism literature and, given that my position departs from this literature, it will receive a more in-depth treatment than those considered in the second section (although the sections themselves are of similar length). As argued in the previous chapter, the varieties of capitalism literature shares many common elements across seemingly contrasting positions. The paradigmatic Varieties of Capitalism framework, as espoused by Peter Hall and David Soskice (2001b), has dominated the debate in recent years, but the contributions to the literature as a whole cannot be reduced to this standpoint. That having been said, while often critical of the Varieties of Capitalism framework, the literature as a whole shares many of its weaknesses – chief of which is a problematic view of the relationship between state and society. The neglect of the fact that the institutions are rooted in the society they are part of, a byproduct of the neglect of capitalism as a particular type of economic system, renders the literature unable to accord culture an integral role in the trajectories of national varieties of capitalism.

I conclude that we need a conceptualization of culture which captures how capitalism shapes and gives content to the thoughts humans hold about the world, plus how national institutions are produced and reproduced over time in capitalist societies. To this end, the second half of the chapter reviews a range of frameworks for their ability to satisfy these requirements. Five broad perspectives on "culture" are identified: political culture; webs of meaning in the local context; cultural embeddedness and cultural constitution; culture industries in and the culturalization of "late capitalism"; and power. I contend that none of these positions captures adequately the role of culture in national varieties of capitalism, because they say little about the material basis for human existence. I conclude by arguing that the neo-Gramscian framework, anchored in Gramsci's discussions of "common sense", developed in the next chapter will be able to conceptualize culture in the manner demanded by this chapter. Only then will it be possible to turn to the role of consensus in the trajectories of European varieties of capitalism.

## The varieties of capitalism literature

The varieties of capitalism literature is indebted to many different sources of inspiration, yet some common themes can be identified. For example, the differences across capitalist countries of similar levels of national income in terms of (for example) state size, the role of organized labour and system of political representation – especially after World War II – means that there is an emphasis on the national varieties of capitalism as opposed to the systemic differences between, for instance, capitalism and communism (for the classic statement see Shonfield 1965). These differences are often driven by the dissimilarities in the institutional configurations governing the national variations, though there is also a parallel tendency to categorize these variations into a few broad "types" of capitalism. Following on from this, there is an often implicit, but notable, normative commitment to the more "humane" versions of capitalism, chief of which are the varieties of capitalism in continental Europe (in particular, northern Europe), where one can find (relative to countries such as the US) generous welfare states, low levels of inequality and significant political participation by organized labour (Albert 1993).

Though important prior to the 1990s, the literature came to prominence through its intervention in the globalization debate, arguing against the assertions that, with the collapse of the Soviet Union and the greater mobility of capital, all economies would converge on a liberal US-style model of political economy (for a review of this debate, see Bruff 2005). The varieties of capitalism literature's argument is two-fold: one, the postulated globalization of the world economy is wildly exaggerated, as is the death of national varieties of capitalism (Berger and Dore 1996; Boyer and Drache 1996); and two, even if the claims were not exaggerated, the historical experiences of small, open economies have demonstrated the possibilities for continued national distinctiveness through the intelligent utilization of national institutions (Katzenstein 1985, 2003).

In addition to this, the varieties of capitalism literature benefited from the rise to prominence of "new institutionalist" perspectives. Like the varieties of capitalism literature, new institutionalism contains within it a number of positions that appear contrasting but in fact share many common assumptions. For example, there is a shared emphasis on the importance of institutions in a relational sense, shaping but not determining both the strategies of actors and also their goals. Institutions thus constrain and also enable the possibilities for change (Peter Hall 1986; Thelen and Steinmo 1992). Furthermore, new institutionalism is best viewed as a series of middle-range theoretical perspectives which achieve a balance between grand theory and empirical research (Campbell and Pedersen 2001: 268–9), since case studies will be required in order to illustrate or test the given model developed (see Campbell and Pedersen (2001) for a discussion of how the competing perspectives can be united around this interplay between empirical research and theoretical reflection).

New institutionalism is a laudable shift away from the behaviouralist- and modernization-inspired approaches dominant in political science in the decades after World War II. These frameworks 'often obscured the enduring socioeconomic and political structures that mold behavior in distinctive ways in different national contexts.' (Thelen and Steinmo 1992: 1), rendering them ahistorical and insensitive to difference. New institutionalism's incorporation of power asymmetries, ideas, agency, unintended outcomes and cross-national institutional diversity has expanded greatly the possibilities for more complex and localized yet lucid analysis. Its attractiveness as a basis for analysing varieties of capitalism has made it possible for scholars from different "schools" of institutionalism to cross-reference each other. For instance, we find a prominent exponent of state-centric historical institutionalist analysis, Linda Weiss, praising the Varieties of Capitalism framework (Weiss 2003), which builds on game theory insights from a firm rather than a state perspective. We also find Fritz Scharpf and Vivien Schmidt, rational choice and discursive institutionalists respectively, synthesizing their approaches in the landmark *Welfare and Work* volumes (Scharpf and Schmidt 2000a, 2000b; Scharpf 2000; Schmidt 2000), which also contained contributions from scholars of various shades of new institutionalism (for instance, Rhodes 2000; Levy 2000; Hemerijck and Schludi 2000).

In consequence, the varieties of capitalism literature, especially since it developed a more precise theoretical outlook – see in particular the Scharpf and Schmidt (2000a, 2000b), Peter Hall and Soskice (2001a), and Streeck and Thelen (2005a) volumes – has combined adroitly its stances on globalization and new institutionalism to make some significant interventions in the debate on the trajectories of European varieties of capitalism. Later in this section I will critique the literature, but for now I will outline what it espouses in relation to European varieties of capitalism:

- Economic performance continues to be good in many European varieties of capitalism. This is particularly the case with regard to small European countries, which are often ignored by commentaries arguing for the declining effectiveness of European-style capitalisms. One specific example is the recovery of the Swedish economy since the early 1990s: while there appears to be agreement that the unique Swedish "model" may no longer exist, it is still a successful capitalism based on high taxation and government spending, significant trade union involvement, low income inequality and a generous welfare state. In other words, there are multiple pathways to economic success (Swank 2002; Steinmo 2003; Auer 2000).

- The domestic institutional environment plays a critical role in the evolution of national varieties of capitalism. Therefore, while it is true that the inability of the national political economy to adapt to contemporary challenges and opportunities underpins poor economic performance, such inability is strongly linked to how different domestic institutions interact with each other. Furthermore, any adaptation is likely to take place along nationally distinctive lines, since the institutional environment shapes how actors respond to contemporary challenges and opportunities. Thus the same set of institutions can be at one point in time unresponsive to change and path-dependent, and at another point responsive to change and the basis for social learning – an example being the turnaround in the Dutch economy's fortunes in the 1980s and 1990s (Visser and Hemerijck 1997; Weiss 1998; Campbell and Pedersen 2007).
- Key to whether the institutional environment is responsive to contemporary challenges and opportunities or not is the crucial relationship between the labour market and the welfare state in European varieties of capitalism. Briefly, the ability of especially central and northern European varieties of capitalism to maintain their welfare states depends to a significant extent on the performance of the labour market. The high floor to wages (due to the emphasis on low inequality) makes it difficult, after a period of higher unemployment in particular, for those on benefits to re-enter the labour market as they are unattractive to employers. Consequently, an insider/outsider dynamic is entrenched, which in the long-term will allow the costs of maintaining the welfare state to outrun the revenues needed to pay for it. Thus the present and future viability of European varieties of capitalism is an open empirical question that is heavily contingent on the effectiveness of the labour market–welfare state nexus. While some scholars emphasize the resistance of welfare programmes to reform (Pierson 1994, 2001), the majority argue that this resistance is declining (van Kersbergen 2000) and that a positive rather than dysfunctional

labour market–welfare state interaction is necessary for the European alternative to US-style capitalism to remain in existence (Hemerijck 2002; Rhodes 1998).

- Finally, a core focus of many scholars, as a result of the emphasis on domestic institutions and the labour market–welfare state nexus, are those domestic institutions which are responsible for the management of this nexus. Therefore, the interaction between the state and the social partners – the trade unions and the employers' associations – in corporatist bargaining processes is at the heart of analyses of European varieties of capitalism. This is the case if the scholar adopts a firm- or production regime-based approach (Estevez-Abe *et al.* 2001) or a politics- or state-based framework (Green-Pedersen 2002). The starting point and locus of analysis may differ, but what that analysis encompasses is strikingly similar across the literature. In essence, countries with fruitful and positive interaction between the tripartite actors – based on a consensus about economic and social policy goals – will in the long-term be more capable of maintaining their European variety of capitalism than those countries characterized by tripartite disagreement and conflict (Hemerijck *et al.* 2000; Kitschelt and Streeck 2003).

It can be seen why the varieties of capitalism literature stresses the need for careful analysis which allows for the possibilities of both institutional stability and change. However, to reiterate the point, for the literature the impact of economic, social and political change makes conditions of consensus a pre-requisite for institutional adaptation to such change – otherwise, the institutions become (or remain) dysfunctional and (continue to) harm economic performance. The importance of consensus for European varieties of capitalism is made clear by Visser and Hemerijck (1997: 67) in their discussion of social learning:

> The institutional format of corporatist governance entails a number of positive effects on learning. These are institutional stability, lengthy time limits, "pacta-sunt-servanda", shared understandings, and a problem-solving style of joint decision-making. The corporatist response to policy failure is founded, in Hirschman's typology, in the development of "voice" (Hirschman, 1970). Participants are obliged to explain, give reasons and take responsibility for their

> decisions and strategies to each other and to the rank and file, but at times also with respect to the public at large; to deliberate a wider range of policy issues; and to take consideration of alternative policy avenues.

Visser and Hemerijck, and many others in the literature, thus modify Peter Hall's (1993) argument on social learning. Hall postulated that processes of policy change can be distinguished between three orders of change. First order change refers to 'the process whereby instrument settings are changed in the light of experience and new knowledge, while the overall goals and instruments of policy remain the same' (278), second order change to 'when the instruments of policy as well as their settings are altered in response to past experience even though the overall goals of policy remain the same' (279), and third order change to 'simultaneous changes in all three components of policy: the instrument settings, the instruments themselves, and the hierarchy of goals behind policy.' (279). Hall, at least in this pre-Varieties of Capitalism formulation, allowed for the role of ideas at the third level of change in particular, because institutions as an explanatory variable lose their salience when the ends *and* means of policy are being questioned. The new direction of state policy is "up for grabs", and competing paradigms attempt to fill the vacuum.

Visser and Hemerijck (1997) argue that while instructive, this approach to social learning was based on an analysis of the Thatcherite transformation of British economic policy: the state in many other political systems possesses more limited powers than in the single-party, unitary, weakly constrained case found in Britain. Therefore, prior to third order change in the UK, policymaking tends to be a closed and exclusionary process. Policymaking in corporatist systems of inclusive negotiation, on the other hand, is from the start a more open process because of the stronger links with society (on account of the involvement of labour and employer representatives), making it possible for the existing institutional framework to incorporate new ideas and realize a third order shift to new policy paradigms without losing its overall salience.

In other words, significant change can be realized through the construction of a consensus on how to proceed, rather than through the imposition of a new settlement, as was the case in Britain. Nevertheless, it is also acknowledged in the literature that policymakers 'are seriously constrained in their capacity to act by prevailing institutions, policy legacies, past commitments of standing programs, and the numerous actors in different policy areas, pursuing multiple and often contradictory goals.' (Hemerijck and Schludi 2000: 132). Moreover, in corporatist systems of governance it is likely that at least some of these groups will hold a veto over proposed changes through their position in the institutional environment (Scharpf 1988). Hence the strong emphasis in the literature on comparative research, which encourages the scholar to be sensitive to cross-country differences while also attempting to draw more general conclusions.

## Varieties of capitalism, varieties of neo-pluralism

Intense debates have taken place within the literature on several key issues. For instance, the Varieties of Capitalism framework, which postulates the existence of two distinct, internally consistent "types" of capitalism (Liberal Market Economies (LMEs) and Coordinated Market Economies (CMEs)) that contain countries who remain with this type over time, has catalysed discussions on how many varieties of capitalism exist, whether we should view the varieties we identify as pure or hybrid varieties, whether a country can move from one variety to another over time, and if internal consistency (termed "institutional complementarity") really exists even if the bifurcation into two types is accepted (see Peter Hall and Soskice 2003; Hay 2004; Höpner 2005; Crouch 2005; Kenworthy 2006; Campbell and Pedersen 2007; Hancké *et al.* 2007).

Unfortunately, this has resulted in the trees assuming a far more important status than the wood itself, with the shared weaknesses among the participants in the debate obscured from view. Indeed, there are implicit, unspoken assumptions shared across the debates. These assumptions revolve around a problematic conceptualization of the relationship between state and society, the consequence of which is to cut off society from the institutions which govern it. As will be explained below, the focus on the institutional configurations at the expense of the society in which they are rooted neglects the *social content* of the national capitalisms. For this reason the literature repeats the errors made by protagonists in earlier debates on the relationship between state and society in capitalist democracies. What we are talking about, in essence, is *varieties of neo-pluralism*.

This may seem a controversial point given my earlier statement that the interaction between the state and the social partners – the trade unions and the employers' associations – in corporatist bargaining processes is at the heart of analyses of European varieties of capitalism. Therefore, it needs to be made clear why the oft-discussed differences between pluralism and corporatism are of little significance when it comes to inspecting the wood rather than the trees. Classically, pluralism focuses on a multitude of interest groups contending for influence on the state, which in turn is neutral and limited in power because power is dispersed throughout society (acting instead as an arbiter of the competing claims), and corporatism emphasizes the importance of a few key interest groups in the policymaking process – which for social and economic policy would be the employers' associations and the trade unions. This is because power is not dispersed equally across society, and the state will include in the policymaking process those groups it deems necessary for the formulation and execution of policy.

This may seem an insurmountable difference in perspective, but the shifts made by pluralism three decades ago and corporatism in the past decade have rendered many of their differences, at least with regard to political economy analysis, negligible. For example, works such as Lindblom (1977) and Dahl (1989) incorporated a more elitist perspective on political participation, which brought the pluralist literature – under its new rubric of neo-pluralism – closer to corporatism's emphasis on the role of key interest groups in the decision-making process. Nevertheless, it may seem that corporatism's inclusion of organized labour is a step too far for pluralism, which in its classical phase highlighted the importance of a myriad of interest groups and thus placed less emphasis on trade unions, and in its elitist phase focused on the strength of business *vis-à-vis* organized labour. Indeed, one of the most famous positions adopted by neo-pluralism is its postulation of the privileged position of business in capitalist democracies (Lindblom 1977).

In the past decade, though, the corporatist literature has moved towards neo-pluralism: there is now a greater stress on the power of business *vis-à-vis* labour. Furthermore, there is also general agreement, as mentioned earlier, that many of the social democratic elements of European political economies are under strain and need to be reformed in order to survive in any form. There is a consensus that securing the future viability of European varieties of capitalism necessitates changes such as increased labour market flexibility, a welfare state more attuned to the needs of the labour market, and so on – technocratic positions which, even if by default, give capital greater weighting than labour. The largely positive writings on social pacts between the social partners in the name of greater national competitiveness and growth, which often entailed substantial concessions from the trade unions – such as labour market flexibilization – in return for the maintenance of tripartite arrangements, are emblematic of the twin emphasis on business power and the desirability of partial liberalization of European varieties of capitalism (termed "competitive corporatism" by Martin Rhodes (1998); see also Auer 2000; Green-Pedersen *et al.* 2001; Katzenstein 2003). Indeed, countries where organized labour has been more able to resist making these concessions, or the state has been unwilling or unable to impose reforms on recalcitrant social partners, are often judged negatively (particularly with regard to Germany – see Kitschelt and Streeck 2003; Manow and Seils 2000; Streeck and Hassel 2003).[1]

Having established the growing similarity between pluralism and corporatism, it is now possible to discuss why the varieties of capitalism literature should be seen as little more than an eloquent repetition of the neo-pluralist position. For this we need to direct our attention to how the relationship between state and society in capitalist democracies is conceptualized, or, to put it more bluntly, how the relationship between state and society is *not* conceptualized. For neo-pluralism this manifests itself, as it did with pluralism, in a failure to discuss the state in any depth (see Martin Smith 2006). For the varieties of capitalism literature it is the other way around: comprehensive discussions of national institutions and the role of the state in tripartite negotiations leave society unexplored. For both literatures the root cause of such blind spots is the inability to accord culture an integral role in the trajectories of national political economies. This is a crucial error, for culture is embodied in all human social practice and thus traverses all parts of the social world – including state and society.

An excellent example is Katzenstein's (1985) study of small European capitalisms. He consistently emphasizes the importance of the greater economic vulnerability faced by small capitalisms as compared to larger countries. This not only means that certain policy biases are built into the system – for example, favouring free trade over protectionism – but also that national institutions have a crucial role in compensating domestic economic and social actors struggling to cope with economic change the country has little or no control over. The most effective way of doing this is to institutionalize political and social conflict through bringing interest groups inside the arena for collective action. There is a particularly inclusive and consensual pattern to how this is done in small countries, which Katzenstein terms "democratic corporatism", and it is characterized by:

> an ideology of social partnership expressed at the national level; a relatively centralized and concentrated system of interest groups; and voluntary and informal coordination of conflicting objectives through continuous political bargaining between interest groups, state bureaucracies and political parties. (32).

For Katzenstein the system of democratic corporatism is characterized by a 'culture of compromise' (*ibid.*). However, he also asserts that small state characteristics such as the culture of compromise have developed within the power nexus located in the institutional arrangements (*ibid.*). Thus the tension in the varieties of capitalism literature, between an affirmation *in principle* of the importance of the society the institutions are part of and the retreat *in practice* to the institutions, is expressed particularly clearly in this work. For example, on the one hand he talks of distinctive national identities in small states due to the perception of smallness (208), the self-dramatization of smallness expressed by those he interviewed (32), and, as stated above, the ideologies of social partnership; on the other, he believes that 'the essence of democratic corporatism lies in its alignment of a territorially based parliamentary system of representation with a particular *functional representation* of interest groups.' (137; emphasis added). A key consequence is the conflation of culture with institutional norms.

However, the location of the explanations within the national institutional environment – ostensibly done because it is only here that actors and ideas can find an organizational means of expression which enables them to have an influence on political, economic and social outcomes – does not cater sufficiently for the integral role of culture in national political economies. If we are interested in institutions as a historical force then we need to know both what conditions gave rise to them in the first place and in what conditions they are reproduced over time. And although it is possible to incorporate both state and society into the theoretical framework while maintaining a focus on national institutions, as will be detailed in the next chapter, this is impossible for the varieties of capitalism literature. For example, Visser and Hemerijck (1997: 182) argue that processes such as welfare state reform require:

> the construction of a political will and long-term commitments [that is, a consensus], built on norms of trust and networks of civic engagement, in order to overcome the inevitable opposition of groups who will lose.

Furthermore, Visser argues that '[c]oncertation often begins with a shared awareness of vulnerability' (2001: 229), which, in turn, is the basis for a consensus. But if we begin to discuss the relevance of "political will" and the "awareness of vulnerability", then we must examine how they are constructed and why certain "wills" and "awarenesses" emerge and others do not. The varieties of capitalism literature is restricted to studying the emergence and perpetuation of wills and awarenesses within institutions. So where do the ideas come from in the first place? To repeat, the presence or absence of consensus depends on interactions *within* the institutional environment. How national institutions are produced and reproduced over time is not considered.

Through this abstention from the crucial issue of how national institutions are produced and reproduced over time, the varieties of capitalism literature commits two errors. Firstly, it ignores the fact that institutions are rooted in the society they are part of. In contrast, *culture is integral to the trajectories of national political economies.* Secondly, it neglects the fact that we live in capitalist societies: this particular means of organizing our material basis of existence saturates our thoughts about the world. Hence *culture is essentially capitalist in content, as are national institutions.* Therefore, culture is not just integral to the trajectories of national political economies; its social content makes it integral in particular ways. As a result, for a framework to provide the theoretical tools necessary for analysing the trajectories of European varieties of capitalism, it must be able to do two things. One, capture how capitalism shapes and gives content to the thoughts humans hold about the world; two, conceptualize how national institutions are produced and reproduced over time in capitalist societies.

To this end, the second half of the chapter reviews a range of frameworks for their ability to satisfy these requirements. I assess five broad perspectives on culture in the social science literatures: political culture; webs of meaning in the local context; culture industries in and the culturalization of "late capitalism"; culture's embedding and constitutive elements; and power. The different perspectives will be considered in turn, though at times they will be compared and contrasted.

## Political culture

> Surveying the topic of political culture...the diligent student is chastened by the amplitude of its definitions, usages, and functions within political inquiry. Political culture has been used as a "conceptual umbrella" covering perceptions, beliefs, and values concerning everything political...At a methodological level, political culture has also been used in a wide variety of ways...The time has come to take stock, to attempt to put the various definitions, approaches and methodologies into an organized framework. (Lane 1992: 362–3).

One of the ironies of Ruth Lane's important contribution is that she inadvertently articulated the commonalities in the political culture literature that had always existed, but had been obscured by battles over the empirical application of the political culture concept. Through highlighting the lineage of political culture from the classic early texts (Almond and Verba 1963; Pye and Verba 1965; Lipset 1960) to modern analyses (Wildavsky 1987; Eckstein 1988; and subsequently Lockhart 2001), Lane demonstrated the unity in diversity that characterizes this literature. Broadly speaking:

> Political culture theory defines political culture in this fourfold way: (1) It consists of the set of subjective orientations to politics in a national population or subset of a national population. (2) It has cognitive, affective, and evaluative components; it includes knowledge and beliefs about political reality, feelings with respect to politics, and commitments to political values. (3) The content of

> political culture is the result of childhood socialization, education, media exposure, and adult experiences with governmental, social, and economic performance. (4) Political culture affects political and governmental structure and performance – constrains it, but surely does not determine it. The causal arrows between culture and structure and performance go both ways. (Almond 2000: 10).

In response to criticisms since its original formulation in the 1950s and 1960s (see Rogowski 1974; Eckstein 1988), Almond concedes that political culture can change over time, though he is at pains to emphasize the persistence of basic political beliefs across different societies. The solution he proposes is to disaggregate political culture in order to gain greater analytical purchase, though in reality this is just an elaboration of the original formulation that political cultures are heterogeneous while also containing a predominant culture type (Almond and Verba 1963). Indeed, Pye's (1965) identification of hierarchy-equality, liberty-coercion and loyalty-commitment continuums has much in common with later typologies found in Inglehart (1977) – for instance, collectivism-individualism – and Douglas and Wildavsky (1982) – for example, individualism-hierarchy.

Thus what we have seen since the original formulation is a stretching of the political culture concept, which now incorporates the possibilities for change among political cultures and the coalescence of multiple and competing subjective orientations towards politics at the national and sub-national level. Nevertheless, such broadening does not alter the core goal of categorizing the country as a cultural type without losing the complexities inherent to that society. In addition, this increasing sophistication does not hide the underlying continuity: the literature is interested in systematically quantifying and/or categorizing human behaviour, mostly achieved through surveys of individual attitudes which are then aggregated, in order to specify in observable and transparent ways the cross-national cultural differences. Moreover, the same categories are applied to a variety of countries despite their differences, forcing various cultural contexts into at most a few types. Therefore, the impulse to make generalizations based on systematic codification – as expressed particularly clearly by Lipset (1960) and Rokkan (1966) – remains strong, whether quantitative anlysis is employed or not (see Lockhart 1999 for a qualitative analysis based on the same impulse).

This is problematic in many ways, because the desire to construct systematic categories that can be applied across different societies inevitably leads to two consequences: one, a tendency to engage in a Dutch auction of new typologies or variables which (allegedly) explain more than previous formulations; and two, more importantly, the obscuring of both local particularities and systemic factors moulding the different countries' cultures. With regard to the second consequence, local particularities are obscured due to the categories imposed on them, for the categories cannot account for the differences within cultures. For example, how would one classify France, with its ideals of fraternity and equality, plus a generous welfare state and relative income equality, co-existing with a strongly elitist educational system, systemic gender discrimination and assimilationist attitude to immigrants?

In addition, the role of capitalism in shaping and giving content to cultural attitudes is conspicuous by its absence. This is curious in view of the consideration given to the role of economic factors, even if it relates to economic performance and nothing more, in both the more programmatic aspects of the literature (see Verba 1965; Almond 2000; Inglehart 1977) as well as the substantive – a case in point being West Germany's political stability after World War II resting on a successful economy (Rogowski 1974; Eckstein 1988; Lockhart 1999). Nonetheless, the economic system is never addressed, making it impossible for the literature to make a direct link between capitalism and culture. Therefore, while on the surface the literature meets the challenge of capturing the social content of the thoughts we hold about the world, the categories laboriously constructed are in fact devoid of social content. There is a neglect of the 'decisive nucleus of economic activity' at the heart of capitalist societies (Gramsci 1971: 161), to the detriment of the literature's potential to conceptualize culture adequately.

## Webs of meaning in the local context

> The concept of culture I espouse, and whose utility the essays below attempt to demonstrate, is essentially a semiotic one. Believing, with Max Weber, that man is an animal suspended in webs of significance he himself has spun, I take culture to be those webs, and the analysis of it to be therefore not an experimental science in

> search of law but an interpretive one in search of meaning. (Geertz 1973a: 5).

Despite Geertz's connection of Max Weber's work with his own, the position he articulated was in fact at considerable variance from Weber's. As Ann Swidler (2000: 271) notes, 'the effect of the Geertzian revolution...has been to break with the Weberian problematic. Rather than looking at the ideas that motivate individual actors (or even collections of individual actors), Geertz's followers examine public symbols and ritual experiences'. Thus the research question should not 'focus on powerful, internalized beliefs and values held by individual actors (what I call culture from the "inside out") [but] culture as operating in the contexts that surround individuals, influencing action from the "outside in".' (*ibid.*: 269–70). Therefore, while the political culture literature stresses the need to study, and aggregate, the subjective experiences of individuals in their particular society, the anthropological approach highlights the intersubjective.

What Raymond Williams (1981) defined as an approach which posits the whole social order as constitutive of all other social activities within that society, this perspective on culture gives us potentially valuable theoretical tools. For instance, the production and reproduction of institutions over time are clearly and explicitly rooted in the webs of meaning prevalent in the local context. Because culture 'is the totality of all that characterises us...[this] includes...the structures and institutions we fashion [and] the concepts and ideas we develop' (Richardson 2001: 2). Moreover, because culture is locally specific, this perspective complements research studying cross-national cultural differences; and, importantly for this book, because institutions are viewed not as culture but as culturally constituted phenomena they are a useful basis for making such cross-national comparisons (Ross 2000; cf. Spiro 1984).

In addition, this perspective gives insights into how the integral role played by culture in the trajectory of the political economy could be conceptualized. Geertz (1973a) cautions against searching forever deeper into the society being studied, for cultural analysis will always be incomplete: as an outsider it will be impossible to absorb every cultural nuance and convention. Instead, the researcher should thickly describe the context being studied, since this will allow him or her 'to support broad assertions about the role of culture in the construction of collective life by engaging them exactly with complex specifics.' (28). Among the complex specifics are:

> the hard surfaces of life...the political, economic, stratificatory realities within which men [sic] are everywhere contained – and with the biological and physical necessities on which those surfaces rest...[We should] train such analysis on such realities and such necessities in the first place.' (30).

Despite this discussion of economic realities, which seemingly allows for the incorporation of a direct link between capitalism and culture, the anthropological approach has its limitations. For instance, the emphasis on historically transmitted meanings, which are intersubjectively held in the local context, privileges a search for semiosis rather than its material underpinnings. Despite Geertz's assertions that culture should not be aestheticized or reified, with regard to the economic context he does just that. For example, he argues that ideas must 'be carried by powerful social groups to have powerful social effects... They have to be institutionalized in order to find not just an intellectual existence in society, but, so to speak, a material one as well.' (1973b: 314). However, this ignores how the powerful social groups and the ideas they support came into existence in the first place. As stated earlier, Geertz would like us to focus in the first instance on complex specifics such as economic reality, but surely this means that economic reality, the material basis for existence, shapes who the powerful social groups are and which ideas become institutionalized?

If this is the case, then the anthropological approach provides us with anything but a direct link to capitalism. It neglects the importance of the material basis for existence – even if this means simply the ability to subsist – for shaping the range and content of the intersubjectively held ideas (see also Crehan 2002, especially 172–207). In other words, the social content of the meanings and ideas, and thus the social content of institutions produced and reproduced over time, can be only partially explained. While the anthropological approach is certainly instructive in several ways – for example, the emphasis on local webs of meaning is relevant for considering nationally intersubjective attitudes about the political economy in European varieties of capitalism – a closer assessment of the relationship between capitalism and culture is necessary for us to make any further progress.

## Cultural embeddedness and cultural constitution

> [T]he arguments developed below rest on two core precepts within economic sociology: that economic arrangements are *embedded* in social contexts, and *instituted* through formal and informal rules, conventions of conduct and exchange, systems of politics and regulation (Tonkiss 2006: ix; original emphasis).

Thus Tonkiss' attempt to update economic sociology to take into account the contemporary nature of capitalism and capitalist societies remains faithful to the influential economic sociology agenda that has been developed over the past three decades (for example, see Granovetter 1985; Swedberg 2003; for overviews of the literature see Granovetter and Swedberg 2001; Smelser and Swedberg 1994). Taking its cue from Max Weber's (1930, 1949) emphasis on the difference and interplay between formal and substantive rationality – that is, the instrumental, goal-driven, maximizing behaviour of economic actors in the market system and the values and systems of meaning that provide the social context for economic action – and from Karl Polanyi's (1944, 1992) focus on the role of non-market institutions in both creating capitalism and also preventing it from sowing the seeds of its own destruction, the economic sociology literature faces in two directions. One, capitalism is a system of market-based economic relations embedded in wider non-economic social relations that shape economic self-interest in accordance with societal norms, networks and values (social/cultural embeddedness); two, the economic relations themselves are socially constituted arenas of action because the institutions which regulate markets – for example, labour market institutions – are the product of social processes (socially/culturally constitutive).[2]

DiMaggio (1994: 28) stresses that economic sociologists tend to emphasize embeddedness over constitution or vice versa, but it is rare to see one take precedence entirely over the other. For instance, Holton (1992: 187) argues that 'culture is simultaneously external and internal to economic life', which he and others (DiMaggio 1990; Alexander 1990) define as the interpenetration of culture and economy. Culture and economy possess their own internal logics and are thus irreducible to each other, but they are only *relatively* autonomous from each other (Parsons' influence is especially apparent here – see Parsons 1949; Parsons and Smelser 1956). So while it is possible for economic sociologists to study how economy shapes culture, the main thrust of the literature is to analyse how economic phenomena are constituted by and embedded in society (Swedberg 1998: 166).

Therefore, the literature's potential contribution to studying how culture is integral to the trajectory of the national political economy is its assertion that 'economic processes have an irreducible "cultural" component.' (DiMaggio 1994: 27). However, the literature is on shakier ground when it comes to *how* economy and culture relate to each other. As Sklair (1997: 242) remarks in his review of the first edition of the monumental *Handbook of Economic Sociology* volume (Smelser and Swedberg 1994):

> [e]mbeddedness must mean something more than the trivial statement that the economy is embedded in society...If you cannot have a phenomenon without its context and the context is the whole of society, then how do you distinguish analytically, let alone empirically, between the economy and its context?

Sklair is at pains to stress that his question is not meant to be rhetorical, and, indeed, if we search beyond economic sociology for texts which distinguish between economy and society but do so in a more analytically directed way, then we find many examples (such as Habermas 1987; Sayer 2001; Jessop 2002). Unfortunately for the economic sociology literature, these texts introduce a line of argument which is conspicuous by its absence: capitalism as an economic system has had a profound effect on the way in which societies operate and function. This simple reversal of emphasis is ignored by the literature, which renders it unable to analyse critically the economic system it has wrapped in a relatively comfortable, benign, em*bed*ding framework (Sayer 2001: 698). In consequence it is impossible, with the economic sociology framework, to make a direct link between capitalism and the worldviews held by the society in question.[3]

While Swedberg (1998) has made the case for economic sociology incorporating a broader "economy and society" focus as conceived in Weber's later work (Weber 1978), he still, like the rest of the literature, holds on to the desire to discuss in general, uncritical terms the interpenetration of economy and culture. For instance, he states that economic sociology should 'look not only at economic behavior alone, but also at economic phenomena that are influenced by noneconomic phenomena...and at noneconomic phenomena that are influenced by economic phenomena' (163). Moreover, Tonkiss' (2006) praiseworthy attempt to provide a more analytically directed framework merely serves to highlight the potential of other literatures. Therefore, while the economic sociology framework is important in many ways – for example, it makes us aware of the potential for the existence and sustainability of national varieties of capitalism due to the distinctive cultural contexts which undoubtedly exist – a consideration of *capitalism itself* is now required.

## Culture industries in and the culturalization of "late capitalism"

> [B]oth theorists and practitioners...understand markets more in terms of the production and flow of signs than simply the selling of goods, and would place cultural knowledges and skills at the centre of both production and consumption. In fact, the extent of this sense of increasing enculturation of markets can be summarized through the term "dematerialization", a word that covers at least four developments: a shift from the production of material to non-material goods, evidenced in the move from manufacturing to service as core industries; the greater non-material consumption of even material goods, in the form of "commodity aesthetics" and "sign values" constructed through design and promotion; the increasing symbolic mediation of goods through objectified cultural forms (advertising, media, retail spectacles); [and] the increasing centrality of non-material raw materials – information, planning, managerial expertise and corporate culture – in economic processes (Slater and Tonkiss 2001: 179–80).

The above quotation captures nicely the points of convergence within this literature. The dividing line tends to be between those who 'view economic forms through a cultural lens...[and those for whom] contemporary capitalist economies really are more "cultural" than they were.' (Tonkiss 2006: 122). Nevertheless, as can be seen from the above quote, it is more than possible to reconcile the two positions. Indeed, whatever the starting point, there tends to be agreement that 'the economy is increasingly culturally inflected and that culture is more and more economically inflected. Thus the boundaries between the two become more and more blurred' (Lash and Urry 1994: 64).

The integration of the cultural and the economic, be it through the culturalization of the economy or the marketizing of the cultural, is an aspect of "late" or "postmodern" capitalism. Taking its cue from the postindustrial society thesis (cf. Bell 1973), which postulated the shift to a new type of capitalism dominated by service industries and knowledge, the literature coalesced around a key paradox. Put simply, there is first of all the emergence of an increasingly "disorganized" capitalism based on the production and consumption of signs and symbols rather than physical goods, in which differentiated and niche markets serve the individualized interests of consumers – in contrast to the mass product markets found in the Fordist, manufacturing-dominated stage of capitalism. Yet, secondly, there is also the emergence of an internationalized or even globalized economic space due to the way in which signs and symbols can flow around the world with little regard for borders. This weakens not only the ties of production and consumption but also of culture to place, encouraging the rise of a universal global culture – or at least the diluting (or hybridization) of local cultures – in the process. (Lash and Urry 1987, 1994; Castells 1996, 1997, 1998; Appadurai 1996; Tomlinson 1999; du Gay and Pryke 2002).

Key to understanding how this process takes place are the culture industries, which have been instrumental in the culturalization of postindustrial, or "late", capitalism (cf. Jameson 1991; Giddens 1990).[4] Generally conceived as inclusive of the arts – art, literature, theatre, music – the mass media – cinema, radio, television, print and most recently the Internet – and often also sectors such as advertising, marketing and product branding, these industries are central to the production and reproduction of signs, symbols and discourses across space. However, this reveals a significant contradiction at the heart of the literature. Presumably the identification of culture industries means that there is a continued need to differentiate between more overtly economic and more overtly cultural areas of social life; yet at the same time there is an emphasis on at least the blurring of economy and culture and in many cases the abolition of the distinction between the two (see Stuart Hall 1989 – a pronouncement he later distanced himself from for its encouragement of perspectives which abandoned the economic as worthy of study (Stuart Hall 1996d, 1997)).

Indeed, attempts to maintain an integral role for culture in the political economy alongside a partial differentiation between economy and culture are often criticized as "reductionist" (see Gregson *et al.*'s (2001) critique of Sayer (1997b)). Nevertheless, the literature is itself, *in its own terms*, reductionist by way of its consistent reference to culture as a certain set of activities. Moreover, it continues to talk of economy and culture as two distinctive terms of use to social scientists (Ray and Sayer 1999: 4). In consequence, theoretical contortions such as the following are commonplace. Gregson *et al.* (2001) criticize Sayer (1997b) for retaining an analytical and substantive distinction between economy and culture, which they believe to signal a retreat 'to the defence of political economy over culture.' (629). Yet they conclude by calling 'for the articulation of economy and culture on the one hand and the continued theoretical primacy accorded to political economy within it on the other.' (639). In a contribution published a couple of years earlier, Ray and Sayer (1999: 4) make the pithy but justified point that surely this means that cultural studies can be called economic studies instead. I would add that surely this means that *culture* industries are *economic* industries.

Thus the literature on culture industries and the culturalization of late capitalism is unable to examine adequately the link between capitalism and culture due to its simultaneous insistence on capitalism's culturalization *and* the distinctive set of culture industries. And, when this link *is* raised, it is done so with regard to the commodification of the arts and to some extent popular culture, not the wider conceptions held about the political economy. Therefore, while the literature is laudable for its insistence on the integral role of culture in the political economy, and thus highlights effectively the way in which any thoughts about the political economy are shot through with cultural beliefs, values and meanings, the manner in which it conceptualizes the capitalism-culture relationship is flawed.

## Power

> As a consequence of the "cultural turn", all social life must be seen as potentially political where politics is the contestation of the relations of power. (Nash 2001: 77).

The final literature to consider is in many ways radically at odds with the above perspectives. Put simply, culture is power: it should not be naturalized and reified as something which is a fixed, immutable part of the society in question, but instead seen as the outcome and medium of power relations. French theorists such as Michel Foucault and Pierre Bourdieu were prominent in articulating the means by which a negation of the subject takes place (for example, see Foucault 1972, 1977, 1980, 1981; Bourdieu 1984, 1990a, 1990b; Bourdieu *et al.* 1998). For both Foucault and Bourdieu, power relations are central to securing the subject's negation and thus the improbability of social progress. This is despite their different starting points: the former begins from a position of epistemic disruption and thus has a certain affinity with the postmodern emphasis on deconstructing "objective truths", while the latter asserts the importance of economic structures in forming "objective" realities which frame how humans develop their dispositions about the world. Nevertheless, both see the way humans view the social world as the outcome of unequal power relations which, while productive of resistance and struggle against such inequality, nevertheless tend to reproduce themselves, and thus the worldviews, over time.

Hence Foucault's power/knowledge formulation (see Foucault 1980). This argues that power is everywhere rather than being in somebody's or some group's possession, and thus implicated in all aspects of human relations. In addition, while many versions of "the truth" exist at any one point in time, a dominant construction forms a "regime of truth". As a result, what is taken to be objective and truthful is actually historically contingent on the power relations existent in the era in question. A similar account, from a different starting point, can be seen in Bourdieu's "misrecognition" concept, whereby humans reproduce through language and action their structures of domination, because these very structures normalize their existence to the extent that emancipation is not only difficult but also virtually impossible to conceive (see Bourdieu 1990a).

Their emphasis on the closing off of alternative forms of knowledge and thus of alternative forms of human relations is a valuable corrective to accounts which discuss "culture" unproblematically as natural to the country in question. It is a reminder that uncontested "facts of life" in different countries had to *become* facts in order to frame the assumptions which flow from them, and this process of becoming would have inevitably been bound up with the unequal power relations and accompanying struggles at that point in time. Therefore, such facts can be unmade and rendered contestable in the future, making culture a historically contingent set of beliefs, attitudes and meanings that needs to be investigated empirically.

Nevertheless, while this perspective is important for tackling critically the means by which institutions are historically grounded, it is on shakier ground when accounting for change. A crucial consequence of such a thorough treatment of social relations is that the logical conclusion must be that 'human beings are fated to be prisoners of the structures of domination.' (Callinicos 1999: 295). Ironically, Foucault's and Bourdieu's political activism suggests that agency does have a role in society's evolution, and their respective discussions of micro-level resistance (Foucault 1981), and durable rather than determining structures (Bourdieu 1990a), appear to reflect this. However, there is little in their theoretical schema to suggest how this takes place – save for the assertion that it does – leaving one to conclude that any resistances or struggles that exist are the functional response of individuals or groups to their situation rather than as the result of human choice (Callinicos 1999: 274–82, 287–95; see also Bruff forthcoming on Foucault).

Furthermore, Foucault and the Foucauldian literature are unable to account for capitalism. For instance, Griffin (2007: 235) argues that neo-liberal economic discourse is 'intrinsically productive of human subjects, behaviours and meanings', yet in the next sentence she argues that '[s]ystems of economic relations structure the formation of human identity/identities, govern human relations and produce human identity.' While this is internally consistent in the sense that, for Griffin and the Foucauldian literature, economic relations are constituted by power/knowledge regimes, it means that we are backed into a corner. Not only is power ubiquitous but it is also *unqualifiable* (Holub 1992: 29). There is no sense of any 'directedness to power relations' (*ibid.*), as Gramsci and others have theorized, leaving the social content of the power relations, and thus the role of capitalism in shaping any "regimes of truth" about the political economy, unexplored.

Bourdieu attempts to avoid this problem through arguing that in every situation there is a plurality of worldviews, which 'provides a base for symbolic struggles for the power to produce and to impose [on others] a vision of the legitimate world.' (Bourdieu 1990b: 134).

However, through his separation of the objective economic structures and our dispositions which internalize, interpret and act within them, and his emphasis on the imprisoning effect of such structures on the dispositions, he reifies the political economy as devoid of social content – save for (unspecified) economic dynamics. Witness his discussion of homologies between different societal sub-systems which are, ultimately, reducible to the economic at the macro-societal level (Grenfell 2004: 178). As a result, how national institutions are produced and reproduced over time is left unanswered, for the separation of object and subject makes it difficult to account for how different societies are recognizably capitalist without taking precisely the same form across space and time.

Ironically, both Foucault and Bourdieu, and their supporters, place great store in human practice as generative of power relations and thus of the structures and institutions which govern us. However, Foucault does not qualify the ubiquitous power relations because of a neglect of the economic, Bourdieu qualifies them too much through an over-emphasis on the economic, and both rely on their vision of power relations to explain away the outcomes of social conflict and struggle (whether they intended to or not). Hence their inability to account adequately for the production and reproduction of these structures and institutions renders their frameworks only partially successful. Thus an account of power relations which can specify their social (that is, essentially capitalist) content, and the struggles and conflicts that are bound up with such content, will be better placed to analyse why and how national institutions are produced and reproduced over time. That is the task of the next chapter.

## Conclusion

To return to the criteria I outlined at the start of the chapter and also before the discussion of the five perspectives on culture, I argued that the theoretical framework needs to capture how capitalism shapes and gives content to the thoughts humans hold about the world, and conceptualize how national institutions are produced and reproduced over time in capitalist societies. In various ways all of the literatures considered in this chapter, including the varieties of capitalism literature, have been found wanting in this task. It is now time to move beyond them and articulate a perspective which is able to satisfy the criteria I have laid down. The next chapter presents Antonio Gramsci's notion of "common sense" as the conceptual apparatus appropriate for the task at hand. Through doing so, I demonstrate its ability to conceptualize culture's integral role in the trajectory of the national variety of capitalism, which in turn enables me to proceed to the subsequent chapters on the role of consensus in the trajectories of the Dutch and German varieties of capitalism.

# 3
# An Alternative Framework: Gramsci's "Common Sense"

The task of this chapter is to outline an alternative framework for analysing the role of culture in the trajectories of European varieties of capitalism. This framework utilizes the conceptual apparatus provided by Antonio Gramsci's discussions of "common sense", in which the sections of this chapter are anchored. I argue that in all aspects of life common sense is the basis for how humans make sense of the situation they find themselves in. Moreover, political struggle centres on the attempts of each group to render *their* version of common sense the basis for how humans in that society think and act. Therefore, several versions of common sense – or culture – can co-exist at any one time, and it is an open empirical question which version becomes ascendant in the society being studied.

At the same time, such attempts can be successful only if they build on the sedimentations of common sense left behind by previous philosophical currents. Thus the dominant version of common sense in a given society is both 'a relatively rigidified phase of popular knowledge in a given time and place' and 'in continuous transformation, becoming enriched with scientific notions and philosophical opinions that have entered into common circulation.' (Gramsci 1985: 421). As a result, it is possible to conceive theoretically and observe empirically both the changes taking place in the given society and the path-dependent elements which distinguish one society from the next. This process of continuously unfolding but path-dependent change is rooted in the manner in which capitalist social relations are embedded in that society. In other words, we must study the common sense opinions which have emerged from 'the material basis for all social existence' in that particular variety of capitalism (Robert W. Cox 1987: 1).

As demonstrated by the declaration that 'it is on the level of ideologies that men [*sic as throughout*] become conscious of conflicts in the world of the economy', Gramsci (1971: 162) – explicitly following Marx – assigns to ideas a critical role in society's evolution. However, for this to be the case there is a need to move beyond the jumble of ideas expressed in the everyday common sense of the masses. Gramsci emphasized the need for moulding, shaping and clarifying the often incoherent, contradictory and amorphous common sense:

> into a more coherent political theory or philosophical current. This "raising of popular thought" is part and parcel of the process by which a collective will is constructed, and requires extensive work of intellectual organisation (Stuart Hall 1996c: 432).

The task of clarification and organization, through which ideas become a material force, are performed by organic intellectuals, who act as the 'deputies' (Gramsci 1971: 12) and representatives of social groups (and for this book include political parties, trade unions and employers' associations).[1] Their task is one of 'organising social hegemony and state domination' (*ibid.*: 12–13) for the group they represent, and to achieve this there is a need to form a system of alliances, or social formation, with other social groups. In so doing the organic intellectuals strive to convert multiple, heterogeneous positions into a common vision – or hegemonic project – which enables the group to gain the consent of those in alliance with it to lead the formation in the attempt to attain societal hegemony. When this occurs the formation is 'able to form a historical bloc whose unity is organised on the institutional terrain provided by the state' (Bruff 2005: 275), thus attaining political hegemony.

The state's status as the sovereign entity in the society gives the formation a position from which it can attempt to implement its version of common sense. This establishes a new (modified) hegemonic order in that country, altering the state's social content, in the form of policy changes and institutional reconfigurations, in the process. However, this process of modification is fraught with potential contradictions, given the need to maintain the coherence of the historical bloc and the existence of different versions of common sense within the state apparatus that were laid down by earlier historical blocs. In addition, '[i]t is also necessary to take into account the fact that international relations intertwine with these internal relations of nation-states, creating new, unique and historically concrete combinations.' (Gramsci 1971: 182). Thus every national state's social content is the historically and spatially specific outcome of national social and political struggle as conditioned by the international context (Morton 2007a: 170). Such interplay between the vertical and the horizontal forms the basis of national varieties of capitalism (see also Bruff 2007), and, as Chapters 5–7 will demonstrate, is key to understanding the different experiences of consensus formation in the Netherlands and Germany.

The aim of this chapter, then, is to chart theoretically the journey made by common sense from the fragmentary, amorphous, uncritical everyday conceptions of the world in society to its embodiment in national institutions in European varieties of capitalism. Firstly, the importance of common sense as an object of study will be established; secondly, the material structure of common sense and thus its link to capitalist social relations will be outlined; thirdly, the role of organic intellectuals in clarifying and organizing common sense into coherent ideas will be discussed; fourthly, the ideological synthesis of various forms of organized common sense form, it will be argued, the basis of the hegemonic project as promoted by the social formation; fifthly, the state will be identified as the institutional terrain upon which the outcome of social struggles is (temporarily) resolved; sixthly, it will be asserted that identifying the version of common sense being implemented by this juridically sovereign entity is a complex process owing to contemporary and historical societal dynamics; and seventhly, the necessary international element of any version of common sense will be discussed.

This alternative framework enables us to make our point of departure from the varieties of capitalism literature on the issue of consensus. As will be made clear in the chapter, different versions of common sense – that is, different cultures – co-exist both in society and in the state. Thus the key issue is the degree to which these different versions overlap and can be synthesized together in a consensus. This is an empirical question, which for this book concerns the Dutch and German varieties of capitalism, and will be dealt with in Chapters 5–7.

## Common sense and its production

The starting point for a discussion of the importance of common sense is Gramsci's observation that 'all men are "philosophers"' because 'the only "philosophy" is history in action, that is, life itself.' (1971: 323, 357). However, this does not mean that by "philosopher" every human has the capacity to formulate a philosophical treatise; rather, that everyone has opinions about the world and, as incoherent and uncritical as they may be, these conceptions should be treated as *their* philosophy (Simon 1991: 26). Common sense is a complex set of ideas from a variety of sources, from the Stone Age to advanced science, 'which, even in the brain of one individual, is fragmentary, incoherent and inconsequential' (Gramsci 1971: 419). Moreover, these fragments of thought are the deposits and traces of popular philosophy that have built up over time to form a set of fragmentary and uncritical yet solid beliefs.

Despite the negative connotations associated with "common sense" (not least by Gramsci himself, as discussed in Chapter 1), it is essential for all ideologies to encounter and negotiate with this 'cultural terrain' if they are to become part of future common sense (Stuart Hall 1991a: 9). This requires an ability to understand the reasons for such common sense opinions, 'up to and including the most reprehensible' (Sassoon 2006: 8), existing and being supported through the actions of the masses in everyday life. This is essential for any social group seeking to achieve hegemony, for their ideas are then connected to the philosophies articulated, however incoherently, in society. The need to negotiate with the cultural terrain does not mean, however, that there is no room for the modification of common sense by new philosophies. As Gramsci argued, it is in fact both path-dependent and dynamic: to recall the quotation at the start of this chapter, '[c]ommon sense is not something rigid and stationary, but is in continuous transformation, becoming enriched with scientific ideas and with philosophical opinions which have entered into common circulation.' (1985: 421). It is therefore *relatively* rigid, shaping without determining the content of future popular philosophies.

The next step in the theoretical journey, having established the importance of common sense in and of itself, is to demonstrate its material structure (cf. Bieler 2001; Crehan 2002). This is not some essentialist notion based on a metaphysical Marxism, but an acknowledgement of the fact 'that the objective possibilities exist for people not to die of hunger and that people do die of hunger, has its importance, or so one would have thought.' (Gramsci 1971: 360). While such a stark picture was more pertinent to Gramsci's time – at least in comparison to the development of rich European capitalisms after 1945 – it is possible to take this notion beyond his context. As Stuart Hall (1996b: 147; emphasis added) states, '[m]aterial conditions are the *necessary but not sufficient* condition of all historical practice.' This is very different from postulating a deterministic economism which seeks to explain *all* human activity with recourse to material conditions (which postmodernists and others accuse historical materialism of doing).

Furthermore, it is one thing to deny the plausibility of such one-dimensional declarations; it is quite another to deny that there is *any* material basis for making social scientific explanations (Sayer 1997a; McLennan 1996). Indeed, it is essentialist, dogmatic and rather reactionary to deny the possibility of the existence of universal human characteristics such as the need for food, drink, clothing and shelter (Sayer 1997a: 482; Nussbaum 1992). Thus the materialism advanced in this book is historical and not theoretical (cf. Stuart Hall 1997: 32; Gramsci 1996: 153): the need to produce is an essential characteristic of human existence. In addition, as Robert W. Cox (1987: 1) famously asserted, '[p]roduction creates the material basis for all forms of social existence, and the ways in which human efforts are combined in productive processes affect all other aspects of social life'. Therefore, how we organize production is also of great importance, for it signifies how humans have attempted to meet the need to produce:

> Work can be defined as action toward the transformation of nature for the purpose of satisfying human needs and desires. The direct satisfaction of human needs and desires is not work, e.g., eating, conviviality, sexual activity, and sleep. Work is what is done to make these direct satisfactions possible – producing the food, building the physical structures within which actions to satisfy human needs take place, creating the symbols that evoke

> such activity, and building the social institutions and moral codes that channel and regulate this activity. (*ibid.*: 13).

Hence the need to produce, and its organization, are analytically distinct but inextricably linked: the act of production is intimately bound up with, for example, the knowledge and institutions necessary for such production to take place (Robert W. Cox 1989: 39). In consequence, we must consider simultaneously the 'economic in the *first* instance...[because] no social practice or set of relations floats free of the determinate effects of the concrete relations in which they are located' (Stuart Hall 1996a: 45) *and* the ideologies that 'are embedded in collective and communal modes of living.' (Simon 1991: 59). This is what Gramsci (1971: 161) refers to as the 'decisive nucleus of economic activity' at the heart of our means of existence.

Stuart Hall (1996a: 44) argues that '[m]aterial circumstances are the net of constraints, the "conditions of existence" for practical thought and calculation about society.' Therefore, the economic in the first instance is restricted to *determinancy* rather than *determinate* status, 'setting limits for defining the terrain of operations' (*ibid.*: 44). The constraining effects of the need to produce provides for the range and categories of thoughts about the social world, but the content of those thoughts can neither be predicted nor fixed across time and space (*ibid.*: 44–5). What this does is leave space for the role of ideas in societal evolution. Hence production is organized through the ideas which respond to, and attempt to make sense of, the need for such production.

Therefore, the interaction between the "what" and "how" of production, if persistent through time, gives rise to its institutionalization in a mode of production which constitutes the material basis for existence – 'the objective world' for those living in it (Robert W. Cox 1996d: 514). Such objectivity is socially constructed by 'persistent patterns of human activity' (*ibid.*: 514) and, conversely, can be reconstructed by present and future patterns of activity. This is why Gramsci (1971: 445) argued that '[o]bjective always means "humanly objective" which can be held to correspond exactly to "historically subjective": in other words, objective would mean "universal subjective".' This way the possibilities of human activity generating new universal subjectives can be accounted for. However, at the same time Gramsci acknowledged the role of the past in shaping the present and future – societal evolution is both open-ended and path-dependent. This point will be considered in more detail later in the chapter, but for now, considering the material structure of common sense, he contended that:

> every real historical phase leaves traces of itself in succeeding phases, which then become in a sense the best document of its existence. The process of historical development is a unity in time through which the present contains the whole of the past and in the present is realised that part of the past which is "essential" – with no residue of any "unknowable" representing the true "essence". The part which is lost, i.e. not transmitted dialectically in the historical process, was in itself of no import, casual and contingent "dross", chronicle and not history, a superficial and negligible episode in the last analysis. (1971: 409).

The issue to consider next, then, is how we can 'analyse why certain ideas have become predominant at a particular time' (Bieler 2006b: 124). By thinking critically about the role of ideas in capitalist societies, we can keep the material structure of common sense in our mind even as we study closely how conceptions of the world become significant.

## Organic intellectuals and ideology

Gramsci's position on intellectuals is directly connected to his declaration that all men [*sic*] are philosophers. Indeed, he opined:

> There is no human activity from which every form of intellectual participation can be excluded: *homo faber* cannot be separated from *homo sapiens*. Each man...outside his professional activity, carries on some form of intellectual activity, that is, he is a "philosopher", an artist, a man of taste, he participates in a particular conception of the world, has a conscious line of moral conduct, and therefore contributes to sustain a conception of the world or to modify it, that is, to bring into being new modes of thought. (1971: 9; original emphasis).

Again, practical activity, by its very nature, implicates conceptions of the world, thus leading Gramsci to articulate a radically different definition of "intellectual" from the one normally associated with such a term. However, he also states that 'not all men in society have the *function* of intellectuals' (*ibid.*: 9; emphasis added), leading him to modify significantly not just who could be an intellectual but also *what* could be an intellectual. When commenting on Machiavelli's work, which posited the individual prince as the mobilizer of society, Gramsci (*ibid.*: 129) argued:

> The modern prince, the myth-prince, cannot be a real person, a concrete individual. It can only be an organism, a complex element of society in which a collective will, which has already been recognised and has to some extent asserted itself in action, begins to take concrete form. History has already provided this organism, and it is the political party – the first cell in which there came together germs of a collective will tending to become universal and total.

Adam David Morton (2007a: 207–8) has argued that although Gramsci's faith in both the *Communist* Party and the Communist *Party* is perhaps inappropriate for the contemporary era, it is important to appreciate 'the way groups of newspapers or reviews (around which individual and collective interests could converge) were incorporated within Gramsci's notion of the "party"'. (see Gramsci 1985: 390–9). Furthermore, he comments that if the "party" is reconceptualized as a "collective intellectual" (cf. Augelli and Murphy 1997), then the organizational status of the organic intellectual can be broadened to include social movements and research centres of global governance (such as the Zapatistas and the World Economic Forum respectively); also individuals – for instance, Carlos Fuentes in Mexico (see Morton 2003b). In this book, trade unions and employers' associations can be brought under the rubric of "organic intellectual" as well as political parties, given that European varieties of capitalism often have tripartite corporatist structures. As a result, the empirical Chapters (5–7) will focus on these three actors, for they are 'the institutional frameworks within and through which different class fractions [or components] of capital and labour attempt to establish their particular interests and ideas as the generally accepted, or "common sense", view.' (Bieler 2000: 13).

It can be seen that for Gramsci, organic intellectuals are, in contrast to "traditional" intellectuals, fundamentally linked to and thus part of social groups. While a traditional intellectual is a man of letters, an artist, a scholarly philosopher, and so on, organic intellectuals are of crucial importance for the passage of common sense from its humble beginnings to something of (potentially) lasting societal significance, for it is they who enable ideas to become a material force. As such, an organic intellectual's 'mode of being... [consists of] active participation in practical life, as constructor, organiser, "permanent persuader" and not just a simple orator... without which one remains "specialised" and does not become "directive"' (Gramsci 1971: 10).

The notion of direction is key to understanding the role of organic intellectuals (Ives 2004: 75), for it demonstrates that, through their activities, organic intellectuals give a sense of purpose to everyday conceptions of the world while also going beyond them. Nevertheless, their ability to construct, organize and persuade is limited by the constant need to remain in touch with the unadulterated common sense conceptions among the social group they have emerged from. Thus organic intellectuals need to organize and develop the conceptions of the world present in their social group into a more coherent and collective ideology that, through going beyond these conceptions, act as a rallying point for and unifier of different social groups (cf. Robert W. Cox 1981: 128; Crehan 2002: 129–30).

Ideology is necessarily, like common sense, a combination of different ideas. The difference is that the ideology is an *active synthesis* rather than a simple conglomeration of different ideas and conceptions. In order to become organic, that is historically effective, the ideology must articulate 'into a configuration of different subjects, different identities, different projects, different aspirations. It does not reflect, it *constructs* a "unity" out of difference.' (Stuart Hall 1991b: 120; original emphasis). In this sense, what matters is less the truth or falsity of such syntheses and more their 'efficacy in binding together a bloc of diverse social elements and acting as cement or as an agent of social unification' (Simon 1991: 61), converting multiple, heterogeneous positions into a common vision, or *hegemonic project*. Moreover, whether the organic intellectuals are able to synthesize and articulate a historically effective ideology is an open empirical question rooted in political and social practice. Therefore, this conception of ideology is dynamic and open-ended since the construction of a unity out of different elements 'is a linkage which is not necessary, determined, absolute and essential for all time.' (Stuart Hall 1996b: 141).

Three consequences of central significance can be noted: one, the conversion of heterogeneous positions into a hegemonic project is a relatively transitory state of affairs, and thus a *process* which requires reproduction over time, sometimes through utilizing ideas of hitherto secondary importance and often through the incorporation of new ideas (leading to the molecular evolution over time of the vision propagated by the same organic intellectuals); two, new ideas can be appropriated to very different causes owing to their unstable anchoring in society (Gramsci 1971: 339–40), and where they settle is to some extent dependent on the outcome of social and political struggle; three, social groups will attempt, despite the periodic need for ideological reproduction through molecular evolution and despite the unstable societal anchoring of new ideas, to secure the process of change for themselves – that is, social groups will intervene in and attempt to stabilize the process of signification in a way which promotes their own interests (Stuart Hall 1997: 30). Hall terms this '[t]he moment of power' (*ibid.*: 30), for whoever manages to secure the process of change for themselves is likely to be the group which achieves societal hegemony – for a certain period of time at least.

What has yet to tackled is the groups themselves. Therefore, with an eye to the next section, it should now be stated that because human existence is rooted in production and its organization, the leading groups in any capitalist society will be comprised of a major social class (that is, capital or labour). This does not mean that the leading group will contain *all* of the class in question; but it will be comprised of at least part of a major social class. Therefore, the process of signification will be stabilized most powerfully by such groups. In turn, this can be achieved only if the organic intellectuals are able to construct ideologies which square the circle between the economic interests of the class they represent and other, non-economic issues such as morality, security and social reform (Bieler 2002: 581).

Such ability to articulate *and* transcend core economic interests is key to the success of the group in securing societal support for its agenda: indeed, 'the programme of economic reform is precisely the concrete form in which every intellectual and moral reform must present itself' (Gramsci 1971: 133). And should the leading social group build a system of alliances with other social groups which makes it possible for its own particular interests to appear equivalent to the interests of society, then it has the opportunity to achieve hegemony in that society.

## Societal and political hegemony

It is the contention of this section that societal hegemony must be achieved before political hegemony can be secured on the state's institutional terrain (see also Bieler and Morton 2003: 482–3, 492 n.9 – cf. Gramsci 1971: 159–60 – on the tight linkages between civil and political society). Hegemony in this sense is understood as not just 'a structure of values and understandings about the nature of order that permeates a whole society' (Robert W. Cox 1996d: 517), but also the means by which such values and understandings '*connect* with a particular constellation of social forces.' (Stuart Hall 1996a: 43; original emphasis). In other words, the moment of hegemony can be observed through an identification of both the ideas *and* the groups propagating these ideas which have achieved societal leadership in relation to other ideas and groups. Thus hegemony is a relational concept and driven by Gramsci's (1971: 238) famous declaration on the nature of Western European capitalisms:

> In the East the State was everything, civil society was primordial and gelatinous; in the West, there was a proper relation between State and civil society, and when the State trembled a sturdy structure of civil society was at once revealed. The State was only an outer ditch, behind which there stood a powerful system of fortresses and earthworks.

While the coercive aspect of societal leadership is not to be forgotten, Gramsci's emphasis on the need for a "war of position" rather than a "war of manoeuvre" – that is, a struggle in civil society that over time enables the class to build a system of alliances with other social groups – brings to the forefront the notion of consent. This is particularly pertinent to this book's agenda, focusing as it does on the role of consensus in the trajectories of European varieties of capitalism. Hence hegemony is conceptualized as primarily the organization of consent by a class which, in alliance with other social groups, leads society (Simon 1991: 22). A class can achieve national leadership only if it takes 'into account the popular and democratic aspirations and struggles of the people which do not have a necessary class character.' (Simon 1991: 43). Therefore, there is not just a synthesis of ideas but also a synthesis of interests. There is a need for any group aspiring to national leadership to take account:

> of the interests and the tendencies of the groups over which hegemony is to be exercised, and that a certain compromise equilibrium should be formed...bringing about not only a unison of economic and political aims, but also intellectual and moral unity, posing all the questions around which the struggle rages not on a corporate but on a "universal" plane, and thus creating the hegemony of a fundamental social group [Gramsci's term for a major social class] over a series of subordinate groups. (Gramsci 1971: 161, 182).

Compromises and concessions to subordinate groups with which the class is seeking to ally can be offered successfully once it is able to transcend its core economic interests and develop a *national–popular* dimension to its hegemonic project. This enables those groups whose interests are not rooted in class to consent to an alliance and thus bring into being a social formation.[2] If the alliance is formed successfully then societal hegemony could be achieved. Nevertheless, the maintenance of the social formation, and of hegemony should it be achieved, requires a continuous renegotiation of the system of alliances comprising the formation – the consent must be actively constructed and reconstructed over time. This requires considerable skill, for despite the need for leading social groups to transcend their core economic interests, any concessions and compromises 'cannot touch the essential; for though hegemony is ethical–political, it must also be economic, must necessarily be based on the decisive function exercised by the leading group in the decisive nucleus of economic activity.' (Gramsci 1971: 161).

Hence the molecular evolution discussed in the previous section is anchored in the economic. Even if the manner in which the core interests of the class are articulated shifts over time, it can still be traced back to these interests (which, too, may alter over time, as will be demonstrated in Chapters 6 and 7 with regard to German capital). Thus the content of *any* hegemony will be predominantly economic (*ibid.*: 259). This means that while it is possible, and indeed probable, that over time the relative weight of various ideas and groups within the hegemonic project will alter – bringing new, or previously subordinate or secondary, ideas and groups to salience (and vice versa) – there is still a certain directedness to these shifts. Indeed, '[t]he language of consensus is a language of common interests expressed in universalist terms, though the structure of power relations underlying it is skewed in favor of the dominant [that is, economic] groups.' (Robert W. Cox 1996c: 421). The hegemonic social formation thus exhibits neither domination of the subordinate groups by the leading group nor parity between the various groups: there are instead constantly shifting, yet constantly unequal, relations of power within the formation. As a result, the version of common sense the formation espouses is skewed towards the economic interests of the leading group while also taking into account those of the subordinate groups.

So far, this section has discussed the process of attaining societal hegemony in relatively broad terms in order to establish how the material structure of common sense is replicated in the material structure of any societal hegemony. It is the task of the remainder of this section to outline how societal hegemony translates into political hegemony, which necessitates a shift to the next stage in common sense's journey, from society to the state – or, in Gramsci's terms, from civil society to political society. As Anne Showstack Sassoon (1987: 117) says, '[t]he achievement of State power can only come after the establishment of a certain hegemony in society.' Once societal hegemony is achieved the social formation is 'able to form a historical bloc whose unity is organised on the institutional terrain provided by the state' (Bruff 2005: 275).

A historical bloc is, as one would expect given its genesis, 'a complex, politically contestable and dynamic ensemble of social relations which includes economic, political and cultural aspects.' (Bieler 2002: 581). As a result, the state is inextricably linked to societal struggles, and is a 'continuous process of formation and superseding of unequal equilibria' (Gramsci 1971: 182). However, although the historical bloc is 'porous and multifaceted' (Sassoon 2000: 102), its institutionalization in the state gives it a 'cohesion and identity... through the propagation of a common culture' (Robert W. Cox 1983: 132) – something which is helped by its anchoring in the economic. Thus the state's institutional terrain gives ample opportunity for a historical bloc to remain hegemonic for an extended period of time, stabilizing its inherent dynamism and giving the state's social content a path-dependence which can be observed and analysed.

As will be made clear below, the organization of hegemony on the state's institutional terrain does not mean that the state is an empty space which is penetrated by leading social forces and bent to their will. For now, though, it is enough to state that the state's social content is shaped by the historical bloc's social content. The bloc, through 'the codification of both prohibitions and positive injunctions' (Poulantzas 1978: 83), has the opportunity to reconstitute society in a manner more favourable to the social forces which comprise it. This allows us to introduce another aspect of the maintenance and perpetuation of societal hegemony by the historical bloc, because the reshaping of the legal framework through, for example, acts of Parliament, institutionalizes a new (modified) hegemonic order in society. By entrenching societal leadership in the legal framework, the historical bloc has the opportunity to frame and thus circumscribe action and thought in accordance with the version of common sense that it supports. This enables its hegemony to appear natural, insulating it from present and future challenges from counter-hegemonic forces (cf. Robert W. Cox 1996d: 517–19). The state thus 'plays a pivotal role in the construction [and maintenance] of hegemony' (Stuart Hall 1996c: 429), because it is:

> absolutely central in articulating the different areas of contestation, the different points of antagonism, into a regime of rule. The moment when you can get sufficient power in the state to organise a central political project is then decisive, for then you can use the state to plan, urge, incite, solicit and punish, to *conform* the different sites of power and consent into a single regime. (Stuart Hall 1991b: 124; original emphasis).

In consequence, '[h]egemony defines the limits within which we can struggle, the field of "common sense" or "popular consciousness".' (Grossberg 1996: 162). Therefore, we must see *reluctant acquiescence* by social groups to hegemonic projects, as embodied in state policies and institutional configurations, to be as likely an outcome as their positive endorsing of the project. As a result, common sense at the state level, while less amorphous, unconscious and contradictory than among the masses, can be based on uncontested assumptions in the same way that the common sense assumptions of the masses are uncontested. The difference is that they might be uncontested not due to agreement but because they have been depoliticized through being placed outside the parameters of debate. This is often done with the compliance of weaker groups: one example pertinent for the book is the reluctant acceptance of sometimes drastic wage moderation by Dutch trade unions, as will be demonstrated in Chapters 5 and 7.

Nevertheless, this does not mean that the state's centrality to the outcomes of social and political struggle enables the victorious group simply to impose its will on either the state's institutional terrain or society at large. Thus a distinction must be made between the *opportunity* to entrench societal leadership in the legal framework and the *outcome*, as the next section outlines.

## The state and common sense

The above discussion indicates that the state is not a given category of analysis that is fixed across space and time. We should instead begin from the observation that the '[t]he objective world of institutions is real because we make it so' (Robert W. Cox 1996b: 149). Employing Gramsci's conceptualization of the connection between the humanly objective and universal subjective, the state is not objective but exudes an aura of objectivity – principally through its possession of *de jure* sovereignty (cf. Bruff 2005: 273). We should therefore expect there to be different forms of state across space and time, for it comprises not just the coercive, legal, narrowly political institutions such as government ministries, but also the social forces – such as political parties, interest groups, and so on – which operate in and through it (Gramsci 1971; Bieler 2002: 580–1). Gramsci terms this the "integral state", which is both civil society and political society, again indicating the state's rootedness in its societal context.

Because of this, Poulantzas (1978) argued that the relations of power characterizing societal struggles are inscribed into the state's institutional structure. Furthermore, the 'law organizes the structure of the compromise equilibrium permanently imposed on the dominant classes by the dominated.' (*ibid.* 91). This does not mean that the subordinate groups are in the ascendancy; more that the law acts as the embodiment of the relations of power between different social groups (92). Therefore, the internal contradictions within the historical bloc, a necessary part of the push for hegemony through the synthesis of different ideas and interests, are inscribed into the state:

> fractions of the power bloc share in political domination only to the extent that they are present *in* the State. Each state branch or apparatus and each of their respective sections and levels...frequently constitutes the power-base and favoured representative of a particular fraction of the bloc, or of a conflictual alliance of several fractions opposed to certain others. In short, it is the specific concentration-crystallization of a given interest or alliance of particular interests. (133).

Thus the concessions made by the leading group are likely to be, as a result of the interests of the ally in question, concentrated in particular parts of the institutional apparatus, *thus detracting from state unity but guaranteeing the (temporary) unity of the historical bloc* through strategic (but not fundamental) adjustments to the hegemonic project. In addition, I argued earlier that the leading social group in a system of alliances will comprise a major social class, but that this group does not contain all of that social class. This means that different components, or fractions, of capital and labour could well be in alliance with, or in opposition to, each other. Therefore, while compromises aimed at maintaining the unity of the historical bloc are of primary importance – for example, industrial capital offering industrial labour improved working conditions in return for a reduction in strike action which has been harming profits – concessions may have to be granted to competing social groups as well.

While of secondary importance to maintaining the historical bloc, this is a useful means of containing counter-hegemonic impulses originating from groups outside the historical bloc, and thus circumscribing action and thought in accordance with the version of common sense that the class fraction supports. This may entail the eventual incorporation of such groups into the bloc (perhaps at the expense of others currently part of it), but neutralization is the first goal. For example, if finance capital is at the head of a historical bloc and industrial capital is outside the bloc, then certain concessions aimed at neutralizing the latter – such as the provision of apprenticeship grants – could be proposed.

As a result, it can now be seen how *different versions of common sense can co-exist in the state*. In terms of contemporary struggles, this is as a result primarily of the relations of power within the historical bloc, but also the relations of power between the bloc and groups outside the bloc, which are inscribed into the state's administrative apparatus. Therefore, the class leading the historical bloc faces the possibility that the implementation of its version of common sense and the need to maintain its system of alliances could be contradictory aims (complicated by the fact that concessions to competing groups may antagonize other groups within the historical bloc). This means that although it is certainly possible for the state to act in a coherent and unified way, this is no more than a tendency (*ibid.*: 137). Thus a key issue is the extent to which the leading social group is able to use privileged centres of power within the state's administrative apparatus – such as the economic ministries – to impose its will on resistant parts of the state apparatus. One means of doing so is through the dissemination of a dominant ideology which acts as a cement across state institutions (*ibid.*: 171; 155–6), holding other social groups in the historical bloc close to the leading class' version of common sense (and, through the greater unity, giving the bloc greater capacity to remain insulated from counter-hegemonic challenges). However, it is not guaranteed that this will happen.

Perhaps more importantly, the state's social content, or its institutional materiality, is also a complex synthesis of differential *historical* accumulations of common sense sediments (Bruff 2007). Thus the historical bloc is, in addition to the above, confronted by a multiplicity of common senses *already within* the state that have been laid down over time as the result of earlier struggles. Moreover, these sediments exhibit varying degrees of possible resistance to, and incorporation into, its vision. For instance, some common sense sediments will have accumulated more heavily than others, depoliticizing more strongly the assumptions regarding a particular area (or areas) of policy. Therefore, the state, through the sediments of common sense that have been laid down over time in different parts of the administrative apparatus, exhibits a path-dependence in terms of both the individual components of the apparatus and the overall direction of policy. A key example in the empirical chapters is the heavy accumulation of common sense sediments in the Netherlands in favour of wage moderation as the means by which economic challenges are met.

In consequence, the state has relative autonomy from the social forces that operate in and through it, because of its institutional materiality and the path-dependence that this entails – path-dependence in a strategic sense and path-dependence in a historical sense. Both of these lead back to common sense, for it is the versions of common sense already existent in the state apparatus, and the contrasting versions of common sense supported by subordinate and competing groups, which gives the state its path-dependent trajectory. I thus distinguish myself from other discussions of relative autonomy, which argue that the state looks after the long-term interests of capital as a whole, and thus is relatively autonomous from the various fractions vying for societal leadership. For example, Bieler and Morton (2003: 486), in keeping with Poulantzas (1973, 1975, 1978), argue that the state imposes 'certain concessions and sacrifices on the dominant classes in order to reproduce long-term domination.' However, this implies a certain causality on the part of the state. In contrast, I would stress that this comes about not through a notion of imposition but through the necessities of social and political struggle and accompanying power relations.

Capital, through its dominant position in the production process (that is, through the ownership of property and the wage enslavement of labour), *does* tend to have its interests looked after by the state, but in the first instance this is through the greater power it enjoys *vis-à-vis* labour in capitalist societies. The state is thus the moment of condensation, the materialization of unequal social power relations in the form of institutional configurations and policies. Nevertheless, this assertion must always be qualified by the observation that this moment has been preceded by earlier moments. Moreover, at any one time there is a need to stabilize and maintain the unequal relations in the form of concessions to subordinate social groups within the historical bloc, and the adoption of agendas which neutralize social groups outside the historical bloc.

## The national and the international

So far the chapter has not addressed the international dimension. Indeed, from the above discussion of path-dependence and relative autonomy it could be inferred that the international dimension is subordinate to the national, or at the very least that a neo-Gramscian perspective is, following Gramsci, suffused by a methodological nationalism (for example, see Germain and Kenny 1998; Shilliam 2004). Morton (2007a, 2007c) has convincingly refuted such notions concerning Gramsci, and this section is in keeping with his assertion (2007a: 170) that we should focus on the national level as our point of departure while remaining aware at all times of the national's conditioning by the international. As such, the trajectories of European varieties of capitalism are the outcome of the manner in which the national and the international intertwine in the given territory (cf. Gramsci 1971: 182). Therefore, when Gramsci (1971: 34–5) argued that the 'contemporary world [is] a synthesis of the past, of all past generations, which projects itself into the future', he is referring to not just a temporal but also a spatial synthesis (cf. Jessop 2006).

This position stands in contrast to those writers who emphasize the transnational dimension of contemporary capitalism (William Robinson 2004; Sklair 2001; Gill 1998; van Apeldoorn 2002; van der Pijl 1998). William Robinson takes this thesis the furthest, arguing that the changes in the world economy since the early 1970s, during which time there has been an explosion of capital, trade and financial flows, and a massive expansion of the reach of transnational corporations, have brought into being a transnational elite united around the goal of extending and entrenching global capitalism. For Robinson this means that the national/international distinction has been transcended by 'transnational social forces and institutions grounded in the global system rather than the interstate system.' (William Robinson 2006: 167). However, his thesis rests on the (putative) penetration of national (as well as transnational) institutions across the world by horizontally integrated transnational forces. This instrumentalist position views national institutions as bending to the will of transnational social forces and the logic of transnational capital. However, he also states:

> Conflict is prone to occur at multiple levels: between transnationally oriented elites and those with a more local, national or regional orientation; between agents of global capitalism and popular forces; among competing groups within the globalist bloc who may foment inter-state conflicts in pursuit of their particular interests; and so on. (*ibid.*: 173).

Suddenly the argument becomes more contingent: institutions and their social content are not simply usurped by transnational social forces and brought to heel. Nevertheless, the totalizing imagery remains intact. While space precludes a detailed exploration of the transnationalization thesis, it was necessary to begin here in order to draw out some of the problems with the literature which discusses national/international interaction from the transnational perspective (see Morton 2007a: 140–50 for an incisive critique; Bruff 2007 for a critical assessment of the "new constitutionalism" aspect of the literature). Neglected are the spatial specificities of capitalist social relations, which date back to capitalism's emergence 'into an anterior international system of state territoriality.' (Morton 2007a: 145; see also Teschke 2003; Lacher 2003, 2006). In consequence, '[t]he existence of territorial sovereign states and the presence of a system of states thus shaped the subsequent geopolitical expression of capitalism.' (Morton 2007a: 146).

Therefore, if it is established that the *origins* of the international system of states were pre-capitalist but the *foundations*, that is the social basis, of the system are capitalist (Poulantzas 1978: 43), then it can be seen that the national state is not dependent on capital's whim to remain in existence. Instead, the national state's institutional materiality gives capitalism a spatial expression and locus that cannot easily be supplanted (cf. Morton 2007a: 148). Thus the manner in which countries became capitalist varies, because the means by which capitalist social relations became their foundation varies. To be sure, capitalism traverses national boundaries, but this is not the same as saying that everywhere capitalism is the same. Societies can be recognizably capitalist without having the same social content or, as a result, the state taking the same form – there can be 'diverse manifestations of the same phenomena' (Gramsci 1992: 151).

This means that there has been in the last three decades a *rebalancing* of the national/international relationship rather than the latter's swallowing up of the former. Such rebalancing is spatially specific in terms of country-country comparisons, and also spatially specific in terms of which institutional "spaces", or parts of the state apparatus, have been more or less affected. Finally, it is also temporally specific, for different countries and different institutional spaces will evolve at variable rates.[3] So how can we conceptualize the national/international relationship in a manner which enables us to conduct empirical research? In a seminal article, Bieler and Morton (2003: 485–90 in particular) utilize Poulantzas' (1973, 1975, 1978), Robert W. Cox's (1981, 1983, 1987) and Gramsci's insights to produce a nuanced yet clear framework for analysis. They couple internationalization with internalization: that is, '[t]he phenomenon now referred to as globalization...represents the transnational organization of production relations which are internalized within states to lead to a modified restructuring (but not retreat) of the state in everyday life.' (487). In other words, because capitalism operates *through* and not *outside* national states, *any* spatial expansion of capitalist social relations must be trans*national* and not global (cf. Poulantzas 1978: 106).

In consequence, any internationalization or transnationalization of capitalism must be accompanied, by way of its spatial expression, by an internalization of this process within national states. Indeed, the term "globalization" is in this sense highly misleading, for it encourages imageries of free-floating capital: in actuality *globalization is a process of the internationalization–internalization of national states* which leaves them restructured but still a key site of economic activity. There can be no expansion of capitalist social relations without their accompanying condensation into the institutional materiality of national state apparatuses (Bruff 2007). Moreover, through identifying fractions of capital it is possible to pinpoint more precisely the form of internationalization–internalization as well as the weighting of the international in the national. For instance, witness the UK's nominally social democratic Labour government – conscious of London's position as perhaps *the* preeminent site of international financial market activity – push for free and unfettered international financial markets (for an examination of the discourse deployed, see Watson 2002).

Taking these points together, an analysis of the national variety of capitalism must assess the degree of internationalization–internalization of the national state – and thus the degree of internationalization–internalization of the sedimentations of common sense that have accumulated in the state's institutional apparatus. Furthermore, the national source of the internationalization–internalization is important. For example, it could be domestic social forces which have expanded, altering the relationship between these and nationally-oriented domestic forces (as was the case in Germany in the 1990s – see Chapters 6 and 7). It could also be foreign social forces that have become part of the national political economy. Moreover, foreign forces that have expanded from a similar variety of capitalism will engender a different form of internalization compared to those expanding from a more contrasting variety (witness the anguished discussions in some of Europe's richer countries about the European "model" of capitalism versus the "Anglo–Saxon" version). Therefore, internationalization–internalization is driven by the expansion of social forces whose form is empirically variable, and whose national origin may be domestic or a range of non-domestic locations. Furthermore, the source of such expansion is likely to be concentrated in certain parts of the international – for example, it may be present in one or more regions more than in others (such as Japanese capital in East Asia, German capital in Europe) or on a global scale but unevenly distributed (US capital).

In addition, the internationalization–internalization of the national state, and thus of common sense, has been a *permanent fixture* in its historical evolution: 'the sovereign state...was *never* truly a container of society, and modern social relations always included crucial global dimensions' (Lacher 2003: 523). This releases us from arguments about the periodization of "globalization" that create, in effect, a "pre-globalization" and "post-globalization" dualism. Morton (2007a, 2007c) and Jessop (2006) have argued that Gramsci is instructive in this regard, for he believes that 'history is always "world history" and that particular histories exist only within the frame of world history.' (Gramsci 1985: 181, cited in Jessop 2006: 31). Hence his emphasis on the intertwining of the vertical (national) and the horizontal (international) in a process of reciprocal interaction and articulation (Jessop 2006; Gramsci 1971: 176, 182). The perspective is international while the point of departure is national (Gramsci 1971: 240).

Crucial for the manner in which the national and the international intertwine is the national's position *in* the international. Referring to Italy's historical development, Gramsci (1996: 314) argued:

> Italy, because of its "cosmopolitan" functions during the period of the Roman Empire and during the Middle Ages, experienced international relations in a passive way; that is to say, in the course of Italian history, international relations prevailed over national relations.

As will be demonstrated in Chapters 5–7, the contrasting positions in the international of the Dutch and German varieties of capitalism is key to their differing experiences with regard to consensus formation. For the Netherlands this has manifested itself in the long-standing assumption that it suffers from economic vulnerability, which has driven the evolution of the Dutch political economy regardless of the weightings of different fractions of capital within it. For Germany this historically manifested itself in the equating of industrial success with general economic success. However, this assumption was based on Germany's territory containing specific locales which provided the most propitious conditions for capital accumulation in the world capital goods industries (see van der Wurff 1993). Hence the increasing ability in the 1990s of German capital – including the industrial fractions – to realize greater value in other countries destabilized Germany's position in the international, leading to a modified intertwining of the vertical and the horizontal. This has reduced the potential for consensus formation, because the growing transnationalization of German capital led its version of common sense away from the version adhered to by German labour, giving less overlap between the different positions. In contrast, the continued weak position of the Netherlands in the international has made it easier for consensus to form – albeit a consensus heavily skewed towards capital's interests – because the shared assumption of vulnerability has provided for considerable overlap between the different positions.

For this reason the book takes the intertwining of the national and the international as its primary point of reference, and the form that this intertwining takes as the secondary point of reference. Therefore, looking forward to the empirical chapters that lie ahead, the framework outlined in this chapter will be utilized to analyse the role of consensus in the Netherlands and Germany primarily with regard to the intertwining of the national and the international.

## Conclusion

This chapter has outlined a neo-Gramscian theoretical framework, anchored in Gramsci's discussions of "common sense". This begins from the assertion that culture is embodied in all social practice, because all humans have conceptions of the world, no matter how fragmentary and composite. The conglomeration of these conceptions is for each person their own version of common sense. There could be many different conceptions of the world within any one society, but these conceptions can only be recognized as a culture if they are intersubjective rather than merely subjective, and thus embodied in persistent collective patterns of human activity and thought. This allows us to acknowledge that there may be several different cultures co-existing at any one point in time.

The different cultures – or different versions of common sense – are neither fixed for all time nor wholly separate from each other. Thus the key issue regarding consensus formation is the degree to which these different versions overlap, and the resulting possibilities for synthesis between them. Hence any synthesis between different cultures is the product of human action and thus an open empirical question. Moreover, the degree of overlap (and the resulting potential for synthesis) can shift over time, depending on the molecular evolution of the different cultures as they come into contact with new ideas, ideas propagated by other versions of common sense, or through the ascendancy within the culture of previously secondary conceptions of the world. At the same time, any such developments are path-dependent, making it possible for the researcher to identify historical trends and to provide explanations for these trends.

In other words, the role of consensus in the trajectories of European varieties of capitalism can be adequately analysed only with recourse to a discussion of culture, which is my point of departure from the varieties of capitalism literature. To this end, armed with the discussion of culture in this chapter, the next four chapters analyse the role of consensus in the trajectories of the Dutch and German varieties of capitalism. The next chapter is concerned with the analyses provided by the varieties of capitalism literature, and as such it provides the basis for Chapters 5 and 6, which utilize the framework outlined in this (and the first) chapter in order to provide a more persuasive explanation. Chapter 7 considers the apparent challenge to the framework posed by post-2001 developments in the Netherlands and Germany.

# 4
# The Netherlands and Germany from the Varieties of Capitalism Perspective

This chapter provides an overview of the historical trajectories of the Dutch and German varieties of capitalism. The chapter is divided into two parts, the first concerning the Netherlands and the second dealing with Germany. 1945 is the starting point because it was after World War II that corporatist institutional structures and the welfare state developed fully in both the Netherlands and Germany.[1] The period after 1979 is discussed in greater depth, for the recession of the early 1980s and the accompanying re-emergence of mass unemployment in both countries presented new and considerable challenges for policymakers to deal with. The manner in which they were faced in the 1980s and 1990s by the Netherlands and Germany has been the subject of much discussion in the varieties of capitalism literature – not least because they are frequently put forward as best and worst practice cases – with the Wassenaar and Alliance for Jobs processes often forming the core of the analysis. The political radicalization in both countries in the post-2001 period is considered in Chapter 7.

A variety of sources is cited in this chapter, and it will be made clear when the perspective of the varieties of capitalism literature is being considered; in particular, the explanations it provides for the contrasting trajectories of the Dutch and German political economies. As was argued in the first two chapters, the literature deems the presence or absence of consensus crucial for the trajectories, because institutional dysfunction can potentially be overcome only with a consensus across the tripartite actors. This chapter considers the concepts of social learning and path-dependence, which are often deployed to analyse the presence or absence of consensus in European varieties of capitalism. The Netherlands is viewed as a prime example of social learning, for the 1982 Wassenaar Agreement catalysed a learning process among the tripartite actors that enabled the institutional environment to act as a stable context for adaptation to new economic realities such as high unemployment. In contrast, Germany – as exemplified by the Alliance for Jobs process in the late 1990s – is a prime example of path-dependence, with disagreement among the tripartite actors on how to face the economic challenges rendering the institutional environment increasingly ill-suited to new economic realities.

The literature's discussions of the Dutch and German varieties of capitalism range more widely than the Wassenaar and Alliance for Jobs processes in the two countries. Nevertheless, the explanations provided for Wassenaar and Alliance for Jobs illustrate clearly the approach taken by the varieties of capitalism literature in general. Therefore, as with the varieties of capitalism literature they represent, the social learning and path-dependence concepts are limited to the institutional environment, for that is what they seek to analyse. As a result, the presence or absence of consensus in the Netherlands and Germany is explained by concepts which take institutions, and not the material basis for existence, as the foundation for analysis.

I argue in the conclusion that although the literature is thorough and comprehensive in its *description* of the trajectories of the Dutch and German political economies, an alternative framework is necessary when seeking to *analyse* the trajectories. For example, it is true that we saw more policy and institutional change in the Netherlands, and that Germany appeared to be weighed down by discord and disagreement, but little is said on the issue of *consensus formation* (which, as stated in Chapter 1, extends to consensus not being formed). That is, instead of searching for whether consensus exists or not – as the varieties of capitalism literature does – we need to enquire into what Silke van Dyk (2006: 409) calls 'the conditions of consensus.' Why and how did consensus form, or not, at that particular time, and why and how did consensus form, or not, over those particular issues? How can consensus itself, or the absence of consensus, be analysed and explained? The chapter ends by asserting that these crucial questions can be answered when utilizing a neo-Gramscian framework to analyse rather than describe the trajectories of the Dutch and German political economies, which is the task of Chapters 5–7.

## The Netherlands

Far-reaching and unprecedented measures were deemed necessary to reconstruct the Netherlands after the devastation of World War II. Initially taking the form of state direction, regulation and planning of wages, production and trade (de Vries 1978), from the early 1950s onwards government intervention became increasingly directed towards the construction of an extensive welfare state (albeit one whose programmes would often be administered by the social partners). By the 1960s it was clear that, in this modified form, 'the intensive ties between the state and economic life were here to stay.' (Blom 1999: 436). The belief that the economic progress made after 1945 was largely achieved through state policies was widespread (Abert 1969). Economic life could and should be influenced by the state and the social partners in the name of the national interest.

During reconstruction many corporatist institutions had been created, most notably the Foundation of Labour (STAR), where bargaining between employers' associations and trade unions over pay and conditions would take place, the Social and Economic Council (SER), a tripartite body established to advise the government on policy (a function shared by STAR in matters of industrial policy), and the Central Planning Bureau (CPB), which, after the early 1950s, planned much less than help coordinate the policy instruments as a means to achieving government goals (Abert 1969). During the 1950s and 1960s one goal was pursued above all others: to maintain a lower price and wage level in comparison to competing countries (*ibid.*). This would, putatively, be of benefit for an economy dependent on international trade for its prosperity, and became once more the main goal in the early 1980s and again in the early 2000s.[2] The system lasted until 1963, by which point the virtual non-existence of unemployment generated pressures for higher wages that could not be contained. No new set of long-term arrangements was instituted until the early 1980s, despite the rising problems facing the economy in the second half of the 1970s. Indeed, in this period wage policy varied 'from almost complete freedom to strong governmental influence.' (Wolff and Driehuis 1980: 43).

Nevertheless, despite such gyrations the discovery and subsequent exploitation of natural gas in the 1960s and 1970s made it possible for the country – for a few years at least – to continue prospering. For example, it allowed the balance of payments to remain in the black despite the deterioration in the Netherlands' international competitiveness – again, for a few years at least (Lubbers and Lemckert 1980). In addition, the welfare state expanded rapidly on the back of the gas revenues. Many new programmes came into existence, such as the latterly-infamous disability benefit scheme in 1967. However, the substantial rise in the energy intensity of the Dutch political economy in the 1963–73 period made the Netherlands particularly vulnerable to the oil shocks of 1973 and especially 1979 (van Zanden 1998). At the same time, economic growth rates after 1973 declined and unemployment began rising – stagflation had hit the economy (*ibid.*).

In addition to this, the varieties of capitalism literature has stressed the significance of 'politically weak coalition governments...[which] were unwilling to act without the agreement of the social partners – which, however, were unable to agree on anything.' (Scharpf 2000: 60). The resulting drift *de facto* reinforced existing trends, meaning that, by the late 1970s, the Netherlands was largely reliant on benign international conditions, for 'rising unemployment, increasing public deficits, declining competitiveness and falling growth rates [had] put the Netherlands in an extremely tight corner.' (Hemerijck and Schludi 2000: 158). As a result, the 1979 oil shock had a major impact on the Dutch economy. By the early 1980s, the budget deficit and unemployment were high, and the recession was longer in the Netherlands than in most other rich countries. It is not surprising that the CPB (1997: 8; original emphasis) concluded that '[i]n the 1970s and early 1980s the Netherlands formed an example of how *not* to deal with stagflation'.

At this point there was a marked shift in the trajectory of the Dutch variety of capitalism. Hemerijck *et al.* (2000: 228) provide a useful overview of the evolution of the political economy after the turning point in 1982:

> Since 1982 a new mix of macroeconomic policy and wage setting emerged that generated a virtuous cycle of price stability, fiscal consolidation, restored profitability, and strong (part-time) job

> creation in private services. Subsequently, supported by welfare and labor market reforms, this virtuous cycle has had important positive feedback effects on female employment and domestic demand, leading in turn to a slow but solid decline in labor market inactivity without having to sacrifice basic social security.

Wage restraint was crucial to breaking the tripartite deadlock: in the years following the path-breaking Wassenaar Agreement of 1982, in which the trade unions and employers agreed to exchange wage moderation for fewer working hours, a series of major reforms were implemented.[3] Moreover, the changes took place from within the existing institutional environment: for example, despite the fall in trade union density from 35–40% to less than 25% of the workforce during the 1980s, almost 100% of the workforce continued to be covered by a collective agreement (Hartog 1999). In effect, then, trade unions agreed to cuts in real incomes in return for the continuation of the collective bargaining system and the belief that the lower labour costs would result in higher employment (Spithoven 2002). The outcome was similar to the 1950s, demonstrating that corporatism could achieve perhaps more restrained wage growth than the free market under monetarism, for there would be no free riders (Visser and Hemerijck 1997). Unit labour costs rose by a mere 5% between 1983 and 1993, and Dutch real wages fell in comparison to other EU countries in the 1980s and early 1990s (van Zanden 1998).[4]

Another key change was the sharp rise in part-time jobs: one-third of the workforce was in such employment by the end of the century. A disproportionate number of them were women, whose participation in the labour market rose from 29% in 1973 to 60% in the mid-1990s (Visser and Hemerijck 1997). Although this form of labour market participation was not a policy goal in the early 1980s, its rise to prominence meant that as time went on it became an increasingly integral part of reducing unemployment and boosting employment. This was demonstrated by the 1993 "New Course" Accord between employers' and unions and also the 1999 Flexibility and Security Act, which sought to improve the position of temporary workers in return for a modest weakening of the rights of permanent staff in order to encourage the growth of flexible work (of which many positions were part-time).[5]

Turning to the welfare system, Hemerijck and Schludi (2000: 162) believe that 'the Dutch welfare state has been transformed from one of the least sustainable in the early 1980s to one of the most by the late 1990s.' An early reform was the delinking of prices from wages and benefits, putting a brake on expenditure growth. Secondly, after the lowering of benefit levels in the late 1980s, the 1990s saw an attempt to reduce the number of claimants via tighter rules on eligibility – particularly with regard to the disability benefits scheme, on whose rolls were more than 10% of the workforce (Hartog 1999; van der Veen and Trommel 1999). In addition, governments increasingly sought to promote labour market participation – through measures such as subsidizing the long-term unemployed to make them more attractive to employers – as a means of guaranteeing the future viability of the still-generous welfare system. This is key for many in the varieties of capitalism literature, who argue that despite the changes, the Dutch welfare state remained extensive and generous, and inequality rose only modestly – a powerful rejoinder to those who believe that only US-style capitalism can deliver economic and employment growth (cf. Visser and Hemerijck 1997; Scharpf 2000; Robert Henry Cox 1998; Auer 2000).

So how can these dramatic changes be explained? As stated earlier, the varieties of capitalism literature utilizes the concept of social learning to explain the formation and perpetuation of consensus on reform. At its simplest, the literature asserts that '[t]he Dutch example shows that corporatist institutions are not synonymous with suffocating rigidity. Instead, they appear to allow for much flexibility.' (Hartog 1999: 484). Hemerijck elaborated on this observation, arguing that learning is problem-induced – that is, catalysed by previous failures (see Hemerijck and Schludi 2000; Hemerijck 2001). The key point is that 'failures not only energize the policy process in a search for new instruments and goals: they also unleash a search for new rules'. (Hemerijck and Schludi 2000: 134). While Hemerijck and Schludi stress that the search may be unsuccessful, their discussion gives a solid foundation for analysing how actors can move from relatively incoherent, tentative notions of what should change to more fundamental reorientations which result in substantial reforms. There does not need to be a "master plan" at the beginning of the process, but the unfolding implications of one set of changes often lead to rethinks in other areas (what they describe as the "sequential logic of policy adjustment").

There has also been a focus on how social learning processes acquire momentum. For although a corporatist environment is important for bringing the actors to the same forum for negotiation, the realization and implementation of reforms depends on the actors being both able and willing to embrace new ideas and solve problems together (Schmidt 2002b). The example frequently cited in this instance is the formation of the "no-nonsense" government in 1982, which used its coalition agreement to state baldly "it is there to govern" – that is, bypass tripartite corporatist structures if necessary. By presenting the social partners with the stark choice of either working more cooperatively when negotiating the wage round or facing the possibility of the erosion of their place in the institutional environment, the government was able to take a stronger, more independent position in the policymaking process (Scharpf 2000).

The Wassenaar Agreement between the trade unions and the employers' associations followed two days after this declaration (Spithoven 2002; Visser and Hemerijck 1997). The varieties of capitalism literature stresses that the action taken by the government was aimed at *revitalizing* and not destroying the corporatist structures. Indeed, the fact that the policy aim was once again wage moderation demonstrates the path-dependent nature of the changes taking place. Visser and Hemerijck (1997) utilize Scharpf's (1993) "shadow of hierarchy" concept to explain this shift, for the reassertion of state independence *vis-à-vis* the social partners was made from within the institutional system's boundaries. Through the augmenting of its capacity *and* willingness to steer corporatist structures towards certain ends, the Dutch state was able to break the deadlock which had prevailed for several years.

Thus, perhaps paradoxically, a stronger state was the prerequisite for an improvement in the functioning of the corporatist framework – reflected by the fact that tripartite consensus was still the goal, and was often achieved – rather than the catalyst for its downgrading (Hemerijck 2001). The net result of the government's assertion of its right to walk away from corporatist fora when it felt that progress was too slow, was to change the relationship between the government and the social partners from conflictual, self-interested bargaining to a more consensual atmosphere in which it was possible to develop a common policy agenda (Visser and Hemerijck 1997). Again, Wassenaar is often used as an illustration of this shift, for it did not contain any quantitative targets for wage growth and working time reduction. Instead, the agreement simply stated that employers and trade unions were committed to achieving these goals.

It may appear paradoxical that wage moderation after 1982 was more successfully achieved under a relatively decentralized, qualitative and non-binding framework, than via the top-down, quantitative and law-based system that had periodically been attempted after the mid-1960s (Robert Henry Cox 2001). However, once we take into account the state's renewed threat to intervene in the collective bargaining process, we can see that it altered the dynamics between the social partners. Green-Pedersen *et al.* (2001: 318) believe that the 'high level of consensual concertation' that developed was based on high levels of trust between various actors at various levels, making it possible for the Netherlands to adjust more smoothly, and less painfully, to new economic realities. In other words, while greater institutional flexibility and adaptivity are important in themselves, the creation of 'a climate of "broad ownership" of the interconnected problems facing the Dutch economy' was a vital element of the adjustment process (Hemerijck and Schludi 2000: 159). Indeed, this sometimes led to the social partners being ahead of the government in the development of reform proposals – for example, the 1999 flexicurity legislation simply confirmed in law a 1996 bipartite agreement on the topic – which demonstrated that the Dutch state's greater capacity for steering did not need to be exercised if the corporatist institutions appeared to be working effectively.

Furthermore, the social learning initiated by Wassenaar demonstrated how long-standing institutions can be put to new uses. For example, the welfare state's long-term viability increasingly came to be seen as dependent on maximizing labour market participation, which necessitated a paradigm shift from absorbing the costs of labour market adjustment to actively helping the unemployed back into the labour market (Robert Henry Cox 1998, 2001). The varieties of capitalism literature stresses that reforms aimed at achieving higher labour market participation – such as the virtual elimination of social security contributions for the low-paid, and any increase in welfare benefits being linked explicitly to the employment rate – were not aimed at dismantling the welfare state but a means for ensuring that it *remained* generous and extensive (see Green-Pedersen *et al.* 2001; van der Veen and Trommel 1999). Hence it was argued that the Dutch welfare state's 'considerable capacity for reform and innovation' had significantly improved its long-term viability by the end of the 1990s (Hemerijck *et al.* 2000: 255). In addition, the need for reform was articulated with reference to well-established national particularisms, which made it easier for the changes to be accepted. For example:

> The Dutch welfare state is...built on an ethic of caring. The Dutch term *verzorgingstaat* translates into English as caring state, not welfare state. Thus when women entered the workforce in large numbers, their claim that they needed assistance to continue caring for their families drew on a well-established principle. This allowed policy entrepreneurs to reconstruct the idea of labor-market flexibility, transforming it from an issue that polarized labor and employers into a principle justifying more innovative labor contracts and allowing men and women equally to care for their families (flexicurity). (Robert Henry Cox 2001: 496–7; original emphasis).

Therefore, a key point for the varieties of capitalism literature is that the Dutch case demonstrated how significant changes can be achieved *through* rather than against corporatist institutions. Toonen and Hendriks (2001: 282, 283) write:

> The institutional set-up and design of the system puts constraints on possible forms of political behaviour so that it forces political interests to actually respect, and not ignore, the pluralistic nature of Dutch society and political system...Paradoxically, the complexity creates limits, but also provides a stable context to the reform.

Indeed, Scharpf (2000: 60) argues that *both* the Dutch "disease" of the 1970s *and* the Dutch "miracle" of the 1990s were brought about by 'a multiparty political system, coalition governments, an independent central bank and institutions for corporatist consultation between a plurality of unions and employers' associations and the government'. This statement, perhaps more than any other, summarizes the varieties of capitalism perspective on the Netherlands. The absence of consensus in the 1970s made it possible for institutional dysfunction to perpetuate, with deleterious consequences for the economy; the presence of consensus in the 1980s and 1990s enabled the dysfunction to be overcome as a result of the extensive learning process embarked upon by the tripartite actors, with positive consequences for the economy. Wassenaar thus illustrates the power of the social learning concept for analysing the evolution of the Dutch variety of capitalism in the 1980s and 1990s. In contrast, the Alliance for Jobs process illustrates the power of the path-dependence concept for analysing the evolution of the German variety of capitalism in the 1980s and 1990s, as the next section discusses.

## Germany

Although Germany faced perhaps even greater need for reconstruction at the end of the Second World War, the policy choices were significantly more market-oriented than in the Netherlands. The social market economy concept, as developed by Alfred Müller-Armack and Ludwig Erhard – Economics Minister from 1949–63 and Chancellor from 1963–6 – believed in:

> a fundamentally free-market economy modified by those measures which could be taken in conformity with market principles...so that it [the market] should operate in the interests of society as a whole. (Nicholls 1994: 143, 145).

For example, the welfare state was accepted as a legitimate part of the economy as long as it was funded out of the surplus generated by appropriate economic policies, since the best route to achieving increased incomes was through the economic growth which resulted from following market-oriented policies (Nicholls 1994). Indeed, 'economic growth in a market economy was the best social policy.' (Braun 1990: 177). Nevertheless, despite the symbolism of legislation such as the 1957 anti-cartel law, 'throughout Germany's industrial history, the academic and governmental attitude towards economic concentration in general, and cartels in particular, had in principle never been one of hostility.' (Hardach 1980: 148). Therefore, a "mixed economy" emerged in West Germany in the decades after 1949, and by the 1960s an extensive *Sozialstaat*, based on continuous support rather than remedial help drawn from surpluses, had been created (Stachura 2003).

Hence Dyson's (2001) characterization of *Modell Deutschland* as a complex and antagonistic combination of the social market and the managed economy. These two elements have since 1945 accommodated each other as well as competed for ascendancy – '[t]he face of German capitalism alters depending on which [advocacy] coalition is ascendant on particular issues at a given time.' (*ibid.*: 138–9). In all, though, the German model rests on 'an underlying coherence defined by market-based adjustment governed by the principle of consensus. Hence consensus remains an essential part of any definition of the efficient secret of the German model.' (*ibid.*: 150). Adjustment via consensus takes place via a corporatist institutional environment, involving the trade unions and employers in many ways (Vitols 2000).

In turn, the social partners are responsible for coordinating the day-to-day running of the private sector (Peter Hall and Soskice 2001b). This is often achieved via quasi-public associations and groups – so-called parapublic associations (Katzenstein 1987) – that effectively govern certain areas of the economy, such as the provision of vocational training, with state approval and sanction (Streeck 1997; Culpepper 1999). In addition, in return for collective bargaining and codetermination – initially applicable to the iron, coal and steel industries, and extended to all firms with more than 2000 employees in 1976 (Overy 2003) – the trade unions agreed in the early 1950s to low wage growth 'on the understanding that this was the means to secure higher levels of welfare and income in the long run.' (*ibid.*: 267). Nevertheless, the commitment to moderate wage growth was not as total as in the Netherlands in the same decade.

The *Wirtschaftswunder* of the 1950s led to, by the early 1960s, the advent of full employment, which, combined with high growth, low inflation, balance of payments surpluses, as well as the progressive expansion of the welfare state, marked Germany out as one of the most significant success stories of the postwar era. Moreover, *Modell Deutschland* appeared highly responsive to political and economic change. This included the swing towards a more managed approach in the late 1960s, with the formation of the tripartite, albeit consultative, *Konzertierte Aktion* (Concerted Action) mechanism plus the government's attempt take a more active role in steering the economy; also the downgrading of these innovations in favour of the shift to monetarism announced by the Bundesbank in the mid-1970s in response to the inflationary impact of the 1973 oil price shock.

Nevertheless, the 1979 oil shock hit Germany, as in the Netherlands, much harder than the 1973 price rise. But unlike the Netherlands, the varieties of capitalism literature stresses that there was no social learning in response to the considerably higher unemployment and low growth. Slowly but surely the aura surrounding *Modell Deutschland* became tarnished, especially in the 1990s. This is despite some indicators remaining in Germany's favour: the budget deficit was under control for most of the time, as was inflation, and the balance of payments surplus often grew year-on-year. These positive indicators, combined with the prestige of *Modell Deutschland*, meant that Germany was still seen as an economic success story at the end of the 1980s (Vitols 2000). However, growth had been low throughout the decade, and the unemployment rate declined only slowly after reaching close to 10% in the early to mid-1980s – continuing the trend for each successive business cycle to begin with a higher unemployment rate than its predecessor (Braun 1990). Therefore, well before unification economic problems were mounting, which for Streeck (1997) were of an increasingly serious nature – not least because, in his opinion, the German model becomes dysfunctional and anachronistic in conditions of high unemployment, since the costs of supporting the unemployed will rise to the extent that it will become unsustainable.

Focusing more closely on the labour market, the 1980s and 1990s saw a continued role for the Bundesbank in coordinating collective bargaining, 'whereby wage demands came to mirror the publicly announced money supply growth target to which the central bank committed itself.' (Hemerijck and Schludi 2000: 151; see also Dyson 2001). Labour's share of national income subsequently declined, as a result of the Bundesbank's fear of wage-induced inflation. Nevertheless, the unemployment rate was unresponsive, which for the varieties of capitalism literature indicated that institutional rather than wage factors were at the heart of the labour market problems. The institutional environment as a whole was structuring economic activity in a non-optimal way, with rising non-wage labour costs and relatively strict employment regulations viewed as barriers to lowering unemployment. Employment growth throughout the two decades was anaemic, turning negative in the 1990s (Funk 2000).

Nevertheless, labour market policy changes, such as the legalization of temporary job contracts in the 1980s, were limited in scope (Manow and Seils 2000). An example of this is the 1985 attempt by the christian democrat-liberal coalition to liberalize the employment law, which was neutralized by discontent within the governing parties' own ranks and by the employers themselves. The result was a heavily watered-down version of the original legislation becoming law, and as such, this was a classic illustration of the institutional environment's path-dependent tendencies (Wood 2001). It was felt by many that the benefits of the institutional arrangements still outweighed the costs, delivering as they did a skilled, productive workforce which insulated Germany from what the DGB and BDA, in a joint 1989 statement, termed 'ruinous competition' based on price rather than value (Silvia 1999: 90; see also Hinrichs 2002; Soskice *et al.* 1998; Thelen 2001).

Many varieties of capitalism scholars emphasize the impact of interlocking institutions, which combine to have clear effects on the policy paths chosen, leading policymakers in certain directions and favouring certain actors, and their goals, over others (Peter Hall and Soskice 2001b; Wood 2001; Pierson 2004). Thus the institutional system, by way of its genesis, has a path-dependent dynamic which militates against substantial change. Indeed, if any change does take place, then, as was the case in the 1980s in Germany, it is steered through well-established institutional channels (Katzenstein 1989). And while Katzenstein was optimistic about the ability of Germany to adjust to socioeconomic change, the weight of opinion in retrospective studies by varieties of capitalism scholars is that the optimism was misplaced (see Manow and Seils 2000 for the clearest exposition). For the literature, the growing institutional dysfunction had already led to a significant decline in economic performance in the 1980s. Furthermore, the most graphic illustration of the increasing problems that this was causing came in the early 1990s, when Germany had to deal with unification and an international recession. The strong tendencies to path-dependence lay behind the routine response to unprecedented times:

> The Bundesbank again insisted on price stability. The government, as in previous recessions, massively shifted the costs onto the social partners' insurance schemes. Older workers, especially in the east, moved into special programs for early retirement. This process of dual externalization led to a considerable rise in contribution rates, itself a major obstacle to smoother structural change. (Manow and Seils 2000: 301).

Therefore, even after the huge overvaluation of the East German mark, much damage was done by the manner in which the institutions responded to the impact of Kohl's populist imposition of a 1:1 exchange rate between the West and East German marks. Manow and Seils argue that the increase in social insurance contributions, needed to fund the social insurance programmes absorbing large numbers of newly unemployed workers, priced the long-term unemployed and the low-skilled out of the labour market through the rise in non-wage labour costs. This in turn further burdened the welfare system as it was forced to bear the costs of the habitual response to the new circumstances (Manow and Seils 2000; Scharpf 2000). There was, in consequence, a perverse interaction between the welfare system and the labour market, but despite the vicious circle encouraged by the institutional framework, it persisted throughout the 1980s and 1990s (Hemerijck and Schludi 2000).

Hence for the varieties of capitalism literature Germany exhibited an inability to adapt when confronted by challenges of a substantial nature (Kitschelt and Streeck 2003). For example, the Bundesrat, the upper house of Parliament which is comprised of regional representatives and has significant powers, was controlled by the SPD in the mid-1990s, which enabled it to block a major tax reform proposed by the government. As Flockton (1996: 213) argues, similar reforms had been suggested at regular intervals since the coalition's accession to power in 1982, meaning that throughout the Kohl era (1982–98) 'very little has been achieved from coalition politics, lobbying and the checks and balances between upper and lower houses of parliament.' (see also Kitschelt and Streeck 2003).

However, despite the significant obstacles to overcoming institutional dysfunction, it needs to be asked why, in contrast to the Netherlands, Germany was unable to form a consensus and embark on a process of social learning. This is a pertinent question because, as in Germany, in the Netherlands 'policymaking is critically dependent upon the agreement of different coalition partners and support from the social partners.' (Hemerijck 2001: 98). Moreover, in the mid-1990s it was believed that substantial change in Germany was 'dependent on prerequisite shifts in the terms of the prevailing consensus' (Gordon Smith *et al.* 1996: 6) – which was also the case in the Netherlands in the early 1980s. So why did this not happen? Why were the tendencies to path-dependence stronger than the tendencies to social learning?

The varieties of capitalism literature often discusses the limited capacity of the German state to act decisively, thus restricting its ability to establish a shadow of hierarchy, *à la* its Dutch counterpart, in the name of the public interest (see Scharpf 2000; Wood 2001). For example, power is dispersed throughout the system by way of its federal political structure, the significant role for the Bundesrat and parapublic institutions such as the Federal Employment Office (Katzenstein 1987), and the autonomy enjoyed by the social partners with regard to collective bargaining (known as *Tarifautonomie*). The potential for reform initiatives to be caught in a "joint decision trap" (cf. Scharpf 1988; Hemerijck and Schludi 2000), when one or more actors veto proposed changes, is thus strong. However, the Dutch state had far from unlimited powers owing to the space for governance it shared with the social partners and, in other policy areas, with a range of interest groups.[6] Indeed, the lesson from the Dutch variety of capitalism would appear to be that state agency, rather than state power *per se*, is key (Hemerijck and Vail 2006). The widespread acceptance of Peter Hall's (1993) appropriation of Heclo's (1974) framework for policy change is a defining feature of this aspect of the varieties of capitalism literature. It is argued:

> Policy adjustment is as much the outcome of "puzzling" – diagnosing the nature and magnitude of the problems at hand, setting priorities, and identifying potentially effective policy solutions – as it is a product of "powering", skilfully rallying political and societal

> support for the selection of particular solutions. (Hemerijck and Schludi 2000: 131).

Thus the state, given its sovereign status, power to set the agenda, and, in some cases, the popular legitimacy enjoyed by the government, has the capacity to make a decisive impact on the trajectory of the political economy – and this includes the German state (cf. Hemerijck and Vail 2006; Timmins 2000). Therefore, the restricted role for the German state is not an adequate explanation. Instead, the literature emphasizes that the state did not exploit the potential to, like its Dutch counterpart, cajole the social partners towards a reform agenda. An excellent example is the Alliance for Jobs process of the late 1990s, in which considerable hopes and expectations were invested. Despite the political capital possessed by the newly elected SPD-Green coalition, which resurrected the moribund Alliance for Jobs process begun in the dying days of the Kohl era, path-dependence again took precedence over social learning.

One of the central criticisms of the Alliance for Jobs process was the lack of direction – or the absence of a "shadow of hierarchy" – given to the social partners by the Chancellor's Office. Despite the outlining of a comprehensive set of topics for discussion, neither the objectives nor the organizational structure were fully defined (Timmins 2000). This is despite the frequent references to the Dutch reform process in political discourse, which, as discussed above, included a significant role for the state. As a result, the literature argues that the social partners were allowed to absolve themselves from responsibility for constructing a consensus on labour market and welfare reform, defensively protecting their own interests instead of considering the national interest (Streeck and Hassel 2003).

The most significant example of this was, in contrast to its central role in the Wassenaar process, the absence of wages from the Alliance agenda out of respect for the tradition of *Tarifautonomie*. Although a two-year wage settlement was agreed between the employers' associations and the unions, the state was not involved in the bargaining. This limitation of the scope and application of the tripartite arena was replicated elsewhere, with negotiations often taking place on a bipartite basis between: the social partners on vocational education issues; the government and the employers on tax reform; and the government and the unions on labour market policy. In addition, some decisions – such as the 2001 pension reform – were made outside the Alliance for Jobs fora entirely (Vail 2003). This significantly restricted the scope for links between different policy and institutional reforms to be made (Timmins 2000), because the shadow of hierarchy could not be cast over the social partners. As a result, the broad ownership of the reform agenda found in the Netherlands did not develop in Germany, limiting significantly the potential for a process of social learning to acquire momentum.

Thus although the institutional system made it difficult for a consensus to emerge, the absence of consensus was, ultimately, the result of the tripartite actors being unable to reach agreement. By way of illustration, Hemerijck and Vail (2006: 79) argue that employers and trade unions wanted very different outcomes: increased labour flexibility and limits to social contributions and taxation for the former, and the protection of industrial jobs over the creation of service employment for the latter. As can be expected, these differing agendas made it difficult for a consensus to be constructed. With little appetite for compromise and the exchange of concessions, consensus could have been, in contrast to the Netherlands, only a *product* and not a *prerequisite* of the negotiations (Timmins 2000). Hence the pessimism in much of the literature in the early 2000s: a consensus would develop only after reforms had proved successful, but the reforms could not be enacted if no consensus existed (see Kitschelt and Streeck 2003 for an example of such pessimism).

The government allowed the Alliance for Jobs process to lapse in early 2003, with the negotiations having been '[d]eadlocked almost from the beginning' (Streeck and Trampusch 2005: 183). Streeck and Trampusch add that nothing was achieved 'apart from the so-called *Job Aqtiv–Gesetz* and two symbolic pilot projects to improve the labour market situation of low-skilled workers, the long-term unemployed and low-income families' (*ibid.*), plus other measures which had no real impact (such as an extension of publicly funded employment programmes).[7] In consequence, the prospects for the German economy, after this major attempt at coordinating a response to the low growth and high unemployment, plus other issues such as welfare state viability, were deemed gloomy. Indeed, the only bright spot was the manufacturing exports sector, which in any case tended not to deliver the needed employment growth by way of the high productivity growth rates crucial to its success (Scharpf 2000).

Therefore, in contrast to the Dutch experience, Germany in the 1980s and 1990s was characterized by an inability to forge a consensus on meeting the growing economic challenges. This was the case even in the late 1990s, by which time sustained economic underperformance – and most notably, persistently high unemployment – had led to the establishment of the Alliance for Jobs process. Thus the Alliance for Jobs, in the same way that Wassenaar illustrates the power of the social learning concept, illustrates the power of the path-dependence concept for explaining why consensus was not formed in Germany in the 1980s and 1990s. While the presence of institutional veto points is undoubtedly part of the explanation, ultimately the tripartite actors themselves bear responsibility for the absence of consensus, and thus the absence of a coherent response to the myriad of economic problems facing the German variety of capitalism.

## Conclusion: towards a "common sense" analysis

This chapter has argued that, for the varieties of capitalism literature, consensus played a crucial role in the trajectories of the Dutch and German political economies in the 1980s and 1990s. The presence of consensus enabled institutional dysfunction to be overcome in the former, and the absence of consensus allowed institutional dysfunction to perpetuate in the latter. It was shown how the concepts of social learning and path-dependence were utilized to explain the presence of consensus in the Netherlands and the absence of consensus in Germany. However, the varieties of capitalism literature's focus on institutions as the source of consensus renders it unable to *analyse* these processes; it can only *describe* them. This is because the literature neglects the issue of consensus formation, which extends to the absence of consensus formation. Its unsatisfactory position on the relationship between state and society makes it impossible for the conditions of consensus (cf. van Dyk 2006: 409) to be explored in any depth. To repeat the questions posed at the start of this chapter, why and how did consensus form, or not, at that particular time, and why and how did consensus form, or not, over those particular issues? How can consensus itself, or the absence of consensus, be analysed and explained?

To reiterate the point made in earlier chapters, to analyse consensus in the manner demanded by these questions one must firstly arrive at a satisfactory conceptualization of culture. The next three chapters will utilize empirical data to argue that, armed with the neo-Gramscian conceptualization of culture outlined in the previous chapter, 'it is then possible to address the question as to *why* a certain set of ideas, rooted within...material relations, dominates at a particular point in time.' (Bieler and Morton 2008: 123). Through doing so my point of departure from the varieties of capitalism literature will be demonstrated, for I will be able to show *why* and *how* consensus did and did not form in the Wassenaar and Alliance for Jobs processes.

# 5
# The Netherlands and Wassenaar

Silke van Dyk's article on consensus in the Netherlands in the 1982–2001 period argues that, especially given the hype in the 1990s about the Dutch "Polder model" – and, moreover, given the traditional view that the Netherlands is intrinsically a consensual or consociational democracy – there is a need 'to reposition consensus from an *explanans* to an *explanandum* by investigating the conditions of consensus.' (2006: 409; original emphasis ).[1] Furthermore, she makes it clear that, through repositioning consensus as something to be explained rather than that which does the explaining, we can politicize the social and economic conditions which the literature takes for granted (*ibid.*). Therefore, as asserted at the end of the previous chapter, we should ask how this process of consensus formation actually took place. Van Dyk writes from a Foucauldian perspective, and thus, as the critique in Chapter 2 would expect, says little about the *material* conditions of consensus. Nevertheless, a neo-Gramscian approach is in accordance with the spirit of van Dyk's contribution to the extent that it seeks to denaturalize the role of consensus in the trajectory of the Dutch variety of capitalism.

This chapter argues that the denaturalization process must be grounded in a discussion of what the economic "facts" of life are from the perspective of the Dutch actors. In particular, the assumption of economic vulnerability forms an anchor for the various versions of common sense which exist in the Netherlands, and thus provides ample scope for their content to overlap. As a result, there is considerable potential for consensus to form through a synthesis of versions of common sense which take vulnerability as their starting point. There is consequently a deep and long-standing internalization of the international into the national. Moreover, the means by which the international has been internalized into the national – highlighting their intertwining in a unique combination of the two – has been via what Uwe Becker (2001a) terms "consensualism", a Dutch policymaking tradition which places great emphasis on agreement being reached between the actors. More specifically, maintaining international competitiveness through wage moderation – and thus generating wealth through exports – has been *the* means by which the Dutch have interpreted the conditioning of the international. This is not to say that wage moderation was pursued or achieved at all times, but it *is* the case that economic difficulties tend to bring this policy back to the forefront of the conceptions of the world held by the tripartite actors.

Accordingly, the crisis in the early 1980s is discussed in this chapter, for the collective perception of crisis led to the Wassenaar Agreement. I also focus on the fact that the unions, after 1982, continually sacrificed income in the name of a belief in the virtues of moderate labour costs for economic and employment growth. While the varieties of capitalism literature uncritically views this significant concession as an example of the multiple pathways that can be taken to economic success, it remains the case that wage moderation commanded, and commands, a remarkable legitimacy in the Netherlands. Thus the consensus that developed in the aftermath of the 1982 Wassenaar Agreement was heavily skewed against the interests of organized labour, yet the tradition of consensualism and the legitimacy of wage moderation led the unions to acquiesce reluctantly to a consensus whose social content was much more favourable to capital. Hence the "shadow of hierarchy" cast by the state over the social partners in 1982 marked the beginning of capital's moment of power in the Netherlands. This moment has been long-lasting, as evidenced by, to give two examples, the continued wage moderation and the flexibilization of the labour market.

The chapter is divided into four main sections. Below I consider the question of consensus in the Netherlands, before demonstrating that the world economy has been a constant reference point for Dutch actors. The third section discusses the impact of the economic crisis in the early 1980s, which not only generated a collective perception of crisis but also a perception that the crisis should be resolved collectively – even though the resulting reforms were much closer to capital's than labour's interests. Subsequently, I assess the reform process itself. I focus on the flexibilization of the labour market, which in the end enjoyed the support of the unions as well as of the employers, as an illustration of the claims made earlier in the chapter. Throughout the chapter I use verbatim quotations, with acronyms used to mask the personal identity of the interviewee. What the acronyms stand for can be found in the notes inserted in the text where the acronym is mentioned for the first time, and also at the beginning of the book.[2]

## Consensus in the Netherlands

When discussing the consensus politics said to exist in the Netherlands, many of the interviewees referred to historical influences that still shape political attitudes:

> The people of Switzerland can all go on their holidays together for 8 weeks, and when they come back they would have some difficulties in restarting their society. If the Dutch population should go on their holidays for 8 weeks, they could not restart the society when they come back because two-thirds of the society would have been drowned under water (VVD#2).[3]

Thus the construction of the dykes centuries ago, when struggling against the recognized ability of the North Sea to cover much of the country, symbolizes the willingness of actors from all sides to reach agreement where possible. In addition, many referred to the history of trading with other countries in order to generate wealth:

> And another historical fact, which I think is important, is the "Golden Age" of the Netherlands in the seventeenth century. The Netherlands was a traders' nation. We earned our money from trade with every part of the world...And our Dutch forefathers were clever enough to discover that if you have to earn your money from trade then you had better be friends with as many people as possible. And you can better try to solve problems by

> discussing them with your opponents than by fighting your opponents. And I think that more than anything else has shaped our Dutch culture (FNV#1).[4]

Several commentators, along with some of the interviewees, have referred to the institutional mechanisms for translating dialogue between opposing views into consensus that all, however reluctantly, subscribe to. For instance, Karsten *et al.* (2008: 41) discuss how a confluence of factors – such as fighting against the water and the Spanish in the Eighty Years' War of 1568–1648 – helped produce a system 'in which social dialogue, consensus seeking and compromise played a central role'. Moreover, '[w]ithin a setting of modern industrial relations it developed into a detailed integration of organized interests in which the state, employers and confederations negotiated over labour issues.' (*ibid.*: 43). FNV#1 gave a similarly positive interpretation of how the system functions:

> in the nineteenth century and the beginning of the twentieth century there were of course the same clashes between labour and capital as in most European countries, but rather soon afterwards you saw the development towards more cooperation and an increasing feeling that, whether you like it or not, you have to live with each other, and you have to deal with each other...And then after the Second World War, there was a rather new mood. We have to cooperate to rebuild the country, we should forget old-fashioned prewar conflicts between the classes...And that also resulted in the new institutions, like the Foundation of Labour, like the Social and Economic Council. In general you could say that from that moment on collective bargaining was accepted as the normal pattern to shape our labour relations. (FNV#1)

However, any consensus that is formed must be maintained and sometimes reconstructed. VNO–NCW[5] asserted:

> every year you have to struggle – the employers and the trade unions – to reach that consensus. Every year you have to deserve that. It is not [enough] on its own...Every year you have to

> prove your attitude, the trust in each other...So you have to struggle every year to reach that consensus.

Therefore, the construction, maintenance and reconstruction of consensus need not be a smooth process. More specifically, consensus does not necessarily entail positive agreement; reluctant acquiescence is as likely. It was argued in Chapter 3 that the need to gain the consent of the other social groups makes it necessary for the leading social group to offer reasons for acquiescing to their hegemonic project. In the Dutch case, Becker (2001a: 29) contends that the culture of consensualism – which he argues is characteristic of Dutch political life – makes it imperative that no party is the 'absolute loser' from the bargaining process. In practice this means that 'the dominant interpretation of the general interest' is rendered the generally accepted opinion and, further, that this is presented by leading and subordinate groups as a joint decision (*ibid.*; see also Becker 2001b: 471–8). Thus the offering of concessions is asymmetrically spread across stronger and weaker groups.[6]

In keeping with this, PvdA#1[7] asserted that 'you have to have a mix of real and symbolic gains' for consensus to be formed, which often requires the pragmatic trading of concessions between the trade unions and employers. In other words, the trade unions managed to extract some concessions from the employers in these two decades. However, on the whole the real concessions tended to flow from labour to capital, and symbolic concessions the other way. Consider this comment by the employers' association representative on the Wassenaar Agreement:

> And if you look back you can say well, the wage costs moderation succeeded, but the shortening of the working time....failed is a strong word...because it doesn't work if you shorten the working week from 40 hours to 34 without reducing the wages. The wage costs per hour are more than otherwise. So that didn't succeed, but that was a concession of ours to the trade unions. (VNO–NCW)

In the varieties of capitalism literature, the exponential rise of part-time work in the 1980s and 1990s is discussed unproblematically as a rational response to economic circumstances that ultimately benefits employers and employees. For example:

> In the early 1980s, employers discovered part-time employment as an alternative for collective working time reduction and countered union demands for a collective reduction of the working week...For employers, part-time employment was the ideal alternative because it is an individual choice and allows differentiation across groups of workers, disconnects operating hours from working hours, brings actual and contractual working hours nearer as part-time workers tend to be sick in their own time, and is reversible. Higher overhead and co-ordination costs are recaptured by lower absentee rates and fringe benefits for part-time workers. (Visser and Hemerijck 1997: 34–5)

This is putatively of benefit for employees as well, since the increased utilization of part-time contracts makes labour more attractive to employers, and thus helps reduce unemployment. Moreover, this is explained by the varieties of capitalism literature as the Netherlands' response to the high unemployment of the early 1980s, and it was far ahead of other countries with respect to part-employment because this strategy was more appropriate in the Netherlands than elsewhere. Nevertheless, it can be seen that this development was not simply an example of the Dutch route to economic success: it was capital's moment of power in the Netherlands, granting trade unions little more than a notional commitment to working time reduction in exchange for a real sacrifice on wages.

It will be argued in the next chapter that the unwillingness of the more powerful German trade unions to accept symbolic concessions when making their own compromise on wages helped prevent the Alliance for Jobs process from acquiring the same momentum as the Wassenaar process did in the Netherlands. This is not, as the varieties of capitalism literature does, to judge harshly such resistance; rather, it is to highlight the need to explain why Dutch trade unions felt it necessary to acquiesce to unequal terms of consensus in the first place. Looking ahead to the rest of this chapter, FNV#2 provided an important temporal qualification to the relationship between capital and labour. The dynamics of consensus politics in the Netherlands are, at least with regard to the political economy, very much driven by economic crisis:

> The Polder model only works when there is a crisis. There was an economic crisis in the early 1980s, and in 1982 there was a national agreement for the mid-term...But it really was a crisis – I told you about the 800,000 unemployed...That was a real problem. Then it works, and then you have an agreement. And in the early 1990s we had another national agreement because there was a crisis again... How can you say it in good English? A little bit opportunistic. Opportunistic from the side of the government and the employers. Only if they need them [the unions], then they use them.

The crisis in the early 1980s will be returned to below. For now, though, I wish to comment on the significance of this quote for Becker's more critical perspective. For example, he (2001a: 29) claims that consensualism is 'a mechanism of sustaining hegemony', but he does not delve any deeper than stating that capital's 'power is rooted in social and political dependency on profitability' (*ibid.*). The full implications of such a statement must be elaborated upon in order to gain a more nuanced insight into why the trade unions acquiesced to wage moderation. So while he provides a compelling overview of consensualism as a means of bargaining and decision-making, the material underpinning of these negotiations is left somewhat understated. In contrast, a neo-Gramscian framework makes it possible to concur with Becker that the creation and maintenance of hegemony resides in its ability not just to produce consent but also to contain dissent. At the same time, it enables us to go beyond Becker in providing a considerably richer account of how and why certain conceptions of the world are produced and reproduced over time.

This is the task of the rest of the chapter. The next section argues that the shared assumption of economic vulnerability is key to analysing the trajectory of the Dutch political economy; subsequently I examine the economic crisis in the early 1980s and the flexibilization of the labour market which followed. Through doing so I demonstrate how alternative conceptions of the world are, in effect, foreclosed by the (depoliticized) common sense assumption that as a small, open economy the Netherlands has little choice in how it adapts to economic change.

## The assumption of vulnerability

This section seeks to show that no interviewee considered the Netherlands to be in a strong position *vis-à-vis* the world economy: it is a country which suffers from a long-standing economic vulnerability.[8] The history of vulnerability was often referred to by the interviewees, and many stressed that even in times of greater Dutch influence on international affairs (such as in the seventeenth century), this was achieved through trade and not through intrinsic power *vis-à-vis* other countries. This provided for a particular insertion into capitalism, giving the Netherlands a material basis for existence that was rooted in the international. In terms of the contemporary era, VNO–NCW highlighted an aspect of vulnerability rarely discussed in the IPE literature, but which nevertheless is significant:

> We are very dependent on Germany, the big countries in Europe. They go their own way – you can see that now with the European Community.[9] So we say well, we are very dependent, so people here have to speak three languages – French, German and English – and to trade in Europe and also in the whole world. So that's an expression of a small country fighting with the water, fighting with the Spaniards, and now recently, you have to speak three languages to make trade with other countries. (VNO–NCW)

In addition, as can be seen in the below quote, the language used to depict such economic vulnerability was often stark:

> there [France] you have a polarized situation between employers and employees. Also in political terms. A polarized situation. Right. Left. Employees against employers. We cannot afford it. We cannot afford it in this country...We [small countries] are small economies, so we have to be more flexible. Otherwise this is disastrous, it would be suicidal. (VVD#1)

As was discussed in the previous chapter, the desire for competitiveness based on moderate labour costs has been a long-standing policy goal. It should now be clear that in the Netherlands moderate labour costs can be justified through invoking the world economy, for economic vulnerability is a "fact" that all actors accept as reality. The varieties of capitalism literature takes for granted that moderate labour costs are, by way of its emphasis on the multiple paths to economic success, the basis for the Dutch route to prosperity. For example, Robert Henry Cox (2001), who exerts considerable energy in asserting the analytical importance of how economic imperatives are socially constructed, states blandly that '[w]age restraint has a long history, serving as the cornerstone of consensus within corporatist negotiations.' (*ibid.*: 483). In contrast, a neo-Gramscian framework makes it possible to demonstrate that the manner in which the international is internalized into the national – Gramsci's unique intertwining of the horizontal and the vertical – is key to understanding why moderate labour costs are viewed to be a necessary condition for Dutch prosperity. To illustrate my position, the below quotes explicitly link the assumption of vulnerability to the policy of wage restraint:

> Well, it is true of course that we earn more than 60% of our national income from exports, and on the other hand we import more than 60% of what we consume. So we have a very open economy, and that means that competitiveness compared to other countries is all-important to us. We simply cannot afford very big differences in wage costs, for instance, in comparison to our main competitors, and our competitors are of course Germany, Belgium and France, and to a little lesser extent the United Kingdom and the United States. And since we have joined the EU, and especially since we have a common currency, our economy is very much tied to other economies. There's no doubt about that. (FNV#1)

> It's [being a small country] not much theorized...But stronger is this idea that we have to adapt. One of the instruments is this wage restraint. It's remarkable how long this tradition goes on, even if you expect that there will be some resistance in certain sectors. And again, even in the trade union movement, which is not very centralized, it goes on. (PvdA#1)

The fact that the relatively decentralized trade union movement was able to adhere to wage moderation across different sectors indicates that the legitimacy of wage moderation is strong. Nevertheless, many interviewees continued to assert the choice the Netherlands had over precisely how moderate labour costs were achieved:

> you must keep in mind that dependency does not mean that you have to be in all respects exactly the same as your neighbour countries. There is still room for manoeuvre regarding how exactly you shape your labour relations. If you take care of the overall labour costs compared to other countries, so that labour costs compared to labour productivity is not out of balance compared to other countries. But there is room for manoeuvre. For instance, if we want more part-time labour in the Netherlands than in other countries, why not? If only it does not lead to a grave imbalance in productivity and labour costs. (FNV#1)

This enables us to construct a more sophisticated picture, based on the above and other comments. The Netherlands, despite the vulnerability, is able to adhere to some of the social norms – such as the desirability of a welfare state – often viewed as characteristic of European varieties of capitalism. Nevertheless, a frequent assertion was that this is *dependent* on moderate labour costs: only if this overarching goal is achieved will the Netherlands generate the economic and employment growth needed for a generous and extensive welfare state. So how did the pursuit of moderate labour costs manifest itself in practice? This question needs to be asked because the periodic drives for wage moderation since 1945 indicate that it has not always been adhered to, especially in good economic times.[10] VVD#2 provided many interesting insights on this point:

> Politicians who are active in the daily political life are looking at things from their own limited kingdom. And they tend to... underestimate all the things that are outside their scope...There is a difference between the instant reaction necessary in the situation, and the permanent array of thinking in which you can operate and flourish.

This quote takes us closer to the *practice* of how, as PvdA#1 put it, 'being a small country is a very important aspect of explaining how things are seen here'. To elaborate, FNV#2's more cynical assessment takes us to the heart of how economic challenges are responded to by actors 'looking at things from their own limited kingdom':

> you can say that the Dutch are at home when the dykes are broken. That really is a crisis, and there is a solution. But as long as the dykes are there, do not believe it. Nothing happens. Living together, between the dykes, discussing all things in life, but doing nothing.

Thus the various versions of common sense overlap to a lesser degree in times of prosperity, because the material basis for existence is increasingly taken for granted. The assumption of economic vulnerability moves away from the forefront of thoughts about the political economy, weakening the anchor that this assumption provides for the various cultures in the Netherlands. In the process, the legitimacy of wage moderation, which is accepted in theory and returns to the limelight in more difficult economic times, diminishes in practice even as it is adhered to in principle. However, when there are economic difficulties there is a heightened awareness of the Netherlands' weak position in the international, strengthening the anchor for the various cultures and narrowing the range of common sense opinions about the political economy. In turn, the depoliticized assumption of economic vulnerability justifies a renewed drive for wage restraint by way of the heavy accumulation of common sense sediments on the state's institutional terrain regarding labour costs.

Thus the reminder of economic vulnerability that such times bring is an essential element of the long-term maintenance and sometime reconstruction of consensus, for it increases the potential for synthesis between the different versions of common sense, with wage restraint acting as the ideological cement holding them together (to the benefit of the ascendant – that is, capital's – version of common sense). Furthermore, certain periods will weaken, or strengthen, the anchor more than others. In the below quote CDA#1[11] contrasts the 1970s, when the discovery of natural gas combined with the impact of the long postwar boom to weaken the anchor provided by the assumption of vulnerability, with the strengthening of the anchor after the crisis of the early 1980s:

> I think one important thing has changed since the 1970s. We all have discovered that radical political ideologies are not helpful for reaching those goals. We have become more pragmatic.

The next section considers the decisive impact of the crisis of the early 1980s on the trajectory of the Dutch political economy. Through the discussion it will be demonstrated that the pragmatism alluded to in the above quote is too neutral a term, obscuring as it does the social content of the pragmatism. The strengthening of the anchor provided by the assumption of vulnerability did not just narrow the range covered by the various versions of common sense: it also created the conditions for capital's moment of power in the Netherlands.

## Crisis and Wassenaar

Colin Hay (2001: 203) asks a question which goes to the heart of studies of the development of a perception of crisis in any political economy: '[i]s the identification of a situation as one of crisis an objective, analytical, or even empirical claim or does it necessarily imply a subjective and hence a normative judgment?' On the next page he provides his own answer to this question:

> if it is narratives of crisis that are responded to and not the contradictions themselves, [then] we cannot in any sense (theoretical or otherwise) derive the response to crisis from a static analysis of the contradictions of the existing system. (*ibid.*: 204)

It must be stressed that Hay was not referring to the Netherlands but to narratives of crisis in general, with an application of his framework to the UK in the late 1970s. For him the subjective dimension was key to the emergence of crisis awareness in the UK at that time:

> economic performance was improving prior to the onset of crisis and it worsened significantly with the turn to monetarism in response to the crisis. The notion that this was a crisis

> of Keynesianism to which monetarism was a (necessary) response is thus difficult to reconcile with the empirical record. (Hay 2007: 193)

While concurring with Hay in the sense that it is through our conceptions of the world that we make sense of the world, he neglects the fact that the conceptions themselves are saturated with references to the material basis for existence. Indeed, later in his discussion Hay claims that the 1978–9 Winter of Discontent was not the result of poor economic performance or economic restructuring. Rather, it was 'a direct consequence of the ever more desperate attempts to manage a stagflationary scenario by passing the costs on to organized labour through ever more punitive incomes policies.' (*ibid.*: 195). However, this is very much in line with a neo-Gramscian and not the constructivist institutionalist outlook that Hay supports, because he explicitly refers to the reaction of trade unions to a more punitive material basis for existence. Acknowledging that crisis awareness is discursively constructed does not preclude a theoretical stance which attempts to elucidate why such awareness emerged *in the first place*, which enables us to identify its social content. As Gramsci (1971: 184; emphasis added) argued:

> It may be ruled out that immediate economic crises *of themselves* produce fundamental historical events; they can simply create a terrain more favourable to the dissemination of certain modes of thought, and certain ways of posing and resolving questions involving the entire subsequent development of national life.

Thus crisis awareness is contingent in terms of its specific timing, but it is also clearly related to the material basis for existence. In the Dutch case the economic difficulties of the early 1980s created a terrain more favourable to the development of crisis awareness. Moreover, the potential for crisis awareness to develop was enhanced by the long-standing internalization of the international into the national. This reminder of vulnerability manifested itself in the macroeconomic situation of the time, with high unemployment and a deep recession narrowing the breadth covered by the various versions of common sense to the point at which a new consensus could be forged. CDA#1 spoke for many when asserting both the importance of the world economy as a reference point and the need for wage-based international competitiveness:

> A small country like the Netherlands has to be very competitive with its surrounding neighbours. In the 1970s, we had forgotten the importance of that notion, so by the end of the 1970s the wage costs in this country had become much higher than in the surrounding countries, especially Germany.

Thus the second oil crisis catalysed the worsening of the difficulties facing the Dutch economy, and the early 1980s saw these problems develop into a 'critical situation' (FNV#1) (as also discussed by FNV#2 earlier in this chapter). And they were not restricted to notionally economic issues:

> the real critical year when I was in Parliament was 1982. That was a very, very crucial year. It was a disaster, a disastrous year. That was the year when we had a very short-lived government...It was a combination of the CDA and leftish elements around den Uyl. Then the government fell down, through in fact the tactics of the socialists who could not master the situation. Then it was really the moment when people said inside the political and outside the political sphere, something has to be done. (VVD#1)

And while the ascription of the blame to the left is unsurprising for a VVD member, later comments reinforced the underlying message, particularly in the way the Netherlands was distinguished from neighbouring countries:

> even between the VVD and the PvdA in the early 1980s, when we were very much against each other in the political sense, there was nevertheless also a common understanding that things had to be changed. There is no doubt about this. It is not a typical polarization as you had [at that time], and still have, in France. (VVD#1)

The feeling of urgency was thus felt across the political spectrum: the reminder of economic vulnerability penetrated deeply.

Moreover, there was a desire to deal with the crisis collectively:

> So we had a lot of unemployed people, rising very fast, but also the trade unions lost a lot of members because they became unemployed. So the membership of the trade unions was downsizing enormously also. And that was the situation in 1981, 1982. And that was the moment that our chairman had informal talks with the chairman of the FNV. How to save the country. And they had interests that were suddenly common. (VNO–NCW)

> we often saw in the period at the end of the 1970s and in the early 1980s, that the sons and daughters of the employers were also unemployed. And that was very important. I remember that in one of the most important meetings...one of the employers told me that his son, who was a good student – he did well at school and at the university – had no job. So it was also important for the employers to have jobs for unemployed people, and for the younger unemployed. It was a common problem for employers as well – how can we solve this? (PvdA#2)

Despite the parity between capital and labour implied by these two quotations, the bargain struck in the Wassenaar Agreement was clearly unequal. There was a painful acquiescence by the trade unions to employer wishes for wage restraint, in exchange for a symbolic promise by capital to reduce working time. Moreover, any small progress made was simply a continuation of a decades-long trend towards decreasing working hours for full-time employees (Becker 2001b: 463). Becker also contends that 'working time reduction of a similar extent was also realized in Germany, Belgium and the Scandinavian countries, where wage restraint was much less drastic.' (*ibid.*: 467)

So why did this happen? Both Becker (2001a, 2001b, 2005) and van Dyk (2006), two of the few critical voices on the trajectory of the Dutch political economy after 1982, make their case in a manner similar to Hay: "truths" about the economy were produced by the powerful actors in order to fix the terms of the debate in favour of their perspective, and over time the weaker actors – principally the trade unions and the PvdA – accommodated themselves to these "facts". Indeed, this process of accommodation and incorporation was often done retrospectively, with the trade unions only in the 1990s supporting fully the reform process set in motion from 1982 onwards (Becker 2001b; van Dyk 2006).

However, short of discussing in general terms the shift in the balance of power between capital and labour towards the former (see Becker 2001a: 28; van Dyk 2006: 413), there is little consideration of *why* certain ideas became truths about the economy and others did not. Here it is appropriate to remind ourselves of the intertwining of the national and the international. On the one hand, the world economy is a constant reference point because of the international material basis for existence. On the other hand, the Dutch traditions of consensualism made it important for labour to acquiesce to the dominant interpretation of how to respond to the challenges posed by economic vulnerability. The manifestation of this intertwining was the consensus on moderate labour costs, a hegemony which did not necessarily gain the consent of organized labour, but at the very least contained dissent on the unequal exchange of concessions imposed on trade unions.

As stated earlier, this does not guarantee the conclusion of agreements such as Wassenaar (see Woldendorp and Keman 2007 for a rigorous overview of the 1965–2000 period), but it does enable us to conceive of how and why agreements, when they occur, are reached. Thus in the case of Wassenaar the employers emerged as the clearly ascendant actor, but this ascendancy necessitated the acquiescence of the trade unions for it to be confirmed. In turn, acquiescence was made possible by the underlying assumption that the Netherlands had to adapt to economic change. Thus the unions reluctantly accepted the notion that wage restraint was the means by which economic and employment growth could be restored. Therefore, *Wassenaar signified capital's moment of power in the Netherlands.*

In addition, the Wassenaar Agreement was mirrored by a shift in direction in the political arena. This helped secure capital's moment of power on the state's institutional terrain:

> [There were] three people of one party and three people from the other party for the [formulation of the conservative–liberal coalition's] economic policies. Other policies also had working groups of three from each party. But the most important working group was [the] working group [for economic policies], and that

> working group had three members from the liberal party and three members from the CDA...A very rigorous government agreement, which could come very much close together with the [Wassenaar] Agreement on the social front [was made]...So that all came together, and the whole thing could, more or less, be brought together in three...tracks. The first track was to reduce the budget deficit, definitely down. The second one was industrial renewal, restructuring of the economy, and the third one was employment – bring down unemployment. (VVD#1)

VVD#1 also referred to the Wagner Commission, which had published a report in 1981 entitled 'A New Industrial Élan'. The commission had been established in the hope that it would make recommendations from outside the deadlocked tripartite negotiations that would nevertheless be accepted by the tripartite actors. As it turned out, the recommendations proved to be very much in favour of capital's agenda, as van Apeldoorn (2008: forthcoming) explains:

> The Wagner Commission issued a number of recommendations – including a reduction of wage costs; a retrenchment of public expenditure; a reform of social security in order to prod people back on to the labour market and an end to...state aids for declining industries – which, as Visser and Hemerijck (1997: 100) conclude, in retrospect 'reads as a catalogue of the policy measures adopted over the next fifteen years'.

Visser and Hemerijck (1997), and the varieties of capitalism literature in general, regard the implementation of these policy measures as the outcome of the social learning process initiated by the establishment of the state's "shadow of hierarchy" in late 1982. However, it was much more than this: there was a marked shift in the state's social content, with significant consequences for the trajectory of the Dutch variety of capitalism. The Wagner Commission acted as the organic intellectual for capital, not least because Wagner was the CEO of Shell (van Apeldoorn 2008), and the condensation of this agenda on the state's administrative terrain was achieved once the conservative–liberal coalition had been elected and the Wassenaar Agreement had been concluded. Thus a transformation of common sense was set in motion. Nevertheless, the reforms were anchored in well-established – that is, path-dependent – conceptions of the world that believed moderate labour costs to be key to generating growth and employment in a small, open economy. An excellent summary of the co-existence of change and continuity was provided by CDA#1 (note again the striking language used):

> We said we had no choice. The public finances were in complete disorder. We had to make savings in public expenditure. We could not raise taxes, because it would be to the detriment of the competitive position of the companies in this country, of the private sector. We had to moderate wages, because our labour force was not competitive. So we said we have no choice, there is no real alternative. Otherwise the process would take much more time and would deteriorate our international position even more. And they [the public] saw that tens of thousands of people were losing their jobs in the beginning of the 1980s.

This section has established that there was a collective perception of crisis in the early 1980s, which brought the assumption of economic vulnerability back to the forefront of various versions of common sense in a manner that made it possible for a consensus to be formed – albeit a consensus that embodied capital's moment of power in the Netherlands. The next section will consider the reform process set in motion by the Wassenaar Agreement, with the flexibilization of the labour market analysed in detail.

## The post-Wassenaar trajectory

Many of the reforms that took place in the years after 1982 were detailed in the previous chapter. Therefore, this section will focus on one particular example of such changes, the flexibilization of the labour market. As can be expected from the above discussion, the employers' association representative viewed positively these developments:

> when looking to the labour market you see that we have a lot of dossiers that are unique compared to the European Community. And that is the temporary work agencies, the flexible labour market,

> and they speak about these things in Germany and France with arguments that we used 20, 25 years ago. (VNO–NCW; emphasis added)

As for the trade union position, FNV#1 expressed more qualified support – but support nonetheless – for the flexibilization of the labour market, invoking the need to adapt to changing circumstances:

> You must be careful in this, for the world is changing rapidly. What was optimal a few years ago is perhaps not optimal any more. And there is a lot of discussion going on about it nowadays, also here in the Netherlands. But it looks like that in the 1990s, indeed we struck a better balance between flexibility and stability than the Germans did in a few respects.

This quotation is a good example of the retrospective accommodation with the consensus that Becker and van Dyk discuss. Although FNV#1 did refer to the sacrifices made by the unions when acquiescing to the consensus, FNV#2 provided a clearer picture of the (lack of) manoeuvre available to the unions in the 1980s:

> the labour market is there. There is temporary work, there is part-time work. The Dutch situation was a paradise for employers [in the 1980s]. And we had to give the answer as the unions. In the end we did two things. First we organized the temporary workers, and had our first collective agreement in 1986. It was made by the services union, but it was not really accepted by the other unions. And the whole discussion took 10 years, until 1996, when there was the Dutch flex law. And that was a very interesting period, because 1986 was the first collective agreement. And then you needed 10 years of struggle, struggle, struggle.

Two conclusions can be drawn from these quotes. First of all, the introduction of greater flexibility was mostly at the behest of the employers who, in an era of mass unemployment, were able to demand, and receive, union acquiescence to their vision. Secondly, the 10 years of struggle are an indicator of the path-dependence of common sense opinions (in this case the trade unions). Although some in the trade union movement had acknowledged by the mid-1980s that acquiescence with the employers' vision was necessary because 'the labour market is there', full acquiescence took much longer to achieve. Such a struggle took place because the changes advocated by the services union implied acceptance of an economy with greater worker insecurity, fewer rights, and less opportunity for unions to organize. However, the services union, and increasingly others, did not see how unemployment could be reduced in any other way because capital was, through the expansion of part-time work, reshaping the labour market in any case. Other domestic factors were also pushing the Netherlands in this direction, as PvdA#2 made clear:

> I remember for example...the discussion of labour time, of part-time work. 10 or 15 years ago in the labour unions we thought that part-time labour was the 'hamburger economy'. Cheap labour, with no social rights, the hire and fire economy. And the only work that you can do is helping people bring their goods from the supermarket to their car. And that's nothing, we need to have serious jobs...[However] a lot of women wanted to have work, but not full-time hours. So they wanted to have part-time jobs in combination with childcare.

Therefore, the rise in both unemployment and female participation contributed to a molecular evolution of the versions of common sense adhered to by trade unions and social democrats, moving towards capital's version of common sense to the extent that they were able to acquiesce to labour market flexibilization. The centre of power within the state established by capital in 1982 had proved able to draw hitherto resistant institutional and policy areas into its orbit. In other words, the expansion of part-time labour, with its origins in the symbolic concession on working time made at Wassenaar, was not part of a benign "social learning" process: it created the opportunity for extracting further union acquiescence on temporary work. Some of the interviewees argued that this was an example of Dutch culture, for the preference was for part-time and not full-time work as in Scandinavia, so children did not spend five days a week at a nursery. However, this "choice", this acquiescence, was the outcome of capital forcing labour's hand:

> The facts are that women are willing to work in part-time jobs. And a lot of the unemployed like to work in temporary work, because they want to work and to educate themselves. And they are the facts. *And now the answer of the union: you cannot say it's no good. The facts are there: it is a real situation. You have to accept it, and then look at how to organize.* So we made this collective agreement, and started discussions with the government about the flex law. And after a lot of discussions we got a flex law in 1995, 1996. And fully agreed in the FNV. The FNV was one of the strongest supporters of the flex law in the end. (FNV#2; emphasis added)

As stated in the previous chapter, the "flexicurity" law, which awarded more rights for temporary employees in exchange for fewer rights for permanent employees in order to encourage the growth of flexible work, was actually drawn up by the social partners themselves. In a revealing passage, VNO–NCW said:

> So we said, well, we will make that law. We know how it works, so we the social partners will make that law. And then we advised the government on the law of flexibility, on the temporary work agencies. And they took that into law...So we again got alongside the government, to work together to let the economy work properly.

Note the use of the term 'we' to describe the social partners: even though trade unions and employers' associations in the Netherlands did not always agree, once the former had acquiesced to the latter's wish for a more flexible labour market it was easy to present themselves as a united front to the government, and demand that the government conformed to the tradition of consensualism. It was stated in Chapter 4 that for the varieties of capitalism literature the common agenda developed after 1982 made it possible for policy proposals to be articulated from different parts of the institutional environment. However, this is uncritically viewed as an indication of a corporatist system which was working well. In contrast, a neo-Gramscian framework makes it possible to argue that the system was working well – *to the extent that the unions were contributing to their own continued subordination* – because of the specific manner in which capital had been able to extract concessions from labour from 1982 onwards.

This is not to say that the concessions made by capital after 1982 were entirely symbolic. As PvdA#1 stated, the trade unions 'weren't able to resist the flexibilization of the labour market and the rise of temporary work. So they adjusted to it, and they got some quite good deals out of it.' In other words, through pushing for a flexicurity law organized labour was able to remain a relevant force in the Dutch political economy. It was more prudent to bend with the wind rather than attempt to stand tall and risk being knocked over; in the process, the tradition of consensualism would make it difficult for employers to walk away from a deal which was largely in accordance with their interests. As a result, in the radicalized political climate of the early 2000s (see Chapter 7), when the trade unions faced a starker choice than those presented to them in the 1980s and 1990s, PvdA#1 could conclude that the greater job security and protection for temporary employees was something that 'employers now are not at all happy with.'

Therefore, union acquiescence could be justified in terms not dissimilar to some of the writings in the varieties of capitalism literature on Germany (and which eventually informed Schröder's Agenda 2010 discourse): that is, a continued refusal to "modernize" could result in market forces blowing apart the institutional structure of the political economy, leaving in its place a much more Anglo–Saxon set of arrangements. As FNV#1 commented:

> There is work to be done in a country like ours which only lasts a few weeks or months, and practically speaking it is better to try and regulate this as best as you can than to sit back and cry that this type of work shouldn't be done.

Nevertheless, it must be recalled that labour's acquiescence to, and retrospective accommodation with, the flexibilization of the labour market was driven by the ascendant position *in general* for capital, in the form of employer and state support for these reforms. In other words, organized labour "learned" to be "more realistic" in the

Netherlands – to use the varieties of capitalism literature's language – because its hand was forced. The flexibilization of the labour market was not a goal of labour but of capital. While the trade unions managed to mount a relatively successful damage limitation exercise, its retrospective accommodation with labour market flexibilization was rooted in a position of considerable weakness *vis-à-vis* the employers. Therefore, as with wage restraint, the exchange of concessions was asymmetrically distributed across the social partners, to the overall benefit of capital. Hence it is of little surprise that the economic and employment boom in the mid to late 1990s was greeted by the unions as a justification of their acquiescence to the reforms of the previous 15 years. Unfortunately for the unions, the subsequent recession and radicalized political climate meant that more concessions were deemed necessary for a return to growth to be achieved. A further condensation of capital's now-lengthy moment of power on the state's institutional terrain appeared imminent. This turbulent period in the recent history of the Dutch variety of capitalism is the subject of the section on the Netherlands in Chapter 7.

## Conclusion

From the vantage point of 2008, it can reasonably be concluded that capital's moment of power in 1982, as symbolized by the Wassenaar Agreement, was of long-lasting significance for the trajectory of the Dutch variety of capitalism. Moreover, this path-dependent transformation of the Dutch political economy is generally believed to have been beneficial, with Wassenaar deemed to have catalysed the improved performance of the Dutch economy in the 1980s and particularly the 1990s. For CDA#1 the crisis of the early 1980s:

> cost us, I think, about 10 years. But we followed that policy fairly consistently, and by the end of the 1980s the total level of labour costs in this country was indeed considerably lower than in Germany, which we considered as our main reference, because that is the country in Europe which is most important as our trade partner. That policy worked, because by the end of the 1980s we saw that employment was growing much faster than in the surrounding countries, and especially in the 1990s we saw that the

> total performance of our country was much better than the bigger countries like France and Germany.

Therefore, even though the role of wage moderation in the improved economic and employment performance is disputed by some (see Becker 2005; Kleinknecht and Naastepad 2005), the co-existence of wage moderation and economic and employment growth in the 1980s and 1990s led many to conclude that the former is the means by which the latter is achieved. The extraordinary legitimacy enjoyed by wage moderation was demonstrated again in the early 2000s, and will be discussed in the section on the Netherlands in Chapter 7. In contrast, the next chapter highlights that shared opinions on economic reality, which was such a strong theme across the interviews in the Netherlands in the form of the assumption of economic vulnerability, was conspicuous by its low profile in the Germany interviews. The consequences for consensus formation were quite different as a result.

# 6
# Germany and the Alliance for Jobs

This chapter demonstrates that in the Alliance for Jobs process there was little overlap between the different versions of common sense, limiting the potential for consensus to form through synthesis. More specifically, it was not possible for agreement about economic "reality" to be reached. This is in contrast to the Dutch experience, where the differing opinions on how best to manage the Dutch economy are rooted in the assumption of vulnerability. This served as a means for forging (asymmetrically constructed) consensus on reform from the early 1980s onwards. Thus there was little scope for assumptions about the political economy to act as an anchor for the various versions of common sense. In addition, the Alliance for Jobs process revealed the difficulty in establishing a common ground even in times of economic difficulty, such as persistently high unemployment.

Perhaps ironically, the need to agree on the "facts" were acknowledged by the social partners, despite their subsequent divergence of opinion on what these assumptions entailed for dealing with challenges such as high unemployment. As BDI[1] stated: 'I think that, as in the Netherlands, both sides have to agree upon the facts. As long as we haven't arrived at this point, then everything will be very difficult.' DGB#1[2] agreed with BDI, arguing that agreement is key to economic success, for these opinions shape how the political economy is viewed: 'what is very important in my opinion is that you reach some general agreement on economic parameters, like the Dutch did...That is a good starting point for measures – that you have the same theory on economic parameters.'

The chapter is divided into four main sections, following a similar pattern to the previous chapter – which will maximize the scope for comparison and contrast between the Dutch and German cases. Below I consider the question of consensus in Germany, before demonstrating that German capital in the 1990s became increasingly dissatisfied with the social market economy, or *Modell Deutschland*. The third and fourth sections discuss the Alliance for Jobs process, which was inaugurated at a time when crisis awareness appeared to have developed to the point at which there was greater potential than in previous years to form a consensus on responding to the prolonged low growth and high unemployment. Two issues central to the absence of consensus – wage moderation and labour market flexibilization – are focused on in order to discuss why the different versions of common sense remained far apart. In particular, the continued resilience of the positions upheld by organized labour in the face of increasingly powerful employers is discussed, for this contrasts with the unions' accommodation with capital in the Netherlands.

As with the previous chapter, verbatim quotations are used throughout, with acronyms used to mask the personal identity of the interviewee. And again, what the acronyms stand for can be found in the notes inserted in the text where the acronym is mentioned for the first time, and also at the beginning of the book.

## Consensus in Germany

Many of the interviewees referred to the tradition of consensual solutions to economic problems, and in some cases gave examples of this approach to policymaking. For instance:

> The Bündnis für Arbeit [Alliance for Jobs] stems from the typical German approach, in accordance with social market policy, to deal with the problem of unemployment. As I said before, there is some typical German cultural way of – maybe I should say continental European way, because the Netherlands are very much the same as the Germans in this case – to deal with the problems. And it is a way of...the principle of consensus. (DGB#1)

The main difference between the German and Dutch interviews in this regard was the shorter history – post-1945 – of consensus alluded to by the German interviewees. Nevertheless, they matched their Dutch counterparts in believing consensus to be central to the functioning of the institutional system. However, it had been more difficult in more recent decades to achieve a consensus on responding to challenges such as high unemployment and low economic growth:

> Maybe, as I said, there was a need for discussing things earlier. There was a need for earlier reforms. And maybe...it would have been better if the so-called consensus-oriented society had reached this consensus in other fields. But maybe we just did not really discuss it. Maybe there was not a need for it...And they [the employers and the trade unions]...had the social partnership. We are very proud of it. It worked, because the economic framework at that time still worked...I do not think that this has changed so much, but the problems we are facing have changed, and maybe we just came to these problems because the consensus before just kept us from certain things. Or from asking certain questions. (BDA[3])

Given the increasing stridency with which the employers were pushing for far-reaching liberalization of the German political economy – this interview was conducted in January 2004, a week after much of the Agenda 2010 programme became law (see the next chapter) – it is unsurprising that the opinion expressed was largely negative. Nevertheless, the underlying message – of Germany being unable to deal satisfactorily with the problems it faced – was a common theme across the interviews. For example, IAB#1[4] argued that while the institutional configuration demanded consensus in order for changes to be made, '[t]here is no true consensus on the actor side.' Therefore, for the Netherlands the ability to forge a consensus was what needed to be explained; for Germany it is the difficulty in forging a consensus that must be explained. As IAB#1 stated, hindering the development of a consensus was disagreement about economic "reality":

> I do not think that there is a consensus on the necessity, the degree and the direction of reforms in Germany. Even today [March 2004 – see the next chapter for more on the transitory consensus

characterizing this period]. There are at least two paradigms. One is more or less the liberal paradigm...And the second one is the more traditional social democratic...or social partnership type of ideology. So I think that consensus is hardly seen. There is still a fundamental debate going on about this point.

The absence of agreement on economic "reality", as can be witnessed by the reference to a "fundamental debate" between "at least two paradigms" makes this clear. Therefore, the potential for synthesis between different versions of common sense has been low. As a result, there has been little appetite for compromise:

At the moment in Germany you have to recognize that there are two problems that we have to face. First of all...you agree to general reforms, but not to reforms that affect you. Much to the others, of course!...this means that there is no movement in society at the moment. Everybody wants to save his own richness... If you go to the BDI or BDA, then they would of course tell you that we have to be more flexible in labour laws, and so on. If you go to DGB, IG Metall [the powerful metalworkers' union], then they tell you that of course we need more security, and so on. (SPD[5])

In addition to the above comments, GRN[6] discussed the debate on labour market reform. From the below quote it is clear that it has proved difficult to forge consensus, even when all sides in the debate agree that reform is needed:

In terms of political debate, it has been really high on the agenda for, I would say, the last 10 years...Actually, it started to become important at the end of the 1980s...[But] it really has become the number one topic from 1994, 1995, 1996 onwards. And I think that it has been the number one priority since then. Which is surprising in a way, because not too much has happened.

Therefore, we have a different situation in Germany compared to the Netherlands. As with the Netherlands, the interviewees referred to the tradition of consensus and the need for a consensus on how to meet economic challenges. However, unlike the Netherlands the potential for synthesizing the different versions of common sense as a means of constructing a consensus was considerably smaller. The lack of an anchor provided by agreement about the economic "facts" made it difficult for this synthesis to take place. Moreover, in addition to this, organized labour in Germany was in a stronger position to resist the employers' agenda. This point is also made by the varieties of capitalism literature, referencing the tradition of *Tarifautonomie* and the absence of a shadow of hierarchy from the state. However, this does not go far enough in explaining the absence of acquiescence, for part of the explanation for Dutch labour moving towards the employers was a desire to place jobs over income. So why, in the context of prolonged mass unemployment, did the trade unions in Germany not make the same concession?

An explanation can be found in the organization of production in the German political economy. It was discussed in the previous chapter that the weak position of the Netherlands in the international provided for a particular insertion into capitalism. The common sense that emerged from this insertion has tended to emphasize the lack of choice in meeting economic challenges, which in turn enhanced the legitimacy of wage moderation for Dutch trade unions. Germany had a different insertion into capitalism: its position in the international has been stronger, owing to the fact that this material basis for existence was largely internal to its territorial boundaries. This is not to say that the Netherlands is wholly dependent on external markets for its prosperity, but that its insertion into capitalism gave its material basis for existence a considerably more international hue. In contrast, the German variety of capitalism contained specific locales which provided the most propitious conditions for capital accumulation in the world capital goods industries (see van der Wurff 1993).

As a result, '[e]mployers – due to the nature of the production process – accorded a high priority to a stable, loyal and well-trained layer of the industrial working class.' (*ibid.*: 167). This gave labour a strength less apparent in the Netherlands, because the specific advantages for the capital goods industries of producing in Germany made it easier for labour to argue that better working conditions, and a more generous welfare state, were not contrary to the interests of the German economy. Combined with the autonomy from state intervention in collective bargaining enjoyed by the social partners, plus codetermination legislation which secured for unions an integral position within companies, and it can be seen how organized labour quickly became after 1945 an indispensable negotiating partner.

However, as noted by Coates (2000: 241), the benefits accruing to the political economy as a whole could be maintained only as long as 'larger and larger shares of world trade in manufactured goods' were captured. This would enable these industries to expand at a rate which would maintain economic growth and full employment. Once this ability to capture ever-larger world market shares began to wane in the 1970s, the consequences for unemployment began to be felt. Nevertheless, as indicated by the persistent growth in balance of payments surpluses, this did not mean that the industrial sector was now unsuccessful. Rather, continued success increasingly rested on value generated by a shrinking workforce. As a result, the equating of industrial success with general economic success became less appropriate.

The next section details how the shift from successful industrial and national economic performance to a successful industrial sector co-existing with declining national economic performance, made it difficult for German actors to modify the conceptions of the world which emerged in the former period. In consequence, the social market economy, even in times of high unemployment, continued to be the reference point. Thus there was a *de facto* consensus in the 1980s across the tripartite actors, but the continued inability of industrial success to equate to general economic success meant that the high unemployment and low growth were not being addressed by these perspectives on the world. And by the 1990s, the greater capacity of the capital goods industries to generate value in production sites outside Germany had catalysed a molecular evolution in the employers' version of common sense, making the formation of a consensus on addressing the economic challenges increasingly improbable.

## German capital and the social market economy

Daniel Kinderman (2005: 438–9) provides an excellent overview of the powerful imagery generated by the success of the

German economy in the decades after the end of the Second World War:

> The social market model is the founding myth of the Federal Republic of Germany, as Haselbach remarks:
>
> > [t]he social market economy constitutes in part West Germany's self-consciousness; it forms the specific "identity" of the West German people. In other words, the "economic miracle" and the "social market economy" constitute the founding myth of West Germany (1997, 158).
>
> The prominence and currency of "social market economy" discourse in Germany is astounding; it would be no exaggeration to say that it is hegemonic as far as economic and social policy is concerned...as Haselbach emphasizes, '[t]he tale of the "social market economy"...is referred to almost every day, somewhere in a German newspaper or political statement; it has become part of the national memory' (1997, 161). The genius of the "social market economy" lies in its versatility: it is both "social" (fair/just) and a "[capitalist] market." By emphasizing different aspects of this totality, Left and Right can endorse the "social market economy" from within their own normative vocabularies.

As will be demonstrated in the next chapter, the term "social market economy" has such currency that the push in the early 2000s for a fundamental modification in the trajectory of the German variety of capitalism argued for a "new" social market economy rather than its abandonment. In the interviews themselves, the actual term was not used very often, but there were many references to a German "model" or German way of doing things. In addition, the powerful impact of the postwar economic success on the "national memory" was discussed:

> after World War II, I think Germany had to find a new self-confidence and we did this through this our strong Dmark... What we could observe was economic growth, and the discussion was how to distribute correctly, and in a just way...That was the discussion in these three decades [1950s, 1960s and 1970s]: how can we distribute what we earn? So when people stopped earning in the 1970s...we still believed that the economic growth that we had, without changes, would be everlasting...And I think in the 1980s,

> we were just so – not just pride, but people of course were proud of their model, it proved to have worked for such a long time...that people did not want to give it [the social market economy] up. Because that is what they were relying on, that is what the first generation after the war grew up with, and things in their mind have always been working. (BDA)

As discussed at the end of the last section, the capital goods industries' growing inability to deliver the desired economic growth and low unemployment did not equate to a crisis in the sector in and of itself. For example, at the end of the 1980s Wolfgang Streeck (1989) was able to talk of "successful adjustment to turbulent markets" in the case of the automobile sector. Therefore, continued industrial success was still believed to equate to continued general success, limiting the potential for a consensus to form on how to deal with the low growth and considerably higher unemployment. A good illustration is the period in the early 1980s, which witnessed the sudden rise in the unemployment rate to high levels and also the fall of the SPD–FDP government in the aftermath of an economic recession. IAB#1 pointed out that the crisis awareness which developed at this time was brief: the much-vaunted *Wende* (turnaround or change) proclaimed by Helmut Kohl and the new CDU/CSU–FDP coalition ground to a halt almost as soon as it had begun. As a result, the high unemployment which characterized all but the final years of the 1980s did not cat-alyse a modification of the versions of common sense. The economy appeared to be continuing to perform well, for the traditional driver of growth, the capital goods industries, continued to perform well.

Therefore, the ability of the "social market economy" concept to have different normative vocabularies attached to it continued well after the divergence between industrial and general economic success had begun. As Sassoon (2000: 6) asserts, 'traditional ways of being and thinking are embedded in institutions and practices which are still influential even when they are being undermined by socio-economic change', because they appear more "real" by way of their longer-established status as a part of the social world (*ibid.*). Hence it is not surprising that there was a *de facto* consensus across the tripartite actors about the ability of the industrial sector to help Germany meet general economic challenges. The common sense sediments that had accumulated heavily over the previous few decades continued to depoliticize thoughts about the economy, despite the considerably worse economic performance in the 1980s. This observation puts us in a better position to explain the response to unification. As Chapter 4 discussed, there was much continuity on the institutional level. For instance, Streeck (1997: 47) argued:

> The West German response to unification was above all designed to protect the West German social order from being modified by the event. Unification was conceived and executed as a giant exercise in *Institutionentransfer*: a wholesale transplantation of the entire array of West German institutions to the former East Germany.

Streeck gives the example of the rapid progress made towards the equalization of wages, which would protect the German social model through the nullifying of wage competition within Germany. He presents this as the protection of the interests of manufacturing industries that are competitive in quality rather than price terms. Nevertheless, the underlying rationale was, as indicated above, the continued belief in the equation of industrial success to general economic success. As GRN stated, 'reunification came, as a sort of interrupting force...And we had a short but very intensive economic high after reunification, and a lot of people had the impression that everything was OK again.' This was recalled with regret by the employers' representative, who in 2004 argued for a considerably different version of common sense compared to capital's outlook in the early 1990s:

> I don't think that employers and trade unions had so different opinions...I can tell you but I don't like to tell you, that even in that time...employers were convinced that job creation programmes could stabilize [the economy after unification]. Again, underestimating the real situation. And in the early 1990s I think employers and employees, the trade unions and the employers' organizations, had quite the same opinion on that. Just more money will do more.

As discussed above, there was not an immediate response to the increasing difficulties experienced in the 1980s, because the continued good performance of the traditional driver of economic growth enabled the equation of industrial to economic success to remain intact. However, whereas the economic recession of the early 1980s confirmed and reinforced the assumption of vulnerability in the Netherlands, the same downturn *challenged* the equating of industrial with general economic success through the considerably lower growth and higher unemployment that followed. And while this did not have much of an impact in the 1980s, from the 1992–3 recession onwards there was a molecular evolution in the version of common sense adhered to by German capital. This came to full fruition with the founding of the New Social Market Economy Initiative in 2000 (*Initiative Neue Soziale Marktwirtschaft* (INSM)) (Kinderman 2005; Menz 2005), which will be discussed in the next chapter. For now, though, it is enough to state that German capital responded to the continued and growing divergence between industrial and economic performance by exporting capital abroad and seeking a more liberal variety of capitalism at home.

This was possible because the 1990s witnessed the growing transnationalization of Germany's material basis for existence (Bieler 2006a), as the advantages of producing in Germany were increasingly challenged by technological diffusion to low-cost competitor countries in East Asia and the fall of communism in eastern Europe. The result was that '[b]etween 1990 and 1997, a *net* total of DM 234 billion new net direct investment flowed out of Germany, DM 47.3 billion (i.e., 1.3 percent of GDP) in 1997 alone, an all-time record' (Silvia 1999: 84; original emphasis). And what is more, 'increasing [outward] FDI [Foreign Direct Investment] occurred precisely in those sectors that used to be the bedrock of Germany's export-led growth strategy'. (Bieler 2006a: 79).

This shift in the material basis for existence was recent enough for Coates (2000: 243) to conclude that 'the jury is still out on the scale and persistence of this capital leakage.' Nevertheless, he provides enough evidence to support the argument that the ties binding Germany's capital goods industries to German territory were weakening throughout the 1990s (see also Flockton 1996: 213), rebalancing the national–international relationship towards the latter. Therefore, the equation of industrial success to general economic success in Germany became increasingly tenuous, for even these industries were losing confidence in Germany as a production location. This was reflected within Germany as well: for example, the postponement of wage equalization between western and eastern Germany from 1994 to 1996, at the behest of employers. In addition, there was an increasing tendency for companies to dilute collective bargaining agreements through the invocation of hardship clauses, which tended to exchange job guarantees or a reduction in working hours for little or no wage compensation (either in total or per hour) (Bieler 2006a). Thus unlike the 1980s, high unemployment and low growth was met with capital export on the one hand, and increasing demands on German labour to make painful concessions (such as wage freezes in exchange for no or fewer redundancies) on the other.

As a result, the varieties of capitalism literature is mistaken when claiming that it was striking to observe 'the lengths to which most employers have been willing to go to manage new pressures for flexibility within traditional institutions.' (Thelen 2001: 85). What is neglected in this analysis is the increasing desire to manage new pressures through *transformed* institutions. For instance, Menz (2005: 199) records the instigation of the *Standortdebatte* (a debate about Germany's attractiveness for investment) by the BDI in the mid-1990s:

> Its rhetoric was designed to de-legitimise the post-war consensus, questioning labour market regulation, the scope of the welfare state, and tax levels in light of the purported need to render the country an attractive site for investment and production.

This attitude was reflected in the aborted Alliance for Jobs negotiations of 1995–6. Suggested by IG Metall as a means of using social partnership to resolve the economic and unemployment difficulties, the talks broke down within six months of their inception. At the heart of the discord was the more radical than hitherto position of the employers' associations, which called for 'a more flexible labour market and, in particular, a reduction in wage costs and taxation levels but failed to respond to union calls for structural initiatives.' (Timmins 2000: 45). Perceiving (correctly) that the government backed the employers, the unions withdrew from the negotiations (*ibid.*). Thereafter they campaigned for a SPD victory in the 1998 elections, with a view to reviving the Alliance for Jobs process under a more favourable government.

The employers' position was only to radicalize further over the coming years, as the next chapter will detail. The potential for consensus to be formed was shrinking, for the transnationalizing basis for Germany's prosperity was reshaping employer perspectives in a way that was increasingly antagonistic to the more traditional interpretation of the social market economy concept adhered to by unions and most social democrats (which remained powerful for these actors: not surprising given the important role for organized labour that this interpretation envisions). Synthesis was becoming ever more elusive, not least because the stronger position of German unions made it less likely that they would reluctantly acquiesce to employer wishes as had their Dutch counterparts – as demonstrated by their withdrawal from the first Alliance for Jobs negotiations in 1996. Nevertheless, the late 1990s, with a new SPD–Green government and continued low growth and rising unemployment, plus the ongoing export of capital and accompanying *Standortdebatte*, was characterized by a sense of urgency and crisis. The new SPD Chancellor, Gerhard Schröder, declared the reduction of unemployment the government's number one priority, and revived the moribund Alliance for Jobs process. Nevertheless, it did not live up to the hopes and expectations invested in it. The next two sections discuss why this was the case.

## The Alliance for Jobs and economic "reality"

The success enjoyed by the Dutch economy, and the high international profile the so-called "Polder model" had achieved, attracted much interest in Germany and can be seen as one of the inspirations for the Alliance for Jobs (Timmins 2000). However, as indicated above, the potential for synthesis between the various versions of common sense was deteriorating throughout the 1990s, thus making it increasingly difficult to forge a consensus. At the heart of the diverging perspectives was disagreement on economic "reality":

> [Wassenaar] was kind of a model for the German Alliance for Jobs in late 1998. But it was obviously not possible to implement or to stabilize such an institutional structure...It was just not possible to establish a certain degree of shared knowledge and confidence...because both the social partners and the government could not reach a common assessment of the basic facts...I think this is very different from the Dutch experience. (IAB#1)

IAB#1 did not mention the two-year moderate wage settlement that was agreed in early 2000, which Streeck and Hassel (2003: 117) declared '[t]he one major accomplishment with which the public credited the Alliance'. Nevertheless, agreement on wages did not unlock the door to consensus formation. This is despite the fact that the agreement met the same objectives for the social partners as did Wassenaar: the stabilization, leading to the hoped-for reduction, of labour costs for the employers, and a continuation of social partnership at the national level for the unions. However, the key difference was that Wassenaar was rooted in shared assumptions about economic reality, which in turn conferred great legitimacy on wage moderation *in and of itself*. In Germany, the employers saw wage moderation as the start of a reduction of labour costs, which they believed would in time revitalize economic and employment growth; for labour it was a concession which required a corresponding response from capital. And this was not forthcoming:

> we had this agreement of course, but there was no real long-term agreement about the frames for wage policy and for the increase of wages...I think that the employers' associations made it very clear from the beginning that we can't guarantee a certain amount of jobs if we agree on something within the Alliance for Jobs. And I think that this was the main point that the DGB didn't accept. We can't talk to our companies and tell them to create 10,000 jobs, and then we have fulfilled the contract. This doesn't work in Germany: we are an association of associations, and our members are not direct enterprises. We can only tell the companies to create jobs – the conditions have improved, so do something about it. But our main task is to have an economic policy framework which pushes competitiveness, and this will lead to a creation of jobs... The associations...can't guarantee a certain amount of jobs. And they can't guarantee that all young people will get work at the beginning of their Ausbildung [vocational training]. (BDI)

The trade unions had a different interpretation:

> There is a quite famous example. The trade unions accepted in the Bündnis für Arbeit that the wage increase increases only very smoothly. They accepted that. And on the other side – the employers – they promised the so-called vocation–education consensus. That every young person that wants to get a vocational education, gets the opportunity...They laid it down like in a contract to offer each person a job or an educational opportunity.

> Which they did for one year, but [then] they failed...So just not a fair amount of give and take. Just one of the most important reasons that the Bündnis failed. (DGB#1)

What in the Netherlands was the foundation for prolonged reluctant acquiescence to the wishes of capital, in Germany was the opening gambit in the negotiations. In both countries the employers' associations were prepared to make only a symbolic concession in exchange for wage moderation. However, in the Netherlands the shared assumptions about economic reality prevented Dutch unions, cowed by their weak position, from demanding reciprocity. In contrast, German unions were able to resist attempts to impose wage moderation with no strings attached – not least because, as will be discussed below, the ascendancy of German capital had yet to be secured on the state's institutional terrain. Therefore, even if *Tarifautonomie* had not existed it is unlikely that the state would have supported such an asymmetric exchange of concessions. BDA expressed disappointment at the outcome:

> The two-year plan was new, and the absolute rate, the growth rate of wages, had been very moderate...We discussed in that context, the overtime work. And the trade unions said, OK, the deal is we agree on moderate wage growth. And you employers guarantee to reduce overtime work, and therefore employ new people. Which just does not work, because it does not work that mechanically in the companies. And though overtime work was reduced, and though we had other agreements on flexible working hours with the trade unions...they just looked at the figures and said, well sorry. So, the next time, bargaining as ever. And this small result, or this small positive effect that the Alliance for Jobs had, these guidelines for the bargaining were dropped.

On the issue of overtime, DGB#1 stated that 'we still have in Germany 1.5 billion paid overtime hours. It is going down a little bit, but it is still way too high...new jobs should be created instead of working overtime.' Unsurprisingly, the employers were not pleased with the attempt to link wage moderation to issues such as vocational education and working time, and viewed this as an example of organized labour's inflexibility and conservatism in the face of new economic realities. In this opinion, they were as one with the varieties of capitalism literature. Consider the clear neo-pluralist tone of this statement from Streeck and Hassel (2003: 121; emphasis added): '[t]oo weak to take risks and too strong to give way, German unions turned into a thoroughly conservative political and industrial force *opposed to experiments of any kind*'. Both DGB#1 and *DGB#2*[7] protested that the image of German trade unions as inflexible resisters of change was not true:

> *There are some limits to where the trade unions can move. But within these limits they are quite flexible. If you take for example the question of negotiations on the shop floor level of a company that is in economic difficulties, and fears that it has to be closed down. Then there might be agreements with the trade unions to say that there have to be some special regulations for this company. So we do have certain limits, but we are flexible within them. I think that is the important point...*They [the employers] say that the [collective bargaining] tariffs are not flexible enough. But a third of all German companies have working conditions that do not fulfil tariffs to 100%. So they are flexible and practical in practice.

A similar chasm between the two sides could also be observed with regard to the labour market, with different modes of labour flexibility emphasized. This will be discussed in the next section; for now I will focus on the employer discontent with the Alliance for Jobs process. Even before the reinstitution of the talks after the SPD's victory, the head of the BDA (Dieter Hundt) declared, in the midst of the *Standortdebatte*, that '[s]ocietal consensus has cost us millions of jobs.' (cited in Menz 2005: 197). Such rhetoric continued during the Alliance for Jobs negotiations, with Hundt arguing that 'an Alliance for Jobs has no point without a basic agreement on wage conditions' (cited in Timmins 2000: 49). In addition, the employers threatened to leave the talks in March 1999 over the issue of taxation (Harlen 2002b: 50), an ultimatum made in response to the labour market reforms implemented by the government after the 1998 victory.

Among other things, the legislation increased the rights of full-time employees and made it less attractive to hire temporary and/or part-time labour through strengthened protection against dismissal and the requirement for low-paid workers to pay higher, or start paying, social insurance contributions (and so making these employees more expensive) (Harlen 2002a: 77). Harlen adds that the subsequent reforms, which abolished capital gains tax on the sale of cross-shareholdings and lowered corporation and income taxation, were part of the balancing act performed by the government. The problem with this strategy – siding with labour on labour market policy and with capital on taxation – was that it assumed parity between the social partners. As has been made clear in this chapter, by the late 1990s German capital was increasingly interested in the transformation of the German institutional set-up to systematically favour its interests over those of organized labour. Therefore, while at this point in time the increasingly unequal relations of power between capital and labour had yet to be condensed on the state's administrative terrain in the form of policy changes and institutional reconfigurations, the likelihood of such a shift taking place seemed to be growing (see the next chapter for more).

Perhaps unsurprisingly, the employer representatives were somewhat reserved about the value of the Alliance for Jobs process, repeatedly stressing disappointment with the outcomes. In contrast, the trade unions had a more sanguine view, claiming that 'the success of the Bündnis in Germany is under-estimated.' (DGB#1) This interviewee then listed some successes and some failures. The successes were:

> a programme against youth unemployment...subsidies for low-wage income...more part-time work for older employees...new vocational and educational opportunities in the information technology field...the so-called Job Aqtiv-Gesetz, which...is a more preventative approach to tackling unemployment.

Regarding the failures:

> The most important failure, in my opinion, is the so-called vocation–education consensus...[plus] the Bündnis didn't create sustainable new jobs...[and] it failed to reduce paid overtime hours.

It can probably be seen that the failures are of a more substantial nature than the successes – particularly the failure to create sustainable new jobs. Nevertheless, the commitment to social partnership as a means of responding to challenges such as high unemployment meant that the principle of the Alliance was not in doubt; it just needed to become more effective. Hence DGB#1's belief (stated in January 2004) that it was 'too early to say that the German Bündnis was a plain failure.' From the employers' side of the negotiating table, though, the Alliance could become more effective only if the social content of any agreements were more in line with their agenda for change. The launch of the New Social Market Economy Initiative in 2000 – the formation of a new organic intellectual to articulate a new (modified) version of common sense which took as its starting point the modified (that is, transnationalizing) material circumstances for German capital – reflected this perspective. Before we move to the next chapter, the issue of labour market flexibility must be dealt with, for the dispute over the type of labour market flexibility that would help improve economic and employment performance illustrates well why it was not possible to form a consensus in the Alliance for Jobs process.

## The Alliance for Jobs and labour market flexibility

As with the previous chapter, I will use the present section to focus on one aspect of the debate about reform – labour market flexibilization. In particular, I will discuss the different paths to flexibility advocated by capital and labour. This topic generated much debate during the Alliance for Jobs process, and was remarked upon by several interviewees. Achieving greater flexibility in the labour market is not an uncomplicated task, because there are different means by which this can be achieved (see Regini 2000). The employers' associations argued in the Alliance for Jobs for an expansion of temporary and low-wage employment outside the stricter regulations governing permanent and better-paid employees, while labour was concerned with the extension of these constraints to part-time work as part of the general orientation towards the redistribution of working time. The interviewees who discussed these differences tended to use the controversy over mini-jobs as a means of setting out their position. Silvia (2002: 14) explains their significance:

> Previously, a German law exempted from any payroll taxation individuals working part-time at a job that paid below a maximum

> monthly ceiling, which in 1998 amounted to 630 deutschmarks per month. Since small job holders did not pay payroll taxes, they received no welfare state benefits unless they held another job that required them to pay payroll taxes. The tax waiver, which had been enacted in the 1970s, made the small jobs quite popular, particularly as German payroll taxes began to creep up in the 1980s and 1990s...In 1998, over 5 million Germans were employed in small jobs, mostly in the service sector.

Part of the government's balancing act, as discussed in the previous section, was the passage of two pieces of legislation in its first year in office which 'required many part-time and self-employed workers to start making social insurance contributions' in return for being eligible for minimum welfare benefits (Harlen 2002a: 77; see also Silvia 2002: 14–15). Vail (2003: 51) notes that the target group of workers were 'employees, disproportionately women, working fewer than 15 hours per week'. In addition, the government passed legislation giving workers in firms of more than 15 employees the right, subject to moderate conditions and without the need for approval from their employer, to move from full-time to part-time work, and also restricted the use of temporary contracts (Silvia 2002: 18; Harlen 2002a: 77). Vail (2003: 52) says that this reflected 'the government's hope to reduce unemployment by increasing the flexibility of labour contracts.' As can be seen, the preference was for a particular mode of flexibility – part-time as opposed to temporary and low-wage modes.[8] Because of this, capital was strongly against the reforms, denouncing them as an instrument to destroy jobs (Silvia 2002: 15).

IAB#1 confirmed this, commenting that the employers' associations 'have not been in favour of part-time work – you could not say that...they are more interested in using these mini-jobs.' The priority accorded to mini-jobs was confirmed by BDA's criticism of the labour market reforms:

> [Mini-jobs are] a means to create jobs in the service sector, to make it easier for people to take these jobs. It's attractive to take them, because you do not have to pay social security contributions to the social security system. And you can do it hour by hour, whatever. And it might be attractive both for employers and employees...[But the government, supported by the trade

> unions] made these mini-jobs more expensive, they made them not very attractive.

In contrast, the trade unions wished to expand service employment in a manner that underpinned rather than bypassed the institutional arrangements. Hence their emphasis on flexible labour that has contractual status – a second tier in the labour market that nevertheless retains many rights and protections:

> In our opinion, the concept of mini-jobs, the working poor, is not appropriate, because it establishes two classes of employees. Employees that have social security, and the have-nots... [Moreover]...it gives employers the idea...to disassemble the job into some mini-jobs...It establishes the wrong incentives for employees plus for employers. Other than that we support part-time. It is just not correct to say that we in the German trade unions believe that it is one man and one lifelong full-time job. It is just not correct to say that...There are a lot of ways of [achieving] flexible jobs, which people – mostly employers – just do not know about. (DGB#1)

In the previous chapter it was argued that significantly overlapping versions of common sense, combined with weaker trade unions, led to a continuation of the consensus on reform initiated by the Wassenaar Agreement. Indeed, the stark pronouncements that 'you cannot say that it is no good' in times of high unemployment led the unions to become the strongest supporters of the flexibilization of the labour market in order to achieve the best deal possible for workers. In contrast, the relatively marginal overlap in Germany was demonstrated by the way in which the employers and the trade unions remained wedded to their preferred mode of flexibility (to the extent that GRN criticized both for their unwillingness to compromise). Moreover, these preferences for different modes of flexibility reflected different perspectives on Germany's material basis for existence. Consider the below comments:

> [Studies show that] the idea of the working poor and very simple service sector jobs is just not appropriate for the changing job world and the economy...Highly qualified, educated labour is the

> appropriate way. I think that there are some small fields in the job market that may be developed for, let's say, low-trained or less-qualified people. For instance, in the private households, cleaning jobs. Simple childcare, very simple childcare...But overall, especially in the German economy, we have to compete in the world market. We depend on exports. What we need is well-trained...and also highly paid employees. (DGB#1)

> trade unions always argue that we have this high export rate, and are the champions, or at least the vice-champions, of exports in the world. But the problem is that the exports aren't really produced in Germany. They are exported from Germany, but they are produced somewhere in Central and East Europe, in Poland and so on. Then they come back, are imported, and the last things are done in Germany and then they are exported. The whole value of these exports of course is really large, but it's not produced in Germany to a large extent. (BDI)

The problem for organized labour was that the government's labour market reforms, which largely adhered to their preferred mode of flexibility, 'drove about one million employment contracts into the undeclared economy.' (GRN) A second unintended consequence of the reforms was the increased use of temporary agency workers to circumvent the strict dismissal protection laws (strengthened by the SPD–Green government) and the restrictions on the use of temporary contracts (Mitlacher 2007). In other words, German capital was attempting to turn into reality the transformation of the German variety of capitalism that it sought, through a combination of pressure from without, in the form of capital export, and pressure from within, in the form of the hollowing out and selective bypassing of the institutional environment (Kinderman 2005).

It can thus be seen that the attempt in the late 1990s to persuade capital to accept the desired taxation reforms, but *not* the desired labour market reforms, was doomed to failure. The growing transnationalization of German capital gave it an ascendancy which, while falling short of securing trade union acquiescence as in the Netherlands, made a significant change in the trajectory of the German variety of capitalism increasingly possible. The government's balancing act can thus be seen in this light: it was a reflection of the sediments of common sense that had accumulated since the *Wirtschaftswunder*, and were resistant to the new (modified) version of common sense supported by capital. Nevertheless, as noted in the last chapter, changes in the material basis for existence are more favourable to certain versions of common sense than others, and for this reason it was unlikely that the Alliance for Jobs would represent the end of capital's campaign for a significantly more liberal, marketized German variety of capitalism.

## Conclusion

This chapter has argued that it was not possible to construct a consensus in the Alliance for Jobs process, because the different versions of common sense were rooted in different interpretations of economic "reality". In particular, the transnationalization of German capital in the 1990s made employers less dependent on Germany for their profits. As a result, it was highly unlikely that a consensus would be forged in the Alliance for Jobs process, for the versions of common sense adhered to overlapped to a considerably smaller degree than in the Netherlands. In addition, labour was still strong enough in the late 1990s to demand real rather than symbolic concessions from capital, and to promote its preferred mode of labour market flexibility. Thus the molecular evolution seen in the Dutch unions' version of common sense, which was driven by the assumption of economic vulnerability and the belief that it was not possible to resist the demands of the employers, was not a feature of the negotiations.

The problem for the trade unions was the enhanced ability of German capital to create new economic "facts" through a combination of pressure from without and pressure from within, which in time could force a shift in the trajectory of the German variety of capitalism, whether the unions liked it or not. In early 2004, in the immediate aftermath of the Agenda 2010 reforms becoming law, DGB#1 said:

> In my opinion it [the Alliance for Jobs] should be reanimated at some time. But the conditions to do that right now are rather bad, because the employers feel and act like they can dominate the economic debate, and also the law-making process. Which they actually can right now...we don't have equal powers, the

> employers stand above the trade unions...To have a successful Bündnis they [the powers] should be levelled.

The task of the next chapter is to explain how Germany moved so swiftly from the Alliance for Jobs to Agenda 2010, the series of legislative reforms which condensed the increasingly unequal capital–labour relations on the state's administrative terrain. Moreover, this shift took place under the same government as in the late 1990s, indicating that the days of attempting to balance the interests of capital and labour were over. I argue that, despite the apparent challenge provided by these developments to the neo-Gramscian framework advocated throughout this book, the post-2001 period has in fact demonstrated the strength of my position.

# 7
# Post-2001 Radicalization

Several factors combined to paint a rosy picture as European varieties of capitalism approached the new millennium. There was a return to higher economic and employment growth in many countries. Moreover, this did not accompany the dismantling of the welfare state or other aspects of the political economy associated with European varieties of capitalism (such as the role of organized labour), in many countries. The most internationally famous example at the time was the Dutch case, but the revival of the Swedish economy, and the improved prospects for the French and German economies, appeared to provide grounds for a more positive assessment.

Moreover, the free-market perspective, which had been a consistent critic of European varieties of capitalism, was damaged by the East Asian crisis and its fallout, proving as it did that markets are not inherently self-equilibrating or judicious in their effects. This gave the opportunity for the beleaguered "Washington consensus" to be replaced by a more humane vision of capitalism – the "Third Way" – as exemplified by countries such as the Netherlands which had (it was argued) married economic efficiency with social justice. In addition, the establishment of the euro area in 1999 was believed to provide the opportunity for Europe to create economies of scale for the private sector without necessitating the abandonment of the European "social model". Symbolic of this was the agenda established at the EU's Lisbon summit in March 2000, which, in the heady atmosphere of the dotcom boom, sought to make Europe the most dynamic economic region in the world by 2010. This would be based on the knowledge industries, creating millions of high-value jobs and thus safeguarding welfare states in the process.

Much of this optimism was shattered in the 2001–3 period. First of all, the collapse of the dotcom boom and the attacks on the World Trade Centre and the Pentagon hit European economies harder than many expected. It seemed that the creation of the euro area had not decoupled European economies from the American economy. In addition, the monetarist stance of the European Central Bank appeared to compound the impact of the downturn, and by 2002 economic stagnation had descended upon most of Europe. Rubbing salt into the wounds was the continued good performance of the British and Irish economies, by some way the two most marketized of Europe's rich economies.

One of the most potent symbols of the shattered hopes was the swift deterioration, beginning in 2001, of the Dutch economy. By 2002 the Netherlands was suffering from considerably higher inflation and worse growth prospects than its competitors. It could have been expected that such stagflationary times would have catalysed a dilution of the consensus discussed in Chapter 5 (for an early warning, see Jones 1999). However, nobody expected the spectacular rise and assassination of the anti-immigration and anti-Islam populist Pim Fortuyn, who not only embodied and helped give rise to widespread discontent with the political establishment, but whose party (Lijst Pim Fortuyn (LPF)) entered government in the aftermath of his murder and the dramatic May 2002 elections (Bruff 2003). Thus the Dutch reputation for either economic efficiency or social justice appeared inappropriate. Furthermore, events such as the massive trade union demonstration in October 2004 against welfare cuts (see below) seemed to prove that the era of consensus was over.

At the same time, the revival of German economic growth was confined to 2000; moreover, the fall in unemployment in the late 1990s was temporary, and resumed its seemingly inexorable climb. In addition, the government was rebuked by the European Commission for breaking the terms of the Stability and Growth Pact on budget deficits – which Germany had itself insisted on as a condition of EMU. Yet the economic gloom, along with the absence of progress in the Alliance for Jobs, was still not enough for the electorate to reject the SPD–Green coalition in the 2002 election. This apparent confirmation of Germany's inability to achieve a consensus on meeting the economic challenges was turned on its head in March 2003, when Gerhard Schröder announced the Agenda 2010 reforms.

Agenda 2010 went well beyond earlier proposals of his government or the 1982–98 conservative–liberal coalition, and thus was the most comprehensive and radical attempt yet to confront the challenges of low growth and mass unemployment. In addition, there was a contemporaneous radicalization of the conservative and liberal parties (see Clemens 2007 on the CDU/CSU), meaning that all four political parties in Parliament, and especially the two main – supposedly "catch-all" – political parties, seemed to take leave of their electoral senses in the name of change. This culminated in the (disjointed) cooperation between the CDU/CSU and the SPD in passing the Agenda 2010 legislation, and the formation of a Grand Coalition after the inconclusive 2005 election. Thus the two main signatories to the Agenda 2010 legislation were now in government and in control of both houses of Parliament. In theory at least, this set the stage for further reforms along the lines of those passed in 2003.

Therefore, the post-2001 era in both the Netherlands and Germany poses a significant challenge to the case established in the previous chapters. The Dutch appeared to abandon consensus in the face of economic crisis, the polar opposite of the argument in Chapter 5, and the German institutional machinery was unexpectedly mobilized in order to implement a programme of substantial reform that was supported by enough actors to make it seem to be the basis of a new consensus. Nevertheless, this chapter will argue that the post-2001 period has in fact demonstrated the strength of my position. To make my case, I will first of all utilize empirical material – comment in the literature has mostly been concerned with the dramatic 2002 elections and/or the rise and decline of the "Polder model" discourse – to highlight the swift re-establishment of consensus in the Netherlands. Organized labour yet again reluctantly acquiesced to its own subordination in return for a place at the bargaining table, agreeing to a *nominal* wage freeze in the process. Nevertheless, I make it clear that the radicalized atmosphere almost prevented such acquiescence from being granted, and, indeed, it was only after the October 2004 demonstration that the conditions for consensus proved more favourable.

With regard to Germany, the Agenda 2010 reforms have generated much comment in the literature; hence the discussion will focus on engaging with the analyses offered by various scholars. I argue that the reforms were the culmination of pressure from German capital rather than simply an act of state unilateralism in response to continued economic difficulties; moreover, the apparent consensus was transitory and built on fragile foundations. Therefore, while the employers' offensive (cf. Kinderman 2005) scored some notable successes, German capital's moment of power was not of the same magnitude as that in the Netherlands in the early 1980s. While it is certainly not the case that there has been a return to the past – the changes were not insignificant – nor has there (yet) been a fundamental shift in the trajectory of the German variety of capitalism.

In other words, both countries exhibited greater continuity than has been perceived. Hence I conclude that while it is certainly possible for common sense opinions to fragment in the Netherlands and cohere in Germany, this and the previous two chapters suggest that over time the reverse is more likely to be the case.

## The Netherlands: the end of consensus?

As Uwe Becker (2005: 1090) notes, 'the call for wage restraint started immediately after the slowdown had become evident in the course of 2001'. Pressure for renewed wage restraint was not possible at this point in time, for the labour market was still working at full capacity. As a result, though, a convenient scapegoat for the myriad of problems which existed at the time – such as massive levels of personal debt which were about to induce a sharp reduction in consumer spending, a house price bubble that was about to burst, and the fact that neither Dutch export performance nor investment levels had responded in the expected manner to the wage moderation of the 1980s and 1990s (*ibid.*) – was established. For example:

> [Because of full employment] we saw that our competitive position in terms of wage costs was deteriorating in the second half of the 1990s again. Wage costs rose too much. And you see that after some delay the economy is performing less well and unemployment is rising again. (CDA#1)

> at [one] point the wage inflation, in about 2000, was enormous. And the...central planning agency, and [the] politicians, they can't say that if we lower taxes then unions and everyone will moderate their wage demands. No, if there is a shortage in the labour market, and you try that, that's not going to happen. So I really believe that the wrong policy choices were made around 2000. (CDA#2)

Note that CDA#2 is criticizing the purple coalition's fiscal policy,[1] which was expansionary at a time of already-high economic growth, for its timing rather than the principle of the policy itself. In other words, the core problem was wages and not the policy *per se*. Although wages were (with regard to this period) discussed to varying degrees across the interviews, it was clear that the assumption of economic vulnerability was, as in 1982, available for the reforging of a consensus on wage moderation, again acting as a strong anchor for various versions of common sense. However, the manner in which this process took place was different to that in the early 1980s, reflecting the radicalized atmosphere in the country.

The formation of consensus, even with an anchor such as economic vulnerability, is not predictable but contingent on human action. And it was not clear that there was much desire for consensus in the government or among employers. For example, although FNV#1 (correctly) stated in November 2003 'the economic situation was worse [in the early 1980s] than it is now' – growth was not as negative, unemployment was considerably lower, and the budget deficit was smaller (compare OECD 2001 and OECD 2004) – the reminder of the internalization of the international into the national provoked a more stringent response from the government compared to 1982. No intertwining of the national and the international is identical across different conjunctures, and in the early 2000s the radicalization and polarization of national politics led to a harsher interpretation of less difficult material circumstances.

The legitimacy of wage restraint, and its perceived success in restoring economic and employment growth after 1982, remained a constant; the difference was the intensity with which this policy was pursued. Therefore, common sense opinions on the Dutch political economy were both path-dependent and transformed, the latter reflecting the harsher political climate compared to 1982. As an illustration, the government announced in 2003 that a *nominal* wage freeze was necessary for both 2004 and 2005 in order to restore competitiveness and (so the logic went) economic growth. Thus, in direct contrast to the qualitative agreement reached at Wassenaar, the state, supported by capital, sought a binding, quantitative commitment to wage restraint from labour.

In addition, it seemed union agreement to such a commitment would entail acquiescence to further condensation of the moment of power that capital secured in the early 1980s on the state's institutional terrain. The government tied agreement to a wage freeze to the right to negotiate on the swingeing welfare retrenchment measures that had already been announced, plus proposed reforms of the welfare system (see Bruttel and Sol 2006 for more on the cuts and other controversial reforms). However, as will be discussed below in a little more detail, there was no intention on the state's part that the negotiations would alter the overall thrust of the agenda. Indeed, VVD#1 noted that the proposed public expenditure cuts were equal as a proportion of Gross Domestic Product (4%) to those implemented by the 1982–6 government. While VVD#1 – no longer active in politics and thus with no personal stake in the coalition's success – backed the agenda as necessary, it can again be seen that a less difficult economic situation was met with a proportionately harsher response. Nevertheless, the trade unions still managed to accommodate themselves to the state's radicalized stance, demonstrating the continued ability of wage restraint to act as the ideological cement holding the different versions of common sense together, to the benefit of capital:

> [The wage negotiations] almost failed this year because the government had so many measures that were negative for the trade unions. And we [the employers] wanted to have two years of zero on the wages. It was very difficult...The FNV said they wanted to have a referendum of the members. Every member – there are 1.2 million members – was asked are you for the consensus with the employers, or are you against? And 56% were for the agreement and 44% were against...it wasn't easy to reach that. And there was the difference between the trade unions on the sectoral level. So you had some trade unions on the sectoral level that were opposed to the agreement on the central level with the employers' organizations. So that resulted in enormous discussion within the

> circle of the trade unions about how to act towards the employers, and then together [with the employers] to the government. (VNO–NCW)

VNO–NCW also commented that the union belief is that it 'is better to have jobs with wages that raise zero and...maintaining jobs, than losing a lot of jobs and have for the remaining jobs a wage rise of 4% or 5%.' Here we can see that this perspective, rooted in the assumption of economic vulnerability, extends beyond the union leadership and into the union membership. Indeed, if any proof were needed of the remarkable legitimacy of wage restraint it is this referendum result. What makes the event even more extraordinary is the context within which the referendum took place. FNV#2 explained the union approach:

> In [the Netherlands we] don't strike about general issues. In [the Netherlands we] make it concrete, say what is my interest, and then I will do it. So if you talk about a social agreement on the national level, then the Dutch people don't strike....It is always that you have to discuss it, and you have to argue about it, and then you find a solution...And [if it fails at the national level] we will strike. And then we pick the strong sectors to make an example, and the rest will follow. That was the strategy. And then the employers said, wait, wait, wait. If we get it on the table later on [in sector negotiations], then it is better to have an agreement now...We [the unions] don't like to strike on the level of the national, because it is not effective to have such a strike. We do it in our own interests on the sectoral and the company level. And it works.

The union threat to strike at the sectoral and branch level, in the name of repairing the damage suffered at the national level, produced a means by which labour could be reincorporated into a consensus which was heavily skewed against its interests. Thus the threat to strike was in fact an expression of considerable weakness, for it represented a last-ditch attempt to gain something, even a small concession, that could justify support for a national agreement that was needed in order to avoid being sidelined in the national-level corporatist institutions. In this economic downturn at least, the employers were discouraged enough to make a deal with the unions.

Nevertheless, a heavy price was still imposed, confirming capital's continued hegemony:

> We were on the side of the government, and the trade unions were very opposed to all of those [welfare] measures. They said well, if the government wants to make those laws and those decisions, then we will get our money back in the agreements at the branch level. And we will demand wages at 4% instead of zero, and we will diminish the measures the government takes at [the national] level. And we will have strikes, and so on...And after that we recounted our steps and said well, they [the proposed reforms and cuts] were good measures, because they were saving the economy, but the most important one is to...fix the wages at zero for 2004 and 2005...That's the main instrument to let the economy function properly again. *But if you want to get the trade unions in your camp, in the core of the business, you have to make concessions on other subjects.*
>
> So we changed our attitude, and we unified again with the trade unions...we were very eager to stick with the government, but we said no, with those strikes and all that kind of stuff...there could be a lot of damage. It's better to again stick together with the trade unions, and to reduce all those measures that the government wanted to take against the trade unions, against the workers... But for that attitude, *from our side, the trade unions have to pay a price, and that is zero wage rises for 2004 and 2005*. So we [the social partners] stuck together against the government. We said to them, if you want to have two years of zero wage rises, then you have to change the measures that you want to take against the social partners, and especially against the trade unions. And by lobbying and making a front we succeeded on 14th October [2003] to make a deal, with the trade unions and with the government. So we were at that time in the middle position. The trade unions have to sacrifice the wages, and the government has to reduce the effects of their measures. And we were in the middle, so we didn't have to make any concessions. And that was a nice position. (VNO–NCW; emphases added)

Note here the two italicized sections of the above quotation. The language of consensus, as expressed in the first set of italics, was predicated on a major concession from organized labour, as highlighted by the second set. VNO–NCW said 'now the trade unions are explaining those results to their sister organizations in Germany, in Belgium, in France. And they can't understand why they [the Dutch unions] agreed to a zero line in the wages.'

It was argued above that the unions reluctantly acquiesced to the wage freeze in order to maintain their position in the institutional environment and retain some influence, even if it was small, on the trajectory of the political economy. However, the exchange of concessions was even more asymmetric than in the 1980s and 1990s. Indeed, the employers did not even need to make a symbolic concession, as was the case in 1982 with regard to working time. And although the government concessions were in some ways against the wishes of the employers' associations, it still resulted in 13 billion euros rather than 17 billion euros of cuts (CDA#2). As demonstrated by these still-substantial welfare cuts, the symbolic concession this time came from the state through its promise of negotiations on the retrenchment.

The budget was back in balance by 2006, a mere three years after the dramatic negotiations of 2003 (OECD 2007). Indicative of the scale and scope of the cutbacks is the fact that this was achieved a massive fourteen years quicker than in the post-1982 period, when the budget was not balanced until 1999 (OECD 2001). The speed with which this turnaround was achieved indicates that not only was the magnitude of the economic challenges not as great as in the early 1980s, but also that the government response was proportionately, and unnecessarily, harsher.[2] In consequence, the trade unions had gained less from acquiescence to the hegemonic version of common sense than in the 1980s and 1990s, making a continued imposition of harsher terms of consensus, in a less difficult economic environment than in the early 1980s, an inevitably conflictual process. For instance, talks on *inter alia* pension reform broke down, leading to a series of sectoral strikes and one of the largest public demonstrations in Dutch history, organized by the trade unions, in October 2004 (Becker 2005). As Karsten *et al.* (2008: 51) explain:

> [The government] decided to restructure the social security system without consulting the social partners: a clear break with the

> essence of the Polder Model...The initiatives for an institutional remodelling took shape during the spring of 2004. Although an agreement with the social partners had been reached in October 2003 to freeze wages and stabilize social security, the government was not satisfied with the progress the reshaping of the welfare state was taking...The social security system with its concomitant laws was to be unravelled through a process of simplification and deregulation...[In the aftermath of the strikes and demonstration] On 6 November, after a night session, the social partners restored social dialogue with the government...Subsequent initiatives have shown that this restoration [of social dialogue based on respect for different perspectives] was indeed at hand.

Karsten *et al.* use neutral language, which masks the fact that just months after the near-breakdown of talks over the demand for a wage freeze, the state reneged on its promise that the unions would have the right to negotiate on the proposed reforms to the welfare system. Once again reflecting the radicalized climate of the time, the state, as in late 2003 regarding the welfare cuts, had made a symbolic concession to labour. And although the employers' associations had also been frozen out of the formulation of the proposals, the government's agenda complemented their perspective, embodying as it did a further condensation of capital's long-standing moment of power. In consequence, autumn 2004 witnessed the stretching of the tradition of consensualism to breaking point.

In the end, consensus was reforged, but it took drastic action from the unions – in being forced to resort to strikes and demonstrations – just to maintain their place in the institutional environment. Furthermore, the agreement reached in early November 2004 was – as with the small changes to the welfare cutbacks in response to the wage freeze a year earlier – still heavily skewed against labour's interests, with many reforms merely postponed rather than abandoned. Nevertheless, the condensation of power relations that had been threatened before the October demonstration did not come to pass, because it was clear that there was widespread public opposition to the proposals. The unions had at least managed to soften the blow of many of the changes (Schaapman 2004).

Although the atmosphere improved after November 2004, in the guise of a restored consensualism and considerably diluted state radicalism, the clock could not be turned back. 2005 saw a convincing rejection of the EU Constitution in a referendum, which for van Apeldoorn (2008: forthcoming) signified not just a rise in Euroscepticism but also the legitimacy crisis faced by the Dutch establishment: 'those on the losing side [of the recent economic recession and welfare cuts]... voted the most against the Constitution.' (*ibid.*). Thus the consensus established at the elite level was more narrowly drawn than in the 1980s and 1990s, giving less scope for neutralizing the counter-hegemonic impulses of competing groups and ideas. Outside policies enjoying great legitimacy such as wage moderation, the state-society relationship is less deferential than had hitherto been the case (Jones 2008).

This was most starkly demonstrated in the 2006 general election, in which the sentiments appealed to by Fortuyn continued to attract support in the guise of the Party for Freedom (PVV) – despite extensive appropriation of Fortuyn's immigration policies by the 2003–6 conservative-liberal government – and the Socialist Party (SP) came close to outpolling the PvdA. Therefore, two parties opposed to consensualism and also the terms of the consensus itself, from the right in the case of the PVV and the left in the case of the SP, managed to establish themselves as significant political players.[3] As a result, the CDA and the PvdA, who had been unable to form a coalition after the similarly inconclusive 2003 election – leading to deep mutual bitterness – were forced to join forces with the small (orthodox Protestant) Reformed Political Party (SGP) in order to shore up the position of the established parties and institutions. Van Apeldoorn (2008) notes that the coalition agreement was strikingly communitarian in tone, emphasizing solidarity and social cohesion over marketization and welfare reform, and in this sense the societal discontent had made an impact. However, he also states that painful labour market and welfare reforms still appeared to be in the offing from the new coalition, despite the communitarian gloss, potentially storing up trouble for the future.

Whether the government will go ahead with such reforms – for example, a proposed relaxation of the dismissal law – is at the time of writing (January 2008) an open question.[4] Both van Apeldoorn (2008) and Jones (2008) believe there is less scope than in the past for conflict to be avoided, not least because, a few years after the recession had passed, the PVV and SP had polled well – signalling a potentially protracted legitimacy crisis for the established parties and institutions owing to their reduced capacity to neutralize competing groups and ideas (van Apeldoorn 2008). Nevertheless, it is my contention that, while more narrowly drawn than before, there continues to be a remarkable coalescence of opinion in the Netherlands around wage moderation as the key to economic success. It therefore seems likely that wage moderation will be central to future responses to economic challenges, continuing to be the means by which various versions of common sense will be synthesized.

Whether this will actually be the case in the future is an open empirical question, and the 2003–4 period demonstrated that sharing the assumption of vulnerability is, on its own, insufficient for consensus to be forged and reforged. Nevertheless, it appears more likely than not that wage moderation will be relatively untouched by future struggles. In other words, the anchor provided by the shared assumption of economic vulnerability will probably still manifest itself most vividly and persistently in the pursuit of wage moderation.

## Germany: consensus on substantial reform?

In early 2002 a scandal erupted when the Federal Employment Office was found to have falsified job placement statistics in order to appear more successful in its activities. The government seized the opportunity to establish a Commission for Modern Services on the Labour Market (known as the Hartz Commission after its chair), taking advantage of the scandal to establish a means by which tripartism, in the form of the deadlocked Alliance for Jobs, could be bypassed. Thus the Hartz commission created the opportunity for a shift in the trajectory of the German variety of capitalism towards a more economically liberal social content. While the literature's discussions of the subsequent legislation focus on either the detail of the reforms or the political manoeuvrings, all too rarely does one find an analysis which takes into account the growing strength of German capital – as highlighted in the previous chapter.

Kemmerling and Bruttel (2006: 93–8) detail the changes that took place, grouping the Hartz I–IV measures which came into effect in the 2003–5 period into three clusters: organizational reform of the Federal Employment Office; reform of the unemployment benefit system; and activation measures in order to increase labour supply (*ibid.*: 93–8). The first cluster refocused sharply training assistance towards short-term rather than long-term programmes, and contracted out some services to the private sector. The second cluster reduced the maximum period (from 18 to 12 months) for which income-related unemployment benefit could be received. It also abolished unemployment assistance, meaning that after the 12 months had expired *all* unemployed persons moved to the most basic social assistance benefit level rather than just those who did not qualify for the intermediate, income-related, assistance level.

The third cluster sought to make it more attractive for people working in mini-jobs by abolishing social security contributions for employees earning less than 400 euros a month, and introducing a sliding scale of increasing contributions for so-called midi-jobs that earned between 400 and 800 euros a month. Thus employers would be able to pay a lower wage due to the fact that workers had greater take-home pay at each level of gross wages. This, combined with stricter rules on the jobs that the unemployed could refuse (which made previous occupational status irrelevant for the majority of unemployed workers, a big change for Germany (Seeleib-Kaiser and Fleckenstein 2007)),[5] encouraged the growth of a low-wage sector. In other words, the legislation signified the state's acceptance of capital's preferred mode of labour market flexibility, a marked change from the Alliance for Jobs process (for more on the Hartz reforms, see Kemmerling and Bruttel 2006; Bruttel and Sol 2006; Seeleib-Kaiser and Fleckenstein 2007).

The Hartz recommendations were part of a wider set of reforms. The September 2002 election, which saw the SPD–Green coalition re-elected with a very small majority, was followed by disastrous regional elections for the SPD. It was clear by February 2003 that the Bundesrat would contain a majority for the opposition parties for the rest of the federal government's term. Nevertheless, by the end of the year 12 bills associated with Agenda 2010 had been passed by both houses of Parliament. In addition to the above, reform of pensions, health care, education and taxation were part of the liberalization programme (Saalfeld 2006: 255). This sequence of events may appear curious, for the government's wafer-thin majority, combined with the opposition majority in the Bundesrat, should have made achieving change even more difficult than usual. In effect, an informal Grand Coalition between the SPD and CDU/CSU was formed, with the former offering the latter:

> a programme of legislation that it could support...The reason why the CDU/CSU accepted that offer – and overcame the temptation to erode the legitimacy of the government by rendering it impotent – was partly the content of the Agenda, partly its own fear of being blamed for political stagnation, and importantly pressure from business, which found Schröder's programme on the whole sympathetic. (Streeck 2006: 80–1)

Analyses of precisely why cooperation took place tend to follow Streeck in focusing on the "game" of political positioning and electoral strategy underpinning the state's unilateralism, with "pressure from business" accorded a *de facto* minor role. For example, Clemens (2007) argues that Agenda 2010 encouraged the CDU/CSU to radicalize their programme so as to appear to the electorate as the real party of reform, while Streeck (2006) and Saalfeld (2006) place greater emphasis on Schröder's skill in negotiating simultaneously with the left in his own party, the Union parties and the Greens. On the other hand, while authors such as Kinderman (2005) do not focus on Agenda 2010, their discussions provide the context necessary for a satisfactory analysis to be made. Kinderman argues that there has been a two-pronged employer offensive, seeking a significantly more marketized political economy, since the late 1990s: 'German employers are challenging the existing system by attacking the legitimacy of existing institutions in the political realm, and by introducing radical new management strategies in the industrial relations realm.' (433–4; see also Menz 2005)

Driving the offensive was, as discussed in the previous chapter, the increasingly transnationalized basis for German prosperity; that is, German capital has become less dependent on Germany for profit, even if this institutional environment has historically been the basis for company success (Bieler 2006a). The increased ability of German capital to exit is prominent in Kinderman's and other discussions (see Raess 2006; Raess and Burgoon 2006; Menz 2005). However, as Raess and Burgoon (2006) clarify, this probably does not go far enough. Through a combination of actual *and* threatened relocation of production and investment, companies have increasingly had the upper hand in collective bargaining negotiations – especially if previous threats were carried out. This position was well-expressed by BDI, who argued:

> Of course we will not have the level of Chinese wages here, but you have to consider that there is China, that this is a production place, and that enterprises have to be there, and are going to go there if the conditions here are not so very good. They [companies] will not wait until they are insolvent.

The strategy of combined actual and threatened relocation was most dramatically executed in the crushing defeat of IG Metall's June 2003 strike in eastern Germany, which sought a reduction in the working week to 35 hours (Raess 2006). The employers' victory against the pre-eminent sectoral union in Germany was achieved through multiple uses of the exit threat: as an economic rationale for resisting IG Metall's demands in the name of a more competitive Germany; as a divide and rule strategy which reduced union solidarity regarding the strike; and as a means of portraying the employers as victims of IG Metall's unreasonable demands, making exit more likely as a result (*ibid.*: 459). This final threat was designed to appeal to wavering strikers and especially public opinion. In the previous four years the latter had shifted from substantial mistrust of business (Kinderman 2005: 438) to a desire for unions to have less influence on government policy (Funk 2003), a change which will be returned to below when I consider the New Social Market Economy Initiative (INSM). Raess (2006) also argues that the employers remained united throughout the dispute because the large firms that have traditionally dominated the employers' associations had undergone a fundamental shift in their outlook in the previous few years, subordinating the desire for social peace to the goal of transforming industrial relations.[6]

In a signal shift from the *Standortdebatte* in the mid to late 1990s, the transnationalizing basis for German prosperity had by the early 2000s led to the emergence of organic intellectuals seeking to achieve a shift in the terms of the debate. This gave greater coherence and clarity to the conceptions of the world that had undergone a molecular evolution in the 1990s. Principal among the developments was the INSM, founded in 2000 in order to bring about a shift in public opinion which would help 'facilitate the implementation of the reforms employers desire and advocate.' (Kinderman 2005: 438). Such reforms include the flexibilization and deregulation of the economy as a whole and the labour market in particular, with job creation deemed more important than debates about their quality or about income inequality (*ibid.*: 439). In other words, the INSM was at the forefront of the push to gain societal acceptance for the new (modified) version of common sense that German capital supported.

Kinderman (*ibid.*: 438–9) also notes that the INSM, like many other groups, utilizes the 'hegemonic' notion of the social market economy, but seeks to tilt decisively the emphasis towards the market rather than society. Thus the *form* of the German political economy may remain the same – for example, the corporatist institutions will continue to exist – but their *social content* should, in the eyes of the INSM, alter significantly (*ibid.*: 452). In so doing, the version of common sense adhered to by German capital was path-dependent – hence the appropriation of the term "social market economy" and the acknowledgement of the corporatist institutions – while also transformed. Kinderman's analysis, although rooted in a social constructivist perspective, indicates clearly that the INSM acted as the organic intellectual for German capital's hegemonic project:

> The [INSM] is non-partisan: it has ambassadors from each of the major political parties, in addition to celebrities and public icons, academics, businesspeople and workers. These figures appear on brochures and billboards, and in television and newspaper ads, online advertisements, television documentaries and opinion pieces, public events, press releases, publications and at conferences, and are supported by a budget of 100 million Euros over 10 years. The campaign focuses on "multipliers", people who are in a position to affect public opinion and who can further disseminate the message. Articles appear almost daily in all major German newspapers and newsmagazines (*ibid.*: 439).

The growing transnationalization of the political economy made possible both the redirection of capital abroad and the articulation of a credible exit threat at home, implying a modified intertwining of the national and the international.[7] Nevertheless, the link between the changing material basis for prosperity and the employers' wishes for a more liberal market economy needed to be made. This was the role of the INSM: its saturation of public debate with the argument that reform was necessary for Germany to prosper once more, its appropriation of the social market economy concept for its own ends, and its success in portraying the trade unions as the obstacles to change (Funk 2003), shifted the terms of the debate towards its version of common sense. In other words, the INSM was instrumental in making it possible for German capital, regardless of the form it took (industrial, finance, and so on), to portray its modified version of common sense as in the interests of Germany as a whole.

To return to my discussion in Chapter 3, key for a hegemonic project such as that propagated by the INSM is the incorporation of its agenda into laws and measures which embody the shift in societal power relations. The condensation took place in this specific conjuncture because the failure of the Alliance for Jobs and the government's powerless political position by early 2003 made the state's incorporation into the INSM's hegemonic project possible. Even though many of the measures implemented were opposed in the September 2002 election campaign by the very same government, the flood of gloomy economic news in autumn and winter 2002 created the conditions for the capitulation of its version of common sense to the new (modified) version supported by capital. Although the *form* of the German state was relatively unchanged – the government had been in power since 1998 – its *social content* had undeniably altered. GRN gave a pertinent example:

> And they [the SPD] claim [Agenda 2010] for themselves. Franz Müntefering [who succeeded Schröder as SPD party chairman in March 2004] says on a lot of occasions, I have been one of the guys who used to think that it is all working and we don't have to do much. And now he literally says, I have learned my lesson and we have to continue. We have to get on with reform.

It is thus not surprising that the employers were so intransigent and united during the June 2003 strike, for their societal hegemony had a few months earlier been secured on the state's institutional terrain through the announcement of the Agenda 2010 measures. Accompanying the legislative changes were important institutional reconfigurations which made it more difficult for resistant parts of the state apparatus to uphold their own version of common sense. In autumn

2002 Wolfgang Clement, a known admirer of the British variety of capitalism, was appointed head of a new super-ministry which was the result of the merging of the ministries of Labour and Economic Affairs. This was an attempt to subordinate the social democratic traditions of the former ministry to the economically liberal bias of the latter. In addition, at the height of the CDU's radicalization it nominated Horst Köhler for the position of President, who is elected by the Bundestag plus delegates from the *Länder* legislatures. These two groups have equal weighting in the voting process, which meant that the CDU/CSU in alliance with the FDP, with a clear majority in the Bundesrat and only a few votes behind in the Bundestag, would be able to win the vote.

Köhler had previously been the head of the International Monetary Fund and was known for his liberal views on the economy. Hence his election in 2004 created another institutional condensation of the altered societal power relations. Köhler exploited this on several occasions in speeches which *de facto* endorsed the INSM (see Schweiger 2006: 246–7). Furthermore, Schröder's request for a dissolution of Parliament over a year before elections were due to be held won Köhler's backing, even though Schröder had disingenuously (and blatantly) interpreted the increasing difficulties facing the Agenda 2010 programme (see below) as a lack of confidence in the government. Surely in Köhler's mind was the presumption that an earlier election represented an earlier accession to power by the CDU/CSU in alliance with the FPD. Therefore, it appeared to bring forward, given their radicalization over the previous years, the potential for not just the defence of Agenda 2010 but its acceleration and intensification.

Nevertheless, the apparent consensus witnessed in 2003 had begun to unravel almost immediately after the Agenda 2010 reforms were passed in the December of that year – that is, well before the September 2005 election. This did not herald a return to the debates of the 1990s, but at the same time the proponents of the reforms were not able to secure a significant enough shift in the terms of the debate: Agenda 2010 was not a strong enough ideological cement. There were many reasons for this. For example, Schröder's immense tactical skills overcame significant opposition from within his own party, but it was only through several threats to resign rather than necessarily winning the argument that this was achieved. This signified the recognition that it was very difficult for concessions to be offered, for these would potentially derail the hegemonic project. Thus the threats to resign demonstrated the highly provisional nature of the consent given by SPD members, not least because the trade unions – implacably opposed to Agenda 2010 – are still an important base of support for the party. Again, as in the Alliance for Jobs process, there was little scope for synthesis between the different positions because the interpretations of economic "reality" remained distinctive.

Schröder resigned as party chairman in February 2004, ostensibly to focus on his job as Chancellor but in reality an admission that he could carry his party no further along the reform path laid down by Agenda 2010. Thus in the same month, mere weeks after the legislation had been passed, he declared 'we have done what was necessary' (Clemens 2007: 244, n. 87). Furthermore, the summer of 2004 witnessed the beginnings of a new party of the left with the formation of the Alternative List for Jobs and Social Justice (later to create the Linkspartei.PDS with the Party of Democratic Socialism (PDS)), which included disaffected social democrats and trade unionists, plus the escalation of public demonstrations against the reforms. The scale of the resistance forced Schröder to reiterate that he would not legislate for any more Agenda 2010 reforms so as to avoid crossing the public's 'threshold of pain' (Streeck 2006: 86). The shift from pressing on with the hegemonic project in the face of resistance, to attempting to neutralize the growth of competing social groups building on such resistance, was now in full swing.

What is more, the CDU/CSU were also affected: voices representing the "catch-all" tradition became louder, forcing the leadership into a series of retreats from the radicalized stance adopted in 2003 (Clemens 2007).[8] As a result, there was at best a fragile defence of Agenda 2010 from the Union parties during the election campaign. In contrast, an apparently amnesia-ridden SPD abandoned the reform platform, building on the widespread public support for Müntefering's April 2005 depiction of private equity firms as locusts. Indeed, the party repeated its 2002 trick of accusing the Union parties of wishing to destroy the welfare state, and its case was helped immeasurably by CDU leader Angela Merkel's choice as prospective finance minister, Paul Kirchhof, who advocated a flat tax for all incomes (*ibid.*). This compounded an already difficult campaign for the Union parties, in which the frictions between the 'market' and 'social' wings had been barely suppressed.

Unsurprisingly, the inconclusive election result and subsequent Grand Coalition were viewed with dismay by supporters of Agenda 2010, to the extent that a major organ of free-market opinion published articles calling for a 'technical caretaker government' to be formed because of democracy's "failure" to produce the "correct" outcome (see Boeri and Castanheira 2005; Kay 2006). As with the Netherlands after the 2006 election, the government was formed reluctantly owing to little other choice for the parties involved – not least because the failure of the CDU/CSU–FDP alliance to win a (widely predicted) majority was viewed as a rejection of further reforms.

Since 2005 the coalition has overseen a balancing of the budget – helped by an economic upswing and a 3% rise in VAT – and reforms to the health and federal systems, but the general shift away from Agenda 2010 has continued. At the time of writing (January 2008), it appears that a disintegration of the coalition could soon be in sight, owing to the SPD's leftward shift under new leader Kurt Beck and the fact that elections are less than two years away. This can be seen in the SPD's push for a country-wide minimum wage, which traditionally would be criticized for its subversion of *Tarifautonomie*, but has commanded widespread public and union support. The momentum behind such a change forced its coalition partner to agree to a minimum wage in some sectors (for example, the postal sector), much to the dismay of the pro-market wing of the Union parties. Thus the stalling of the reform drive may become permanent, ending the transitory consensus on significant liberalization of the German variety of capitalism that existed in 2003–4.

The reasons for this can be traced back to the previous chapter: the different versions of common sense offer little potential for synthesis in a new consensus. The inability of the INSM and Agenda 2010 to detach a large enough portion of social democratic and trade union opinion from their version of common sense was a crucial factor in the consensus remaining provisional only. Indeed, the fact that, for instance, the postal sector's minimum wage has been set at a high level indicates the tenacious hold the "industrial success = general economic success" equation, and the "social" aspect of the social market economy concept, still have on German conceptions of the world. Nevertheless, although the economic upswing that began in 2006 has dampened the radicalism of German capital, it is likely that the next economic downturn will be the spark for a further push for liberalization. Hence interesting times lie ahead for the German variety of capitalism.

## Conclusion

This chapter concludes the discussion from Chapter 5 onwards of the role of consensus in the Dutch and German varieties of capitalism from a neo-Gramscian perspective. The utilization of Antonio Gramsci's notion of "common sense", which enabled us to connect consensus and culture, has yielded significant and original insights into the trajectories of the two political economies. In particular, the chapters have demonstrated that out of the different material bases for existence in the Netherlands and Germany have emerged contrasting possibilities for consensus. It has proved more likely that consensus on overcoming institutional dysfunction will be formed in the Netherlands than in Germany, due to the greater overlap between the different versions of common sense provided for by the shared opinions about economic "reality".

The present chapter has shown that this observation is not a predictive, general law that can be applied to the Netherlands and Germany in all cases. Indeed, in the radicalized atmosphere of the early part of the post-2001 period there was a breakdown of consensus in the Netherlands and the formation of consensus on reform in Germany. Nevertheless, the swift return to consensus in the former and the unravelling of consensus in the latter demonstrates the strength of my case. For this reason I believe that while it is certainly possible for common sense opinions to fragment in the Netherlands and cohere in Germany, over time the reverse is still more likely to be the case.

# 8
# Conclusion: "Critical" IPE?

This book has made the case for the superiority of a neo-Gramscian framework when analysing the trajectories of European varieties of capitalism. It has done so through engaging with the varieties of capitalism literature with regard to the role of consensus in these trajectories. I have argued that through delimiting the formation of consensus to the institutional environment, the varieties of capitalism literature cuts institutions off from the society they are rooted in. In contrast, I asserted that we need to consider culture in order to conceptualize adequately the role of consensus. The conceptual apparatus provided by Antonio Gramsci's notion of 'common sense' makes it possible for a thorough analysis to be offered, for the degree of overlap between different versions of common sense – or cultures – shapes the possibility for synthesis between different perspectives in the form of a consensus. This was demonstrated through the utilization of the theoretical framework to analyse the empirical data presented in Chapters 5–7, and is summarized by Table 8.1.

Rather than repeating at length the insights and arguments of previous chapters, I will use this chapter to discuss the relevance of the book for the IPE literature more generally. In particular, I wish to use this chapter to focus on the reception and application of Robert W. Cox's work. Put simply, while certainly an eclectic and unorthodox historical materialist, Cox is nevertheless a historical materialist (Robert W. Cox 1996a: 58). For instance, he states that his outlook is a 'historicist Marxism that rejects the notion of objective laws of history and focuses upon class struggle as the heuristic model for the understanding of structural change.' (*ibid.*: 57–8) This

**Table 8.1** Summary of the book's argument

| | **Varieties of capitalism perspective** | **Neo-Gramscian perspective** |
|---|---|---|
| *Point of departure* | Institutions | Material basis for existence (capitalism) |
| *State-society relationship* | Separate from each other | Intimately linked; methodologically distinctive |
| *Source of consensus* | Institutional environment | Culture |
| *Lens for analysing presence/absence of consensus* | Social learning (presence); path-dependence (absence) | Potential for synthesis between different versions of common sense shapes whether consensus is present or absent |
| *Wassenaar process in the Netherlands* | Social learning through exchange of concessions | Union acquiescence to capital's moment of power + capital's common sense |
| *Alliance for Jobs process in Germany* | Path-dependence through unwillingness to compromise + union intransigence | Transnationalizing capital; no union acquiescence to capital's modified common sense |
| *Post-2001 in the Netherlands* | Decline of "Polder model" and of consensus politics | Re-established consensus overcomes state radicalism; labour again acquiesces |
| *Post-2001 in Germany* | Agenda 2010 and state unilateralism / political manoeuvrings | Transitory consensus on substantial reform; fragile support for Agenda 2010 |

gives a directionality to his work on ideology, civilizations and world order. The apparent straddling of different theoretical perspectives that this has entailed has led to criticism for *inter alia* being either excessively materialistic or for not being materialistic enough (see Schechter 2002).

For the purposes of the chapter I will concentrate on the mainstream literature rather than debates within historical materialist scholarship (see Bieler *et al.* 2006 for the latter). This is because, in a similar manner to the varieties of capitalism literature – which is critical only through a contrast with the naïve globalization literature, neo-classical economics, neo-liberal policy prescriptions, and so on – the IPE literature has a tendency to award itself the label "critical". This enables the scholar to market themselves as someone set apart from the mainstream IPE literature, a distancing which is often justified through an assertion that the mainstream literature takes the role of ideas and norms for granted. However, this radicalism is considerably overstated and only goes so far. As with the varieties of capitalism literature, the elephant in the room – *capitalism* – is left unexplored.

In consequence, what has come to pass is the appropriation by the IPE literature of Cox's writings on modes of thinking plus a simultaneous rejection of his work on production, class and social forces (compare and contrast Germain 2007 with Morton 2007b). This separation of ideas from the material conditions out of which they emerged – a dichotomy which Cox (2002: 31) continues to reject – has not discouraged IPE scholars from utilizing a one-sided interpretation of Cox in order to declare themselves "critical". In the process, "critical" scholarship has come to be defined as – *and defines itself as* – an enquiry into the role of ideas in constituting interests, identities and institutions (Morton 2006). This, whether explicitly stated or not, accepts Weber's depiction of ideas as the determinants of the tracks along which interests are defended and articulated. However, this plainly ignores what the tracks are made of – that is, their material structure (cf. Bieler and Morton 2008). As has been asserted repeatedly in this book, our conceptions of the world can never escape the material circumstances in which we live: they are saturated with references to the need to produce and how to organize production.

To take two recent examples, consider the recent special issue of *Review of International Studies* on critical International Relations theory and the debate in *Review of International Political Economy* on the differences between American and British IPE scholarship (Cohen 2007; Higgott and Watson 2008; Ravenhill 2008; Cohen 2008). In the former, the editors' introduction (Rengger and Thirkell-White

2007: 5) refers to Cox's 1981 *Millennium* article as one of the contributions which enabled critical theory to have 'a huge impact on the study of international relations over the last twenty-five years.' And while it is true that historical materialist perspectives were and are by no means the only example of critical theory, in the special issue a constructive discussion of historical materialism is largely conspicuous by its absence.

For example, Kratochwil (2007: 37) argues that 'the relatively sophisticated conceptual tools of Cox's approach are no longer sufficient for capturing the dynamics of the system.' Bizarrely, the justification for this assertion is the formation of a transnational capitalist class not being accompanied by the formation of its labour equivalent – which is precisely what a neo-Gramscian perspective would be able to explain through *inter alia* a discussion of hegemony and its role in containing labour's orientations to national territories. In two other contributions, Palan (2007) and Hobson (2007) laud certain aspects of, respectively, Marx's and Cox's work – but Marx and Cox are useful only if they are combined with, and ultimately subsumed by, heterodox (Palan) and post-racist (Hobson) frameworks.

A more dismissive approach can be observed in the recent debate in *Review of International Political Economy*. Benjamin Cohen's (2007) first article discusses Cox's contributions to the development of IPE, arguing that the warmer reception of his work in the UK compared to the US was due to the influence of the English "school" of International Relations theory (212), a wholly different approach to historical materialism. The reason for dovetailing Cox with a considerably less radical perspective becomes clear over the subsequent pages, when Cohen attributes to UK universities 'a more relaxed attitude toward Marxism or other leftist doctrines' (213). To complete the condescension, he repeats the phrase 'Marxism or other leftist doctrines' on the next page. In other words, historical materialism is not a serious theoretical framework; it is dogma.

Cox is reprieved from such judgement because of his 'grand eclecticism' (210), but this in turn is deemed a weakness of British IPE, for it prevents the attainment of the methodological rigour adhered to by American IPE. Hence Cohen's conclusion that UK IPE should become more "rigorous" and US IPE should entertain a wider range of theoretical perspectives, which potentially could lead to a synthesis between the two schools (217). Unfortunately, this framing of the debate provoked responses that took the reader further away from critical reflection. For instance, Higgott and Watson (2008) are concerned with the fact that any synthesis of British and American IPE will, given size and prestige factors, inevitably take place on the terms of the latter. For this reason they defend the role of political philosophy in British IPE scholarship, but, crucially, the political philosophy they cite is strictly non-Marxist. Moreover, Ravenhill (2008) is at pains to stress the diversity within the American and British academic communities. As a result, the discussion – which extends to Cohen's (2008) reply – centres on the form rather than the substance of IPE scholarship. Hence historical materialism is ignored yet again.

When commenting on the IPE field in general, Paul Cammack (2007: 15) argues that '[t]he effect is to draw a line between (included) "neo-Gramscians", who may be assimilated to the debate which reinforces the mainstream, and (excluded) "Gramscians" and other assorted Marxists, who cannot be tolerated'. It is undoubtedly true that some scholars believe they are engaging constructively with historical materialism – for instance, in the contributions of Germain and Hobson – but the effect has been as Cammack describes. Therefore, we must ask the question: what is the social content of "critical" IPE scholarship? For this author, it is clear that the version of common sense adhered to by "critical" IPE is characterized by a downplaying or even ignorance of the material basis of existence on the grounds of rejecting "determinism" or "reductionism" – a trait shared by the more conventional social constructivist and the more polemical post-structural variants. Yet "critical" IPE is itself reductionist by way of the causal role assigned to ideas: the material conditions out of which ideas emerge are neglected in favour of the ideas in and of themselves. This is a fundamental theoretical error, for the material conditions are the conditions of our existence, and as such are the essential basis for human social practice:

> People can contest their identity discursively but if their material situation including their social relations remains the same, the claimed new identity might reasonably be said to be spurious. You can proclaim yourself free when in fact you are still in chains: not all social constructions work out...why else does the sight of large, calloused hands with swollen joints make us assume their

> owner has had a life of hard, manual labour? (Sayer 1997a: 484, n.22).

As McLennan (1996: 67; original emphasis) argued, 'some degree of essentialism is unavoidable. The disputes are usually over *which* essences we should accept as important' – whether, I might add, this is acknowledged explicitly or not. To this end, this book has argued that the essence of life is the material basis for our existence. The conceptions of the world which attempt to make sense of this material basis for existence are together a version of common sense opinions about reality. If enough conceptions of the world overlap, some versions of common sense are intersubjective and thus a culture because they are modes of thought that are embodied in collective human social practice. The degree of overlap, and potential for synthesis, between different cultures indicates the possibilities for consensus in that society. Thus the role of consensus in European varieties of capitalism can be analysed only via a discussion of culture, which in turn can be studied only through an appreciation of the material basis for existence in the given society. In other words, historical materialism is central to the study of capitalist societies and must be taken seriously in its own right.

# Notes

## 1 Introduction

1 This does not cover all of the institutionalisms – although their number depends on the author writing about them (see Peters 1999; Lowndes 2002 for differing approaches). It also does not include sociological institutionalism, which is often mentioned (see Peter Hall and Taylor 1996; Schmidt 2006). From my point of view, sociological institutionalism is very similar to the framework utilized by economic sociologists, whose work I consider in Chapter 2. In addition, to continue subdividing the literature into different institutionalisms would obscure my key point: that they are still *institutionalisms* and as such have much in common with each other. Hence the discussion of the three main strands – rational choice, historical, and discursive/constructivist – with regard to political economy analysis.

2 It is for this reason that Raymond Williams' seminal work on culture is not considered appropriate for the framework developed in this book, because, despite his wide-ranging theoretical discussions of culture, he was at heart a literary theorist. As a result, the more substantive aspects of his work repeatedly centre on more traditional notions of culture – that is, as "the arts" – which contrasts with Gramsci's consistent emphasis on the political implications of his discussions of literature, plays, and so on. See, for example, Williams (1977; 1980; 1981). See also Crehan (2002: 166–76) for an assessment of the problematic implications of utilizing Williams' work.

3 It can be seen that, through the use of the term path-dependence, there is a superficial convergence between my approach and that of the varieties of capitalism literature. However, the latter can only *describe* the path-dependence; in contrast, a neo-Gramscian framework enables us to *analyse* the path-dependence.

4 The interviewees are referred to in Chapters 5–7 as a "representative" of the organization through which they were contacted, as denoted by the acronym assigned to them. This generic term is used to protect the identity of the interviewees. Moreover, where more than one representative of the organization were interviewed, the interviewees are labelled #1 and #2, an order which is chronological only.

## 2 Culture in the Literatures

1 This is not to say that all writers on the challenges facing the German economy in the 1990s and 2000s emphasize this, at least in the first instance. For example, David Soskice (2000) has contended that a combination of the costs of unification and of conforming to the fiscal

requirements laid down in the Maastricht Treaty were chiefly responsible for Germany's woes in the 1990s. Nevertheless, he argues elsewhere that the failure to overcome these challenges was due to the inability of the institutional environment to adapt sufficiently well (Carlin and Soskice 1997). Moreover, in Peter Hall and Soskice (2001b) it becomes clear how the institutional environment needs to adapt: while 'markets do not necessarily generate superior outcomes' in CMEs (of which Germany is the archetype) (65), they nevertheless predict 'some, if more limited deregulation in CMEs [than in LMEs in the contemporary era of globalization] because, alongside non-market institutions, they also use market mechanisms whose operation can be improved by a measured amount of deregulation' (60, fn.41). This default bias towards marketization is thus assumed to be the solution to the economic challenges faced by CMEs, *whatever the cause of the challenges and problems.*

In addition, the interaction between Bundesbank policies and the tripartite actors is mentioned in some contributions. However, the literature emphasizes the need for the government and especially the social partners to adapt to non-accommodating monetary policies or else the institutional dysfunction will continue. Thus, even if the immediate cause of the economic downturn was the raising of interest rates, the solution is not monetary easing but reduced labour costs, welfare reform and so on. The *Welfare and Work* volumes contain the most eloquent arguments thus far on the topic – see Scharpf (2000); Hemerijck and Schludi (2000); Manow and Seils (2000).

2 The literature uses culture and society interchangeably when discussing embeddedness and constitution. While writers tend to use one term instead of the other, the analysis is strikingly similar – for instance, DiMaggio (1990: 113) states that 'economic behavior is embedded not only in social structure...but also in culture', but then acknowledges that '[t]he analytic distinction between culture and social structure...is in many ways artificial.' Therefore, the distinction between culture and society is unclear, despite attempts to delineate culture as constructed social scripts and structure as patterns of social relations, for the terms are used to make the same theoretical points about embeddedness and constitution. Because of this, the review of the literature will also use culture and society interchangeably, depending on the scholar being cited.

3 This also makes it impossible to take into account the unequal power relations which are part and parcel of capitalism and, indeed, if we wish to consider it in isolation, of the cultural context as well (Sayer 2001: 697–702).

4 The issue will not be considered in this book, but it seems a little bizarre to describe the contemporary era as "late" capitalism. This implies a belief that capitalism is near its end – unless, that is, there are "very late" or even "almost exhausted" stages of capitalism to come. Although the term "late capitalism" is a neat heuristic device with which one can sum up the contemporary form of capitalism, its ahistoricism is something that should be avoided.

## 3 An Alternative Framework: Gramsci's "Common Sense"

1 For Gramsci the function of the organic intellectual is performed by the political party, but later in the chapter I will argue that other actors can also perform this function.
2 As will be discussed later in the chapter, the offering of concessions can be made by one class fraction to another. However, for now the necessary non-class aspect of the social formation will be concentrated on.
3 See Hay 2004 for an exemplary argument along these lines, albeit from a – constructivist institutionalist – varieties of capitalism perspective.

## 4 The Netherlands and Germany from the Varieties of Capitalism Perspective

1 For the pre-1945 period see de Vries 1978, van Zanden 1998 for the Netherlands; for Germany see Blackbourn 2002, Overy 2003.
2 The repeated emphasis on wage restraint, justified on the grounds of economic vulnerability, forms a key part of the analysis of the Dutch variety of capitalism that I offer in the chapters subsequent to this one. The difference between my position and that of the varieties of capitalism literature is that I examine the reasons for its considerable legitimacy, while the varieties of capitalism literature views it as an example of the different paths to economic success that can be taken by European political economies.
3 Both Hartog (1999) and Becker (2005) provide evidence that wage restraint had in fact begun in 1979 and thus preceded the Wassenaar Agreement. However, for the varieties of capitalism perspective this places too little emphasis on the institutional realignments and policy reforms triggered by the agreement. From a more critical perspective, such as my own and van Apeldoorn's (2008), Wassenaar was a key moment in the trajectory of the Dutch variety of capitalism because it signified capital's long-standing moment of power in the Netherlands.
4 Therefore, a classic "beggar-thy-neighbour" policy based on increased price competitiveness relative to other countries, and particularly Germany, had been implemented.
5 The "New Course" agreement was signed by the trade unions and employers' associations in December 1993. It agreed to greater decentralization and flexibility in bargaining, a reduction in working hours, plus the promotion of employment and the recommendation of 'part-time work as a possible solution to the combined pressure of work and child care.' (Visser and Hemerijck 1997: 108).
6 Andeweg and Irwin (2002) discuss the paradox of a unitary political structure being combined with functional decentralization of many responsibilities to non-state actors.
7 The *Job Aqtiv-Gesetz*, inspired by the Dutch and Danish examples, sought to make Germany's labour market policy more active – that is, instead of absorbing the costs of labour market difficulties, the employment service

should be more proactive in helping the unemployed find work. Like other active labour market policies, there was a mixture of incentives to return to employment and sanctions for refusing job offers.

## 5 The Netherlands and Wassenaar

1 For the more traditional perspectives on consensus in the Netherlands, see Lijphart (1968); Andeweg (2000); Koole and Daalder (2002).

2 To remind the reader of a note from Chapter 1, the interviewees are referred to in Chapters 5–7 as a "representative" of the organization through which they were contacted, as denoted by the acronym assigned to them. This generic term is used to protect the identity of the interviewees. Moreover, where more than one representative of a given organization was interviewed, the interviewees are labelled #1 and #2, an order which is chronological only.

3 *Volkspartij voor Vrijheid en Democratie* (People's Party for Freedom and Democracy), the Dutch conservative liberals; henceforth **VVD**; two interviewees – **VVD#1** (interviewed 2 December 2003) and **VVD#2** (interviewed 11 December 2003).

4 *Federatie Nederlandse Vakbeweging* (Federation of Dutch Trade Unions), the main umbrella organization for Dutch trade unions; henceforth **FNV**; two interviewees – **FNV#1** (interviewed 1 December 2003) and **FNV#2** (interviewed 10 December 2003).

5 *Vereniging VNO–NCW* (Confederation of Netherlands Industry and Employers), the main umbrella organization for Dutch employers' associations; henceforth **VNO–NCW**; one interviewee – **VNO–NCW** (interviewed 4 December 2003).

6 The asymmetric spread of concessions across the different groups was discussed in Chapter 3. However, as will be detailed later in the chapter, Becker does not assess fully why the exchange of concessions was asymmetric after 1982, downplaying as he does the material conditions out of which ideas emerge and perpetuate.

7 *Partij van de Arbeid* (Labour Party), the Dutch social democrats; henceforth **PvdA**; two interviewees – **PvdA#1** (interviewed 1 December 2003) and **PvdA#2** (interviewed 3 December 2003).

8 Chapter 3 discussed the limitations of the debate about "globalization", and in particular the erection of the "pre-globalization" and "post-globalization" dualism. The redundancy of such an approach is starkly illustrated in this section, for while the Dutch interviewees all agreed that the "global economy" is a fact, it has been a fact for a long time. Therefore, "globalization" has few implications for the different versions of common sense in the Netherlands, rooted as they are in the assumption of economic vulnerability.

9 Here VNO–NCW is referring to the downfall of the Stability and Growth Pact because of the unwillingness of France and Germany to adhere to the rules. This again indicates a contrast between the Netherlands and

Germany for, along with many other small members of the eurozone, the Netherlands was one of the strongest supporters of the Pact.

10 Chapter 7 discusses how less moderate wage rises in the late 1990s became the scapegoat for the recession in the early 2000s.

11 *Christen Democratisch Appèl* (Christian Democratic Appeal), the Dutch christian democrats; henceforth **CDA**; two interviewees – **CDA#1** (interviewed 2 December 2003) and **CDA#2** (interviewed 10 December 2003).

## 6 Germany and the Alliance for Jobs

1 *Bundesverband der Deutschen Industrie* (Confederation of German Industries), one of the main umbrella organizations for German employers' associations; henceforth **BDI**; one interviewee – **BDI** (interviewed 2 April 2004).

2 *Deutsche Gewerkschaftsbund* (Confederation of German Trade Unions), the main umbrella organization for German trade unions; henceforth **DGB**; two interviewees – **DGB#1** and **DGB#2** (interviewed 6 January 2004).

3 *Bundesvereinigung der Deutschen Arbeitgeberverbände* (Confederation of German Employers' Associations), one of the main umbrella organizations for German employers' associations; henceforth **BDA**; one interviewee – **BDA** (interviewed 7 January 2004).

4 *Institut für Arbeitsmarkt- und Berufsforschung* (Institute for Employment Research), the research institute for the Federal Employment Office; henceforth **IAB**; two interviewees – **IAB#1** and **IAB#2** (interviewed 29 March 2004).

5 *Sozialdemokratische Partei Deutschlands* (Social Democratic Party of Germany), the German social democrats; henceforth **SPD**; one interviewee – **SPD** (interviewed 31 March 2004).

6 *Bündnis 90/Die Grünen* (Alliance '90/The Greens), the German green party; henceforth **GRN**; one interviewee – **GRN** (interviewed 2 April 2004).

7 In the below quote all italicized comments were made by **DGB#2.**

8 An example of this is the government's rejection of a report by the benchmarking committee established as part of the Alliance for Jobs process. Ironically, several of the suggested reforms, which were considerably closer to the version of common sense adhered to by capital (hence labour's insistence that the government reject the report), were also proposed by the Hartz Commission, and subsequently implemented as part of the Agenda 2010 programme.

## 7 Post-2001 Radicalization

1 The "purple" coalition acquired its name through the combining of conservative (blue) and social democratic (red) parties, and comprised the VVD, PvdA, and the small centre party Democrats 66. Once the impact of the LPF had subsided, the 2003–6 government in effect swapped the PvdA for the CDA, although this coalition's social content was considerably different to that of the 1994–2002 government.

2 Some may argue that the response was proportionately harsher in the early 2000s because of the limits placed on the government's room for manoeuvre by the Stability and Growth Pact on budget deficits. This overlooks two key points: one, the pact was abandoned in November 2003, meaning that, in the aftermath of the FNV referendum, there was plenty of scope for the welfare cuts to be reduced in size and scope; and two, even if the pact had remained in place, the budget deficit as a percentage of Gross Domestic Product reached its peak, of a little over 3%, in 2003 (OECD 2007). Therefore, while it is true that in 2003 the future state of public finances was not known, the swift fall in the deficit after 2003 was not accompanied by an adjustment in the government's fiscal stance until a balanced budget was achieved as swiftly as possible.

3 The SP moderated its stance in the months before the general election, thus indicating the potential for its future incorporation into consensualism and the terms of consensus. This did not happen in the aftermath of the 2006 election, when it was quickly concluded that it would not be possible to have both the SP and the CDA in the coalition. Nevertheless, the fact that the SP is now almost as popular as the PvdA means that there is a good possibility that future coalition negotiations will involve the SP. Whether these talks will result in the SP becoming part of the government, which will almost certainly include the CDA due to its position as the centre party, is an open, and intriguing, empirical question.

4 I would like to thank Mara Yerkes for keeping me informed about this issue.

5 Thus within a few years of the *Job Aqtiv–Gesetz* becoming law, this significant change to German welfare policy had already been surpassed. This is a good example of the radicalism of Agenda 2010, for it went well beyond what had previously been considered an important reform.

6 Thus the INSM was successful in providing the basis for employers' associations to overcome the divisions which had emerged in the 1990s, a decade marked by the withdrawal of many, often small, companies from the associations (Silvia 1997). Underlying this trend was the increasing difficulty with which these companies felt able to fulfil their part of collective bargaining agreements. In response, different gradations of membership were offered in order to bring companies back into the fold, and reassure wavering members of the associations. Principally, the status *ohne Tarifverbindung* was key, offering membership with partial benefits compared to full members, but, in exchange, no obligation to respect collective bargaining agreements. In some regions of Germany a majority of association members have *ohne Tarifverbindung* status (Kinderman 2005: 442). Silvia and Schroeder (2007) feel that this shift may render employers' associations redundant in the long-term, with company-level agreements taking on the role historically performed by collective bargaining at the sectoral level. In contrast, Kinderman (2005) and Raess (2006) contend that this strengthens the associations through uniting employers behind the agenda articulated by the INSM, a position that this author finds more persuasive.

7 It should be noted that I have not said that the German economy is transnationalized – there is a *growing* transnationalization leading to an increasingly but by no means fully transnationalized political economy. Thus it is a process rather than an end-state, marking the modified intertwining of the national and the international, *not* the complete transnationalization of the German variety of capitalism. Furthermore, while German capital is in the 2000s much more willing to invoke "globalization" in order to reinforce the push for a "new social market economy", it is notable that labour is of a rather different perspective – in contrast to the shared assumption of economic vulnerability found in the Netherlands. For instance, **DGB#2** emphasized that, given the importance of the German economy for the European and the world economy, Germany will never need to assume vulnerability in the way that small countries do. Therefore, the contrasting opinions about "globalization" mirrored the differences about economic "reality" discussed in Chapter 6.

8 This was the case for the CDU leadership in particular; the CSU's support for the reform agenda had been half-hearted at best (Clemens 2007).

# Bibliography


Abert, J.G. (1969) *Economic Policy and Planning in the Netherlands, 1950–1965*. New Haven and London: Yale University Press.

Albert, M. (1993) *Capitalism against Capitalism* (trs. P. Haviland). London: Whurr.

Alexander, J.C. (1990) 'Analytic Debates: Understanding the Relative Autonomy of Culture', in J.C. Alexander and S. Seidman (eds) *Culture and Society: Contemporary Debates*. Cambridge: Cambridge University Press, 1–27.

Almond, G.A. (2000) 'The Study of Political Culture', in L. Crothers and C. Lockhart (eds) *Culture and Politics: A Reader*. New York: St. Martin's Press, 5–20.

Almond, G.A. and Verba, S. (1963) *The Civic Culture: Political Attitudes and Democracy in Five Nations*. Princeton: Princeton University Press.

Andeweg, R.B. (2000) 'From Dutch Disease to Dutch Model? Consensus Government in Practice'. *Parliamentary Affairs*, 53:4, 697–709.

Andeweg, R.B. and Irwin, G.A. (2002) *Governance and Politics of the Netherlands*. Basingstoke: Palgrave Macmillan.

Anderson, P. (1976) *Considerations on Western Marxism*. London: New Left Books.

Appadurai, A. (1996) *Modernity at Large: Cultural Dimensions of Globalization*. Minneapolis: University of Minnesota Press.

Auer, P. (2000) *Employment Revival in Europe: Labour Market Success in Austria, Denmark, Ireland and the Netherlands*. Geneva: International Labour Organization.

Augelli, E. and Murphy, C.N. (1997) 'Consciousness, Myth and Collective Action: Gramsci, Sorel and the Ethical State', in S. Gill and J.H. Mittelman (eds) *Innovation and Transformation in International Studies*. Cambridge: Cambridge University Press, 25–38.

Barnet, R.J. and Cavanagh, J. (1994) *Global Dreams: Imperial Corporations and the New World Order*. New York: Simon and Schuster.

Becker, U. (2001a) 'A "Dutch Model": Employment Growth by Corporatist Consensus and Wage Restraint? A Critical Account of an Idyllic View'. *New Political Economy*, 6:1, 19–43.

—— (2001b) '"Miracle" by Consensus? Consensualism and Dominance in Dutch Employment Development'. *Economic and Industrial Democracy*, 22:4, 453–83.

—— (2005) 'An Example of Competitive Corporatism? The Dutch Political Economy 1983–2004 in Critical Examination'. *Journal of European Public Policy*, 12:6, 1078–1102.

Bell, D. (1973) *The Coming of Post-Industrial Society: A Venture in Forecasting*. New York: Basic Books.

Bellamy, R. (1990) 'Gramsci, Croce and the Italian Political Tradition'. *History of Political Thought*, 11:2, 313–37.

Bellamy, R. and Schecter, D. (1993) *Gramsci and the Italian State*. Manchester: Manchester University Press.

Berger, S. and Dore, R. (eds) (1996) *National Diversity and Global Capitalism*. Ithaca and London: Cornell University Press.

Bieler, A. (2000) *Globalisation and Enlargement of the European Union: Austrian and Swedish Social Forces in the Struggle over Membership*. London: Routledge.

—— (2001) 'Questioning Cognitivism and Constructivism in IR Theory: Reflections on the Material Structure of Ideas'. *Politics*, 21:2, 93–100.

—— (2002) 'The Struggle over EU Enlargement: A Historical Materialist Analysis of European Integration'. *Journal of European Public Policy*, 9:4, 575–97.

—— (2006a) *The Struggle for a Social Europe: Trade Unions and EMU in Times of Global Restructuring*. Manchester: Manchester University Press.

—— (2006b) 'Class Struggle over the EU Model of Capitalism: Neo-Gramscian Perspectives and the Analysis of European Integration', in A. Bieler and A.D. Morton (eds) *Images of Gramsci: Connections and Contentions in Political Theory and International Relations*. London: Routledge, 119–32.

Bieler, A. and Morton, A.D. (2003) 'Globalisation, the State and Class Struggle: A "Critical Economy" Engagement with Open Marxism'. *British Journal of Politics and International Relations*, 5:4, 467–99.

—— (2008) 'The Deficits of Discourse in IPE: Turning Base Metal into Gold?' *International Studies Quarterly*, 52:1, 103–28.

Bieler, A., Bonefeld, W., Burnham, P. and Morton, A.D. (2006) *Global Restructuring, State, Capital and Labour: Contesting Neo-Gramscian Perspectives*. Basingstoke: Palgrave Macmillan.

Blackbourn, D. (2002) *History of Germany 1780–1918: The Long Nineteenth Century* (2nd ed.). Oxford: Blackwell.

Blom, J.C.H. (1999) 'The Netherlands since 1830', in J.C.H. Blom and E. Lamberts (eds) *History of the Low Countries* (trs. J.C. Kennedy). New York and Oxford: Berghahn, 387–460.

Blyth, M. (2002) *Great Transformations: Economic Ideas and Institutional Change in the Twentieth Century*. Cambridge: Cambridge University Press.

Boeri, T. and Castanheira, M. (2005) 'Germany Needs a Technical Caretaker Government'. *Financial Times*, 27 September.

Bourdieu, P. (1984) *Distinction: A Social Critique of the Judgement of Taste* (trs. R. Nice). London: Routledge.

—— (1990a) *The Logic of Practice* (trs. R. Nice). Cambridge: Polity.

—— (1990b) *In Other Words: Essays Towards a Reflexive Sociology* (trs. M. Adamson). Cambridge: Polity.

Bourdieu, P. *et al.* (1998) *The Weight of the World: Social Suffering in Contemporary Society* (trs. P. Parkhurst Ferguson). Cambridge: Polity.

Boyer, R. and Drache, D. (eds) (1996) *States Against Markets: The Limits of Globalization*. London and New York: Routledge.

Braun, H-J. (1990) *The German Economy in the Twentieth Century*. London: Routledge.

Bruff, I. (2003) 'The Netherlands, the Challenge of Lijst Pim Fortuyn, and the Third Way'. *Politics*, 23:3, 156–62.

—— (2005) 'Making Sense of the Globalisation Debate When Engaging in Political Economy Analysis'. *British Journal of Politics and International Relations*, 7:2, 261–80.

—— (2007) 'Utilising Gramsci When Analysing European Models of Capitalism: Combining the Horizontal and the Vertical', presented at the *8th European Sociological Association conference*, Glasgow Caledonian University and the University of Strathclyde, 3–6 September.

—— (forthcoming) 'The Totalisation of Human Practice in Open Marxist/ Foucauldian Perspectives on Class/Power Relations'.

Bruttel, O. and Sol, E. (2006) 'Work First as a European Model? Evidence from Germany and the Netherlands'. *Policy & Politics*, 34:1, 69–89.

Callinicos, A. (1999) *Social Theory: A Historical Introduction*. Cambridge: Polity.

Cammack, P. (2007) 'RIP IPE'. *Papers in the Politics of Global Competitiveness*, No. 7. Institute for Global Studies, Manchester Metropolitan University: e-space Open Access Repository.

Campbell, J.L. (2004) *Institutional Change and Globalization*. Princeton: Princeton University Press.

Campbell, J.L. and Pedersen, O.K. (2001) 'The Second Movement in Institutional Analysis', in J.L. Campbell and O.K. Pedersen (eds) *The Rise of Neoliberalism and Institutional Analysis*. Princeton: Princeton University Press, 249–81.

—— (2007) 'The Varieties of Capitalism and Hybrid Success: Denmark in the Global Economy'. *Comparative Political Studies*, 40:3, 307–32.

Campbell, J.L., Hall, J.A. and Pedersen, O.K. (eds) (2006) *National Identity and the Varieties of Capitalism: The Danish Experience*. Montreal: McGill-Queen's University Press.

Carlin, W. and Soskice, D. (1997) 'Shocks to the System: The German Political Economy under Stress'. *National Institute Economic Review*, 159:1, 57–76.

Castells, M. (1996) *The Information Age: Economy, Society and Culture. Vol. I: The Rise of the Network Society*. Oxford: Blackwell.

—— (1997) *The Information Age: Economy, Society and Culture. Vol. II: The Power of Identity*. Oxford: Blackwell.

—— (1998) *The Information Age: Economy, Society and Culture. Vol. III: The End of the Millennium*. Oxford: Blackwell.

Chaney, D. (1994) *The Cultural Turn: Scene-setting Essays on Contemporary Cultural History*. London: Routledge.

Clemens, C. (2007) 'Two Steps Forward, One Step Back: Merkel's CDU/CSU and the Politics of Welfare State Reform'. *German Politics*, 16:2, 222–46.

Coates, D. (2000) *Models of Capitalism: Growth and Stagnation in the Modern Era*. Cambridge: Polity.

Cohen, B.J. (2007) 'The Transatlantic Divide: Why are British and American IPE so Different?' *Review of International Political Economy*, 14:2, 197–219.

Cohen, B.J. (2008) 'The Transatlantic Divide: A Rejoinder'. *Review of International Political Economy*, 15:1, 30–4.

Cox, R.H. (1998) 'From Safety Net to Trampoline: Labor Market Activation in the Netherlands and Denmark'. *Governance*, 11:4, 397–414.

—— (2001) 'The Social Construction of an Imperative: Why Welfare Reform Happened in Denmark and the Netherlands but Not in Germany'. *World Politics*, 53:3, 463–90.

Cox, R.W. (1981) 'Social Forces, States and World Orders: Beyond International Relations'. *Millennium*, 10:2, 126–55.

—— (1983) 'Gramsci, Hegemony and International Relations: An Essay in Method'. *Millennium*, 12:2, 162–75.

—— (1987) *Production, Power and World Order: Social Forces in the Making of History*. New York: Columbia University Press.

—— (1989) 'Production, the State and Change in World Order', in E-O. Czepiel and J.N. Rosenau (eds) *Global Changes and Theoretical Challenges: Approaches to World Politics for the 1990s*. Lexington, MA.: Lexington, 37–50.

—— (1996a) 'Realism, Positivism, and Historicism', in R.W. Cox (with T. Sinclair) *Approaches to World Order*. Cambridge: Cambridge University Press, 49–59.

—— (1996b) 'Towards a Posthegemonic Conceptualization of World Order: Reflections on the Relevancy of Ibn Khaldun', in Cox, *Approaches to World Order*, 144–73.

—— (1996c) 'Labor and Hegemony', in Cox, *Approaches to World Order*, 420–70.

—— (1996d) 'Multilateralism and World Order', in Cox, *Approaches to World Order*, 494–523.

—— (2002) 'Reflections and Transitions', in R.W. Cox (with M.G. Schechter) *The Political Economy of a Plural World: Critical Reflections on Power, Morals and Civilization*. London: Routledge, 26–44.

CPB Netherlands Bureau for Economic Policy Analysis (1997) *Challenging Neighbours: Rethinking German and Dutch Economic Institutions*. Berlin, Heidelberg and New York: Springer-Verlag.

Crehan, K. (2002) *Gramsci, Culture and Anthropology*. London: Pluto.

Crothers, L. and Lockhart, C. (eds) (2000) *Culture and Politics: A Reader*. New York: St. Martin's Press.

Crouch, C. (2005) 'Models of Capitalism'. *New Political Economy*, 10:4, 439–56.

Culpepper, P.D. (1999) 'The Future of the High-skill Equilibrium in Germany'. *Oxford Review of Economic Policy*, 15:1, 43–59.

Dahl, R.A. (1989) *Democracy and its Critics*. New Haven: Yale University Press.

de Vries, J. (1978) *The Netherlands Economy in the Twentieth Century: An Examination of the Most Characteristic Features in the Period 1900–1970* (trs. D.J. Jordan). Assen: Van Gorcum.

de Wolff, P. and Driehuis, W. (1980) 'A Description of Post War Economic Developments and Economic Policy in the Netherlands', in R.T. Griffiths (ed.) *The Economy and Politics of the Netherlands since 1945*. The Hague: Nijhoff, 13–60.

Devine, F. (2002) 'Qualitative Methods', in D. Marsh and G. Stoker (eds) *Theory and Methods in Political Science* (2nd ed.). Basingstoke: Palgrave Macmillan, 197–215.

DiMaggio, P. (1990) 'Cultural Aspects of Economic Action and Organization', in R. Friedland and A.F. Robertson (eds) *Beyond the Marketplace: Rethinking Economy and Society*. New York: Aldine de Gruyter, 113–36.

—— (1994) 'Culture and Economy', in N.J. Smelser and R. Swedberg (eds) *The Handbook of Economic Sociology*. Princeton: Princeton University Press, 27–57.

Douglas, M. and Wildavsky, A. (1982) *Risk and Culture: An Essay on the Selection of Technological and Environmental Dangers*. Berkeley: University of California Press.

du Gay, P. and Pryke, M. (2002) *Cultural Economy: Cultural Analysis and Commercial Life*. London: Sage.

Dyson, K. (2001) 'The German Model Revisited: From Schmidt to Schröder'. *German Politics*, 10:2, 135–54.

Eckstein, H. (1988) 'A Culturalist Theory of Political Change'. *American Political Science Review*, 82:3, 789–804.

Estevez-Abe, M., Iversen, T. and Soskice, D. (2001) 'Social Protection and the Formation of Skills: A Reinterpretation of the Welfare State', in P.A. Hall and D. Soskice (eds) *Varieties of Capitalism: The Institutional Foundations of Comparative Advantage*. Oxford: Oxford University Press, 145–83.

Femia, J.V. (1981) *Gramsci's Political Thought: Hegemony, Consciousness, and the Revolutionary Process*. Oxford: Clarendon.

Flockton, C. (1996) 'Economic Management and the Challenge of Reunification', in G. Smith, W.E. Paterson and S. Padgett (eds) *Developments in German Politics 2*. Basingstoke: Macmillan, 211–32.

Forgacs, D. and Nowell-Smith, G. (1985) 'General Introduction', in A. Gramsci, *Selections from Cultural Writings* (eds D. Forgacs and G. Nowell-Smith; trs. W. Boelhower). London: Lawrence and Wishart, 1–15.

Foucault, M. (1972) *The Archaeology of Knowledge* (trs. A.M. Sheridan Smith). London: Tavistock.

—— (1977) *Discipline and Punish: The Birth of the Prison* (trs. A. Sheridan). London: Allen Lane.

—— (1980) 'Truth and Power', in M. Foucault, *Power/Knowledge: Selected Interviews and other Writings, 1972–1977* (ed. C. Gordon; trs. C. Gordon, L. Marshall, J. Mepham and K. Soper). Brighton: Harvester, 109–33.

—— (1981) *The History of Sexuality. Vol. I: An Introduction* (trs. R. Hurley). Harmondsworth: Penguin.

Friedman, T. (2005) *The World is Flat: A Brief History of the Globalized World in the Twenty-first Century*. London: Allen Lane.

Funk, L. (2000) 'Economic Reform of Modell Deutschland', in R. Harding and W.E. Paterson (eds) *The Future of the German Economy: An End to the Miracle?* Manchester: Manchester University Press, 16–35.

—— (2003) 'Public "Want Less Influence for Unions"'. Published on the *European Industrial Relations Observatory* website, at http://www.eurofound.europa.eu

Garrett, G. (1998) *Partisan Politics in the Global Economy*. Cambridge: Cambridge University Press.

Geertz, C. (1973a) 'Thick Description: Toward an Interpretive Theory of Culture', in C. Geertz, *The Interpretation of Cultures: Selected Essays*. New York: Basic Books, 3–30.

—— (1973b) 'The Politics of Meaning', in Geertz, *The Interpretation of Cultures*, 311–26.

Germain, R.D. (2007) '"Critical" Political Economy, Historical Materialism and Adam Morton'. *Politics*, 27:2, 127–31.
Germain, R.D. and Kenny, M. (1998) 'Engaging Gramsci: International Relations Theory and the New Gramscians'. *Review of International Studies*, 24:1, 3–21.
Gerson, K. and Horowitz, R. (2002) 'Observation and Interviewing: Options and Choices in Qualitative Research', in T. May (ed.) *Qualitative Research in Action*. London: Sage, 199–224.
Giddens, A. (1990) *The Consequences of Modernity*. Cambridge: Polity.
Gill, S. (1998) 'European Governance and New Constitutionalism: Economic and Monetary Union and Alternatives to Disciplinary Neo-liberalism in Europe'. *New Political Economy*, 3:1, 5–26.
Gramsci, A. (1971) *Selections from the Prison Notebooks* (eds/trs. Q. Hoare and G. Nowell-Smith). London: Lawrence and Wishart.
—— (1985) *Selections from Cultural Writings* (eds D. Forgacs and G. Nowell-Smith; trs. W. Boelhower). London: Lawrence and Wishart.
—— (1992) *Prison Notebooks. Vol. I* (ed. J.A. Buttigieg; trs. J.A. Buttigieg and A. Callari). New York: Columbia University Press.
—— (1996) *Prison Notebooks. Vol. II* (ed. and trs. J.A. Buttigieg). New York: Columbia University Press.
—— (2007) *Prison Notebooks. Vol. III* (ed. and trs. J.A. Buttigieg). New York: Columbia University Press.
Granovetter, M. (1985) 'Economic Action and Social Structure: The Problem of Embeddedness'. *American Journal of Sociology*, 91:3, 481–510.
Granovetter, M. and Swedberg, R. (eds) (2001) *The Sociology of Economic Life* (2nd ed.). Boulder, CO.: Westview Press.
Green-Pedersen, C. (2002) *The Politics of Justification: Party Competition and Welfare-state Retrenchment in Denmark and the Netherlands from 1982 to 1998*. Amsterdam: Amsterdam University Press.
Green-Pedersen, C., van Kersbergen, K. and Hemerijck, A. (2001) 'Neo-liberalism, the "Third Way" or What? Recent Social Democratic Welfare Policies in Denmark and the Netherlands'. *Journal of European Public Policy*, 8:2, 307–25.
Gregson, N., Simonsen, K. and Vaiou, D. (2001) 'Whose Economy for Whose Culture? Moving Beyond Oppositional Talk in European Debate about Economy and Culture'. *Antipode*, 33:4, 616–46.
Grenfell, M. (2004) *Pierre Bourdieu: Agent Provocateur*. London and New York: Continuum.
Griffin, P. (2007) 'Sexing the Economy in a Neo-liberal World Order: Neo-liberal Discourse and the (Re)Production of Heteronormative Heterosexuality'. *British Journal of Politics and International Relations*, 9:2, 220–38.
Grossberg, L. (1996) 'History, Politics and Postmodernism: Stuart Hall and Cultural Studies', in D. Morley and K.-H. Chen (eds) *Stuart Hall: Critical Dialogues in Cultural Studies*. London: Routledge, 151–73.
Habermas, J. (1987) *The Theory of Communicative Action. Vol. II: Lifeworld and System: A Critique of Functionalist Reason* (trs. T. McCarthy). Cambridge: Polity.

Hall, P.A. (1986) *Governing the Economy: The Politics of State Intervention in Britain and France*. Cambridge: Polity.
—— (1993) 'Policy Paradigms, Social Learning and the State – The Case of Economic Policy-making in Britain'. *Comparative Politics*, 25:3, 275–96.
Hall, P.A. and Soskice, D. (eds) (2001a) *Varieties of Capitalism: The Institutional Foundations of Comparative Advantage*. Oxford: Oxford University Press.
—— (2001b) 'An Introduction to Varieties of Capitalism', in Hall and Soskice, *Varieties of Capitalism*, 1–68.
—— (2003) 'Varieties of Capitalism and Institutional Change: A Response to Three Critics'. *Comparative European Politics*, 1:2, 241–50.
Hall, P.A. and Taylor, R.C.R. (1996) 'Political Science and the Three New Institutionalisms'. *Political Studies*, 44:4, 937–57.
Hall, S. (1980) 'Nicos Poulantzas: *State, Power, Socialism*'. *New Left Review*, 119 (I), 60–9.
—— (1988) *The Hard Road to Renewal: Thatcherism and the Crisis of the Left*. London: Verso.
—— (1989) 'The Meaning of New Times', in S. Hall and M. Jacques (eds) *New Times*. London: Lawrence and Wishart, 116–33.
—— (1991a) 'Reading Gramsci', in R. Simon (1991) *Gramsci's Political Thought: An Introduction* (revised and reset edition). London: Lawrence and Wishart, 7–10.
—— (1991b) 'Gramsci and Us', in Simon, *Gramsci's Political Thought*, 114–30.
—— (1996a) 'The Problem of Ideology: Marxism without Guarantees', in Morley and Chen, *Stuart Hall*, 25–46.
—— (1996b) 'On Postmodernism and Articulation' (interview by L. Grossberg), in Morley and Chen, *Stuart Hall*, 131–50.
—— (1996c) 'Gramsci's Relevance for the Study of Race and Ethnicity', in Morley and Chen, *Stuart Hall*, 411–40.
—— (1996d) 'When Was the "Post-colonial"? Thinking at the Limit', in I. Chambers and L. Curti (eds) *The Post-colonial Question: Common Skies, Divided Horizons*. London: Routledge, 242–60.
—— (1997) 'Culture and Power' (interview by P. Osborne and L. Segal). *Radical Philosophy*, 86, 24–41.
Hancké, B., Rhodes, M. and Thatcher, M. (eds) (2007) *Beyond Varieties of Capitalism: Conflict, Contradictions, and Complementarities in the European Economy*. Oxford: Oxford University Press.
Hardach, K. (1980) *The Political Economy of Germany in the Twentieth Century*. Berkeley and London: University of California Press.
Harlen, C.M. (2002a) 'Schröder's Economic Reforms: The End of *Reformstau*?' *German Politics*, 11:1, 61–80.
—— (2002b) 'Globalisation and German Labour Market Policies', in L. Funk and S. Green (eds) *New Aspects of Labour Market Policy*. Berlin: Verlag für Wissenschaft und Forschung, 39–53.
Hartog, J. (1999) 'Wither Dutch Corporatism? Two Decades of Employment Policies and Welfare Reforms'. *Scottish Journal of Political Economy*, 46:4, 458–87.

Haselbach, D. (1997) 'Social Market Economy and West German Identity', in M. Zimmer (ed.) *Germany: Phoenix in Trouble?* Edmonton: University of Alberta Press, 157–82.

Hay, C. (2001) 'The "Crisis" of Keynesianism and the Rise of Neoliberalism in Britain: An Ideational Institutionalist Approach', in Campbell and Pedersen, *The Rise of Neoliberalism and Institutional Analysis*, 193–218.

—— (2004) 'Common Trajectories, Variable Paces, Divergent Outcomes? Models of European Capitalism under Conditions of Complex Economic Interdependence'. *Review of International Political Economy*, 11:2, 231–62.

—— (2006) 'Constructivist Institutionalism', in R.A.W. Rhodes, S.A. Biner and B.A. Rockman (eds) *The Oxford Handbook of Political Institutions*. Oxford: Oxford University Press, 56–74.

—— (2007) 'Whatever Happened to Thatcherism?' *Political Studies Review*, 5:2, 183–201.

Heclo, H. (1974) *Modern Social Politics in Britain and Sweden: From Relief to Income Maintenance*. New Haven: Yale University Press.

Hemerijck, A. (2001) 'The Dutch Negotiating Economy: Learning Through Concertation', in F. Hendriks and T.A.J. Toonen (eds) *Polder Politics: The Re-invention of Consensus Democracy in the Netherlands*. Aldershot: Ashgate, 95–113.

—— (2002) 'The Self-transformation of the European Social Model(s)', in G. Esping-Andersen (ed.) *Why We Need a New Welfare State*. Oxford: Oxford University Press, 173–213.

Hemerijck, A. and Schludi, M. (2000) 'Sequences of Policy Failures and Effective Policy Responses', in F.W. Scharpf and V.A. Schmidt (eds) *Welfare and Work in the Open Economy. Vol. 1: From Vulnerability to Competitiveness*. Oxford: Oxford University Press, 125–228.

Hemerijck, A. and Vail, M.I. (2006) 'The Forgotten Center: State Activism and Corporatist Adjustment', in J.D. Levy (ed.) *The State after Statism: New State Activities in the Age of Globalization and Liberalization*. Cambridge, MA.: Harvard University Press, 57–92.

Hemerijck, A., Unger, B. and Visser, J. (2000) 'How Small Countries Negotiate Change: Twenty-five Years of Policy Adjustment in Austria, the Netherlands and Belgium', in F.W. Scharpf and V.A. Schmidt (eds) *Welfare and Work in the Open Economy. Vol. II: Diverse Responses to Common Challenges*. Oxford: Oxford University Press, 175–263.

Higgott, R. and Watson, M. (2008) 'All at Sea in a Barbed Wire Canoe: Professor Cohen's Transatlantic Voyage in IPE'. *Review of International Political Economy*, 15:1, 1–17.

Hinrichs, K. (2002) 'What Can Be Learned from Whom? Germany's Employment Problem in Comparative Perspective'. *Innovation*, 15:2, 77–97.

Hirschman, A.O. (1970) *Exit, Voice and Loyalty: Responses to Decline in Firms, Organizations and States*. Cambridge, MA.: Cambridge University Press.

Hirst, P. and Thompson, G. (1999) *Globalization in Question: The International Economy and the Possibilities of Governance* (2nd ed.). Cambridge: Polity.

Hobson, J.M. (2007) 'Is Critical Theory Always *for* the White West and *for* Western Imperialism? Beyond Westphilian to a Post-racist Critical IR'. *Review of International Studies*, 33:1–2, 91–116.

Holton, R.J. (1992) *Economy and Society*. London: Routledge.

Holub, R. (1992) *Antonio Gramsci: Beyond Marxism and Postmodernism*. London: Routledge.

Höpner, M. (2005) 'What Connects Industrial Relations and Corporate Governance? Explaining Institutional Complementarity'. *Socio-economic Review*, 3:2, 331–58.

Hunt, L. and Bonnell, V.E. (eds) (1999) *Beyond the Cultural Turn: New Directions in the Study of Society and Culture*. Berkeley, Los Angeles and London: University of California Press.

Inglehart, R. (1977) *The Silent Revolution: Changing Values and Political Styles among Western Publics*. Princeton: Princeton University Press.

Ives, P. (2004) *Language and Hegemony in Gramsci*. London: Pluto.

Jameson, F. (1991) *Postmodernism, or, The Cultural Logic of Late Capitalism*. London: Verso.

Jessop, B. (2002) *The Future of the Capitalist State*. Cambridge: Polity.

—— (2006) 'Gramsci as a Spatial Theorist', in Bieler and Morton, *Images of Gramsci*, 27–43.

Jones, E. (1999) 'Is "Competitive" Corporatism an Adequate Response to Globalisation? Evidence from the Low Countries'. *West European Politics*, 22:3, 159–81.

—— (2008) *Economic Adjustment and Political Transformation in Small States*. Oxford: Oxford University Press.

Karsten, L., van Veen, K. and van Wulfften Palthe, A. (2008) 'What Happened to the Popularity of the Polder Model? Emergence and Disappearance of a Political Fashion'. *International Sociology*, 23:1, 35–65.

Katzenstein, P.J. (1985) *Small States in World Markets: Industrial Policy in Europe*. Ithaca and London: Cornell University Press.

—— (1987) *Policy and Politics in West Germany: The Growth of a Semisovereign State*. Philadelphia: Temple University Press.

—— (1989) 'Stability and Change in the Emerging Third Republic', in P.J. Katzenstein (ed.) *Industry and Politics in West Germany: Toward the Third Republic*. Ithaca and London: Cornell University Press, 307–53.

—— (2003) '*Small States* and Small States Revisited'. *New Political Economy*, 8:1, 9–30.

Kay, J. (2006) 'Europe Will Never Vote for Reform'. *Financial Times*, 17 April.

Kemmerling, A. and Bruttel, O. (2006) '"New Politics" In German Labour Market Policy? The Implications of the Recent Hartz Reforms for the German Welfare State'. *West European Politics*, 29:1, 90–112.

Kenworthy, L. (2006) 'Institutional Coherence and Macroeconomic Performance'. *Socio-economic Review*, 4:1, 69–91.

Kinderman, D. (2005) 'Pressure from without, Subversion from within: The Two-pronged German Employer Offensive'. *Comparative European Politics*, 3:4, 432–63.

Kitschelt, H. and Streeck, W. (2003) 'From Stability to Stagnation: Germany at the Beginning of the Twenty-first Century'. *West European Politics*, 26:4, 1–34.

Kjær, P. and Pedersen, O.K. (2001) 'Translating Liberalization: Neoliberalism in the Danish Negotiated Economy', in Campbell and Pedersen, *The Rise of Neoliberalism and Institutional Analysis*, 219–48.

Kleinknecht, A. and Naastepad, C.W.M. (2005) 'The Netherlands: Failure of a Neo-classical Policy Agenda'. *European Planning Studies*, 13:8, 1193–1203.

Koole, R. and Daalder, H. (2002) 'The Consociational Democracy Model and the Netherlands: Ambivalent Allies?' *Acta Politica*, 37:1–2, 23–43.

Kratochwil, F. (2007) 'Looking Back from Somewhere: Reflections on What Remains "Critical" in Critical Theory'. *Review of International Studies*, 33:1–2, 25–45.

Kvale, S. (1996) *InterViews: An Introduction to Qualitative Research Interviewing*. London: Sage.

Lacher, H. (2003) 'Putting the Capitalist State in Its Place: The Critique of State-centrism and Its Limits'. *Review of International Studies*, 29:4, 521–41.

—— (2006) *Beyond Globalization: Capitalism, Territoriality and the International Relations of Modernity*. London: Routledge.

Lane, R. (1992) 'Political Culture: Residual Category or General Theory?' *Comparative Political Studies*, 25:3, 362–87.

Lash, S. and Urry, J. (1987) *The End of Organized Capitalism*. Cambridge: Polity.

—— (1994) *Economies of Signs and Space*. London and Thousand Oaks: Sage.

Lawson, S. (2006) *Culture and Context in World Politics*. Basingstoke: Palgrave Macmillan.

Levy, J.D. (2000) 'France: Directing Adjustment?', in Scharpf and Schmidt, *Welfare and Work in the Open Economy. Vol. II*, 308–50.

Lijphart, A. (1968) *The Politics of Accommodation: Pluralism and Democracy in the Netherlands*. Berkeley: University of California Press.

Lindblom, C. (1977) *Politics and Markets: The World's Political and Economic Systems*. New York: Basic Books.

Lipset, S.M. (1960) *Political Man: The Social Bases of Politics*. London: Heinemann.

Lockhart, C. (1999) 'Cultural Contributions to Explaining Institutional Form, Political Change, and Rational Decisions'. *Comparative Political Studies*, 32:7, 862–93.

—— (2001) *Protecting the Elderly: How Culture Shapes Social Policy*. University Park, PA.: Pennsylvania State University Press.

Lowndes, V. (2002) 'Institutionalism', in Marsh and Stoker, *Theory and Methods in Political Science*, 90–108.

Lubbers, R.F.M. and Lemckert, C. (1980) 'The Influence of Natural Gas on the Dutch Economy' (trs. R.T. Griffiths), in Griffiths, *The Economy and Politics of the Netherlands since 1945*, 87–113.

Manow, P. and Seils, E. (2000) 'Adjusting Badly: The German Welfare State, Structural Change, and the Open Economy', in Scharpf and Schmidt, *Welfare and Work in the Open Economy. Vol. II*, 264–307.

March, J.G. and Olsen, J.P. (1989) *Rediscovering Institutions: The Organizational Basis of Politics*. New York: Free Press.

McLennan, G. (1996) 'Post-Marxism and the "Four Sins" of Modernist Theorizing'. *New Left Review*, 218 (I), 53–74.

Menz, G. (2005) 'Old Bottles – New Wine: The New Dynamics of Industrial Relations'. *German Politics*, 14:2, 196–207.

Mill, J.S. (1991) *On Liberty and Other Essays* (ed. J. Gray). Oxford: Oxford University Press.

Mitlacher, L.W. (2007) 'The Role of Temporary Agency Work in Different Industrial Relations Systems – a Comparison between Germany and the USA'. *British Journal of Industrial Relations*, 45:3, 581–606.

Morton, A.D. (2003a) 'Historicizing Gramsci: Situating Ideas in and Beyond Their Context'. *Review of International Political Economy*, 10:1, 118–46.

—— (2003b) 'The Social Function of Carlos Fuentes: A Critical Intellectual or in the "Shadow of the State"?' *Bulletin of Latin American Research*, 22:1, 27–51.

—— (2006) 'The Grimly Comic Riddle of Hegemony in IPE: Where is Class Struggle?' *Politics*, 26:1, 62–72.

—— (2007a) *Unravelling Gramsci: Hegemony and Passive Revolution in the Global Political Economy*. London: Pluto.

—— (2007b) 'Unquestioned Answers/Unanswered Questions in IPE: A Rejoinder to "Non-Marxist" Historical Materialism'. *Politics*, 27:2, 132–6.

—— (2007c) 'Waiting for Gramsci: State Formation, Passive Revolution and the International'. *Millennium*, 35:3, 597–621.

Motta, S. (2006) 'Utopias Re-imagined: A Reply to Panizza'. *Political Studies*, 54:4, 898–905.

Nash, K. (2001) 'The "Cultural Turn" in Social Theory: Towards a Theory of Cultural Politics'. *Sociology*, 35:1, 77–92.

Nicholls, A.J. (1994) *Freedom with Responsibility: The Social Market Economy in Germany, 1918–1963*. Oxford: Clarendon Press.

Nussbaum. M.C. (1992) 'Human Functioning and Social Justice: In Defense of Aristotelian Essentialism'. *Political Theory*, 20:2, 202–46.

Ohmae, K. (1990) *The Borderless World: Power and Strategy in the Interlinked Economy*. London: Collins.

Organisation for Economic Cooperation and Development (2001) *Historical Statistics: 1970–2001*. Paris: Organisation for Economic Cooperation and Development.

—— (2004) *Main Economic Indicators: August 2004*. Paris: Organisation for Economic Cooperation and Development.

—— (2007) *Main Economic Indicators: August 2007*. Paris: Organisation for Economic Cooperation and Development.

Overy, R. (2003) 'Economy and State in Germany in the Twentieth Century', in S. Ogilvie and R. Overy (eds) *Germany: A New Social and Economic History. Vol. III: Since 1800*. London: Arnold, 251–78.

Palan, R. (2007) 'Transnational Theories of Order and Change: Heterodoxy in International Relations Scholarship'. *Review of International Studies*, 33:1–2, 47–69.

Parsons, T. (1949) *The Structure of Social Action: A Study in Social Theory with Special Reference to a Group of Recent European Writers* (2nd ed.). Glencoe, IL.: Free Press.

Parsons, T. and Smelser, N.J. (1956) *Economy and Society: A Study in the Integration of Economic and Social Theory*. Glencoe, IL.: Free Press.

Peters, B.G. (ed.) (1999) *Institutional Theory in Political Science: The "New Institutionalism"*. London: Pinter.

Pierson, P. (1994) *Dismantling the Welfare State? Reagan, Thatcher, and the Politics of Retrenchment*. Cambridge: Cambridge University Press.

—— (ed.) (2001) *The New Politics of the Welfare State*. Oxford: Oxford University Press.

—— (2004) *Politics in Time: History, Institutions and Social Analysis*. Princeton: Princeton University Press.

Polanyi, K. (1944) *The Great Transformation: The Political and Economic Origins of Our Time*. Beacon Hill: Beacon Hill Press.

—— (1992) 'The Economy as Instituted Process', in Granovetter and Swedberg, *The Sociology of Economic Life*, 29–51.

Poulantzas, N. (1973) *Political Power and Social Classes* (trs. T. O'Hagan). London: New Left Books.

—— (1975) *Classes in Contemporary Capitalism* (trs. D. Fernbach). London: New Left Books.

—— (1978) *State, Power, Socialism* (trs. P. Camiller). London: New Left Books.

Pye, L.W. (1965) 'Introduction: Political Culture and Political Development', in L.W. Pye and S. Verba (eds) *Political Culture and Political Development*. Princeton: Princeton University Press, 3–26.

Pye, L.W. and Verba, S. (eds) (1965) *Political Culture and Political Development*. Princeton: Princeton University Press.

Radice, H. (2004) 'Comparing National Capitalisms', in J. Perraton and B. Clift (eds) *Where Are National Capitalisms Now?* Basingstoke: Palgrave Macmillan, 183–94.

Raess, D. (2006) 'Globalization and why the "Time is Ripe" for the Transformation of German Industrial Relations'. *Review of International Political Economy*, 13:3, 449–79.

Raess, D. and Burgoon, B. (2006) 'The Dogs that Sometimes Bark: Globalization and Works Council Bargaining in Germany'. *European Journal of Industrial Relations*, 12:3, 287–309.

Ravenhill, J. (2008) 'In Search of the Missing Middle'. *Review of International Political Economy*, 15:1, 18–29.

Ray, L. and Sayer, A. (1999) 'Introduction' in L. Ray and A. Sayer (eds) *Culture and Economy after the Cultural Turn*. London: Sage, 1–24.

Regini, M. (2000) 'The Dilemmas of Labour Market Regulation', in G. Esping-Andersen and M. Regini (eds) *Why Deregulate Labour Markets?* Oxford: Oxford University Press, 11–29.

Rengger, N. and Thirkell-White, B. (2007) 'Editors' Introduction'. *Review of International Studies*, 33:1–2, 3–24.

Rhodes, M. (1998) 'Globalization, Labour Markets and Welfare States: A Future of "Competitive Corporatism"?', in M. Rhodes and Y. Mény (eds) *The Future of European Welfare: A New Social Contract?* Basingstoke: Macmillan, 178–203.

—— (2000) 'Restructuring the British Welfare State: Between Domestic Constraints and Global Imperatives', in Scharpf and Schmidt, *Welfare and Work in the Open Economy. Vol. II*, 19–69.

Richardson, M. (2001) *The Experience of Culture*. London, Thousand Oaks and New Delhi: Sage.

Robinson, A. (2006) 'Towards an Intellectual Reformation: The Critique of Common Sense and the Forgotten Revolutionary Project of Gramscian Theory', in Bieler and Morton, *Images of Gramsci*, 75–87.

Robinson, W.I. (2004) *A Theory of Global Capitalism: Production, Class and State in a Transnational World*. Baltimore: John Hopkins University Press.

—— (2006) 'Gramsci and Globalisation: From Nation-state to Transnational Hegemony', in Bieler and Morton, *Images of Gramsci*, 165–80.

Rogowski, R. (1974) *Rational Legitimacy: A Theory of Political Support*. Princeton: Princeton University Press.

Rokkan, S. (1966) 'Comparative Cross-national Research: The Context of Current Efforts', in R.L. Merritt and S. Rokkan (eds) *Comparing Nations: The Use of Quantitative Data in Cross-national Research*. New Haven: Yale University Press, 3–25.

Ross, M.H. (2000) 'Culture and Identity in Comparative Political Analysis', in Crothers and Lockhart, *Culture and Politics*, 39–70.

Rupert, M. (2005) 'Reflections on Some Lessons Learned from a Decade of Globalisation Studies'. *New Political Economy*, 10:4, 457–78.

Saalfeld, T. (2006) 'Conflict and Consensus in Germany's Bi-cameral System: A Case Study of the Passage of the Agenda 2010'. *Debatte*, 14:3, 247–69.

Sassoon, A.S. (1987) *Gramsci's Politics* (2nd ed.). London: Hutchinson Education.

—— (2000) *Gramsci and Contemporary Politics: Beyond Pessimism of the Intellect*. London: Routledge.

—— (2006) 'Gramsci and the Secret of Father Brown', in Bieler and Morton, *Images of Gramsci*, 1–11.

Sayer, A. (1997a) 'Essentialism, Social Constructionism, and Beyond'. *Sociological Review*, 45:3, 453–87.

—— (1997b) 'The Dialectic of Culture and Economy', in R. Lee and J. Wills (eds) *Geographies of Economies*. London: Arnold, 16–26.

—— (2001) 'For a Critical Cultural Political Economy'. *Antipode*, 33:4, 687–708.

Schaapman, M. (2004) 'Tripartite "Autumn Agreement" Covers Broad Social Reform Agenda'. Published on the *European Industrial Relations Observatory* website, at http://www.eurofound.europa.eu

Scharpf, F.W. (1988) 'The Joint Decision Trap: Lessons from German Federalism and European Integration'. *Public Administration*, 66:3, 239–78.

—— (1993) 'Coordination in Hierarchies and Networks', in F.W. Scharpf (ed.) *Games in Hierarchies and Networks: Analytical and Empirical Approaches to the Study of Governance Institutions*. Frankfurt and Boulder, CO.: Campus and Westview, 125–65.

—— (2000) 'Economic Changes, Vulnerabilities, and Institutional Capabilities', in Scharpf and Schmidt, *Welfare and Work in the Open Economy. Vol. I*, 21–124.
Scharpf, F.W. and Schmidt, V.A. (eds) (2000a) *Welfare and Work in the Open Economy. Vol. 1: From Vulnerability to Competitiveness*. Oxford: Oxford University Press.
—— (eds) (2000b) *Welfare and Work in the Open Economy. Vol. II: Diverse Responses to Common Challenges*. Oxford: Oxford University Press.
Schechter, M.G. (2002) 'Critiques of Coxian Theory: Background to a Conversation', in Cox, *The Political Economy of a Plural World*, 1–25.
Schmidt, V.A. (2000) 'Values and Discourse in the Politics of Adjustment', in Scharpf and Schmidt, *Welfare and Work in the Open Economy. Vol. I*, 229–309.
—— (2001) 'The Politics of Economic Adjustment in France and Britain: When Does Discourse Matter?' *Journal of European Public Policy*, 8:2, 247–64.
—— (2002a) *The Futures of European Capitalism*. Oxford: Oxford University Press.
—— (2002b) 'Does Discourse Matter in the Politics of Welfare Adjustment?' *Comparative Political Studies*, 35:2, 168–93.
—— (2006) 'Institutionalism', in C. Hay, M. Lister and D. Marsh (eds) *The State: Theories and Issues*. Basingstoke: Palgrave Macmillan, 98–117.
Schweiger, C. (2006) 'The Role of the *Modell Deutschland* in the Enlarged European Union'. *Debatte*, 13:3, 243–63.
Seeleib-Kaiser, M. and Fleckenstein, T. (2007) 'Discourse, Learning and Welfare State Change: The Case of German Labour Market Reforms'. *Social Policy & Administration*, 41:5, 427–48.
Shilliam, R. (2004) 'Hegemony and the Unfashionable Problematic of "Primitive Accumulation"'. *Millennium*, 33:1, 59–88.
Shonfield, A. (1965) *Modern Capitalism: The Changing Balance of Public and Private Power*. London: Oxford University Press.
Silvia, S.J. (1997) 'German Unification and Emerging Divisions within German Employers' Associations: Cause or Catalyst?' *Comparative Politics*, 29:2, 187–208.
—— (1999) 'Every Which Way but Loose: German Industrial Relations since 1980', in A. Martin and G. Ross (eds) *The Brave New World of European Labor: European Trade Unions at the Millennium*. New York: Berghahn, 75–124.
—— (2002) 'The Fall and Rise of Unemployment in Germany: Is the Red-Green Government Responsible?' *German Politics*, 11:1, 1–22.
Silvia, S.J. and Schroeder, W. (2007) 'Why Are German Employers' Associations Declining? Arguments and Evidence'. *Comparative Political Studies*, 40:12, 1433–59.
Simon, R. (1991) *Gramsci's Political Thought: An Introduction* (revised and reset edition). London: Lawrence and Wishart.
Sklair, L. (1997) 'Review Essay – The Nature and Significance of Economic Sociology'. *Review of International Political Economy*, 4:1, 239–47.

—— (2001) *The Transnational Capitalist Class*. Oxford: Blackwell.
Slater, D. and Tonkiss, F. (2001) *Market Society: Markets and Modern Social Theory*. Cambridge: Polity.
Smelser, N.J. and Swedberg, R. (eds) (1994) *The Handbook of Economic Sociology*. Princeton: Princeton University Press.
Smith, G., Paterson, W.E. and Padgett, S. (1996) 'Introduction', in Smith *et al.*, *Developments in German Politics 2*, 1–12.
Smith, M. (2006) 'Pluralism', in Hay *et al.*, *The State*, 21–38.
Smith, N.J. (2006) 'Mapping Processes of Policy Change in Contemporary European Political Economies: The Irish Case'. *British Journal of Politics and International Relations*, 8:3, 519–38.
Soskice, D. (2000) 'Macroeconomic Analysis and the Political Economy of Unemployment', in T. Iversen, J. Pontusson and D. Soskice (eds) *Unions, Employers and Central Banks: Macroeconomic Coordination and Institutional Change in Social Market Economies*. Cambridge: Cambridge University Press, 38–76.
Soskice, D., Hancké, B., Trumbull, G. and Wren, A. (1998) 'Wage Bargaining, Labour Markets and Macroeconomic Performance in Germany and the Netherlands', in L. Delsen and E. de Jong (eds) *The German and Dutch Economies: Who Follows Whom?* Heidelberg and New York: Physica-Verlag, 39–51.
Spiro, M.E. (1984) 'Some Reflections on Cultural Determinism and Relativism with Special Reference to Emotion and Reason', in R.A. Schweder and R.A. LeVine (eds) *Culture Theory: Essays on Mind, Self, and Emotion*. Cambridge: Cambridge University Press, 323–46.
Spithoven, A.H.G.M. (2002) 'The Third Way: The Dutch Experience'. *Economy and Society*, 31:3, 333–68.
Stachura, P.D. (2003) 'Social Policy and Social Welfare in Germany from the Mid-nineteenth Century to the Present', in Ogilvie and Overy, *Germany. Vol. III*, 227–50.
Steinmo, S. (2003) 'Bucking the Trend? The Welfare State and the Global Economy: The Swedish Case Close Up'. *New Political Economy*, 8:1, 31–48.
Streeck, W. (1989) 'Successful Adjustment to Turbulent Markets: The Automobile Industry', in Katzenstein, *Industry and Politics in West Germany*, 113–56.
—— (1997) 'German Capitalism: Does it Exist? Can it Survive?', in C. Crouch and W. Streeck (eds) *Political Economy of Modern Capitalism: Mapping Convergence and Diversity*. London: Sage, 33–54.
—— (2006) 'A State of Exhaustion: A Comment on the German Election of 18 September'. *Political Quarterly*, 77:1, 79–87.
Streeck, W. and Hassel, A. (2003) 'The Crumbling Pillars of Social Partnership'. *West European Politics*, 26:4, 101–24.
Streeck, W. and Thelen, K. (eds) (2005a) *Beyond Continuity: Institutional Change in Advanced Political Economies*. Oxford: Oxford University Press.
—— (2005b) 'Introduction: Institutional Change in Advanced Political Economies', in Streeck and Thelen, *Beyond Continuity*, 1–39.

Streeck, W. and Trampusch, C. (2005) 'Economic Reform and the Political Economy of the German Welfare State'. *German Politics*, 14:2, 174–95.

Swank, D. (2002) *Global Capital, Political Institutions, and Policy Change in Developed Welfare States*. Cambridge: Cambridge University Press.

Swedberg, R. (1998) *Max Weber and the Idea of Economic Sociology*. Princeton: Princeton University Press.

—— (2003) *Principles of Economic Sociology*. Princeton: Princeton University Press.

Swidler, A. (2000) 'Cultural Power and Social Movements', in Crothers and Lockhart, *Culture and Politics*, 269–83.

Teschke, B. (2003) *The Myth of 1648: Class, Geopolitics and the Making of Modern International Relations*. London: Verso.

Thelen, K. (2001) 'Varieties of Labor Politics in the Developed Democracies', in Hall and Soskice, *Varieties of Capitalism*, 104–44.

Thelen, K. and Steinmo, S. (1992) 'Historical Institutionalism in Comparative Politics', in K. Thelen, S. Steinmo and F. Longstreth (eds) *Structuring Politics: Historical Institutionalism in Comparative Analysis*. Cambridge: Cambridge University Press, 1–32.

Timmins, G. (2000) 'Alliance for Jobs: Labour Market Policy and Industrial Relations after the 1998 Elections', in Harding and Paterson, *The Future of the German Economy*, 36–53.

Tomlinson, J. (1999) *Globalization and Culture*. Chicago: University of Chicago Press.

Tonkiss, F. (2006) *Contemporary Economic Sociology: Globalisation, Production, Inequality*. London: Routledge.

Toonen, T.A.J. and Hendriks, F. (2001) 'The Embarrassment of Success: Institutional Underpinnings of Polder Politics', in Hendriks and Toonen, *Polder Politics*, 265–89.

Vail, M.I. (2003) 'Rethinking Corporatism and Consensus: The Dilemmas of German Social-protection Reform'. *West European Politics*, 26:3, 41–66.

van Apeldoorn, B. (2002) *Transnational Capitalism and the Struggle over European Integration*. London: Routledge.

—— (2008) 'A National Case-study of Embedded Neoliberalism and its Limits: The Dutch Political Economy and the "No" to the European Constitution', in B. van Apeldoorn, L. Horn and J. Drahokoupil (eds) *Contradictions and Limits of Neoliberal European Governance: From Lisbon to Lisbon*. Basingstoke: Palgrave Macmillan, forthcoming.

van der Pijl, K. (1998) *Transnational Classes and International Relations*. London: Routledge.

van der Veen, R. and Trommel, W. (1999) 'Managed Liberalization of the Dutch Welfare State: A Review and Analysis of the Reform of the Dutch Social Security System, 1985–1998'. *Governance*, 12:3, 289–310.

van der Wurff, R. (1993) 'Neo-liberalism in Germany? The "Wende" in Perspective', in H. Overbeek (ed.) *Restructuring Hegemony in the Global Political Economy: The Rise of Transnational Neo-liberalism in the 1990s*. London: Routledge, 162–87.

van Dyk, S. (2006) 'The Poldermodel and its Order of Consensus: A Foucauldian Perspective on Power and Discourse within the Process of Consensus Creation'. *Acta Politica*, 41:4, 408–29.
van Kersbergen, K. (2000) 'The Declining Resistance of Welfare States to Change?', in S. Kuhnle (ed.) *The Survival of the European Welfare State*. London: Routledge, 19–36.
van Zanden, J.L. (1998) *The Economic History of the Netherlands 1914–1995: A Small Open Economy in the "Long" Twentieth Century*. London: Routledge.
Verba, S. (1965) 'Comparative Political Culture', in Pye and Verba, *Political Culture and Political Development*, 512–60.
Visser, J. (2001) 'Industrial Relations and Social Dialogue', in P. Auer (ed.) *Changing Labour Markets in Europe: The Role of Institutions and Policies*. Geneva: International Labour Organization, 184–242.
Visser, J. and Hemerijck, A. (1997) *"A Dutch Miracle": Job Growth, Welfare Reform and Corporatism in the Netherlands*. Amsterdam: Amsterdam University Press.
Vitols, S. (2000) 'Globalization: A Fundamental Challenge to the German Model?', in R. Stubbs and G.R.D. Underhill (eds) *Political Economy and the Changing Global Order* (2nd ed.). Oxford: Oxford University Press, 373–81.
Watson, M. (2002) 'Sand in the Wheels, or Oiling the Wheels, of International Finance? New Labour's Appeal to a "New Bretton Woods"'. *British Journal of Politics and International Relations*, 4:2, 193–221.
Weber, M. (1930) *The Protestant Ethic and the Spirit of Capitalism* (trs. T. Parsons). London: Allen & Unwin.
—— (1949) *On the Methodology of the Social Sciences* (eds/trs. E.A. Shils and H.A. Finch). New York: Free Press.
—— (1978) *Economy and Society: An Outline of Interpretive Sociology* (eds G. Roth and C. Wittich; trs. E. Fischoff *et al.*). Berkeley: University of California Press.
Weiss, L. (1998) *The Myth of the Powerless State: Governing the Economy in a Global Era*. Cambridge: Polity.
—— (2003) 'Introduction: Bringing Domestic Institutions Back in', in L. Weiss (ed.) *States in the Global Economy: Bringing Domestic Institutions Back in*. Cambridge: Cambridge University Press, 1–33.
Wildavsky, A. (1987) 'Choosing Preferences by Constructing Institutions: A Cultural Theory of Preference Formation'. *American Political Science Review*, 81:1, 3–22.
Williams, R. (1977) *Marxism and Literature*. Oxford: Oxford University Press.
—— (1980) *Problems in Materialism and Culture: Selected Essays*. London: Verso.
—— (1981) *Culture*. London: Fontana.
—— (1983) *Keywords: A Vocabulary of Culture and Society*. London: Fontana.
Woldendorp, J. and Keman, H. (2007) 'The Polder Model Reviewed: Dutch Corporatism 1965–2000'. *Economic and Industrial Democracy*, 28:3, 317–47.
Wood, S. (2001) 'Business, Government, and Patterns of Labor Market Policy in Britain and the Federal Republic of Germany', in Hall and Soskice, *Varieties of Capitalism*, 247–74.

# Index